CW00927371

EL CID

THE MAKING OF A LEGEND

EL CID

THE MAKING OF A LEGEND

M.J. TROW

SUTTON PUBLISHING

First published in 2007 by
Sutton Publishing Limited · Phoenix Mill
Thrupp · Stroud · Gloucestershire · GL5 2BU

The extracts from *In the Arena* are reprinted by permission of
HarperCollins Publishers Ltd. *In the Arena*, Charlton Heston, 1996.

British Library Cataloguing in Publication Data
A catalogue record for this book is available from the British
Library.

Hardback ISBN 978-0-7509-3909-6
Paperback ISBN 978-0-7509-3910-2

Typeset in Sabon
Typesetting and origination by
Sutton Publishing Limited.
Printed and bound in England.

Contents

Acknowledgements

I would like to express my thanks to all who have contributed to the making of this book. First and foremost to my editor Jaqueline Mitchell and her team at Sutton, in particular Anne Bennett and Jane Entrican. To my agent Andrew Lownie for all the years of friendship and unflagging support. To my day-job colleague Eva Campama-Pizarro for her invaluable translation work. To all who have allowed me to use their pictorial images and permitted me to quote from their works. If, in spite of my best efforts, I was unable to contact you, please be assured that this omission will be corrected in future editions. But most of all, as always, to my wife Carol, johanna factotum, without whom this book would not have been possible.

And a special word of thanks to Charlton Heston, who in a cinema in Southport long, long ago, introduced a small boy to the magic of the Campeador, El Cid.

M.J. Trow
2007

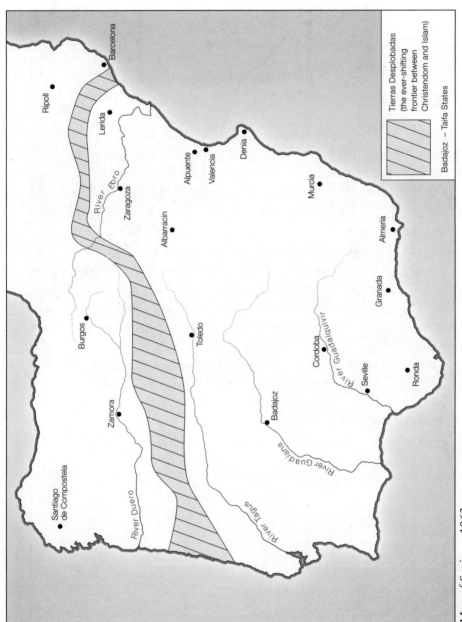

Map of Spain, *c.* 1063.

Tierras Desplobadas
(the ever-shifting
frontier between
Christendom and Islam)

Badajoz – Taifa States

Ripoll

Barcelona

Lerida

Alpuente

Valencia

Denia

Murcia

River Ebro

Zaragoza

Albarracin

Almeria

Granada

Burgos

Toledo

Cordoba

River Guadalquivir

Seville

Ronda

Zamora

Badajoz

River Guadiana

Santiago
de Compostela

River Duero

River Tagus

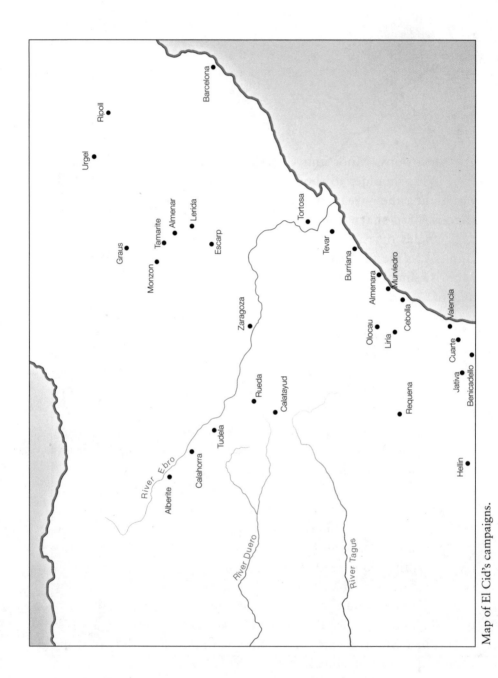

Map of El Cid's campaigns.

1

Out of the Gates of History . . .

The troops, Moor and Christian, wait in the dawn's rays to fight, shoulder to shoulder, in the battle that is to come, the sun gilding their weapons in the outer courtyard in Valencia. The shadows are sharp from crenellations and buttresses, throwing dark angles on to the ancient stones. One by one, the Christian counts kiss the tall cross that Bishop Jeronimo brings to them; the Moorish amirs nod in respect. Alfonso VI, king of Léon, of Castile and of Asturias, is watching the great gates of the inner curtain wall at the top of the hill. His great helm is tucked into the crook of his arm and both he and his horse are bright with the lions and castles of his kingdom. There is no sound among those thousands of waiting men, except the jingle of bits and the snort of horses, high-saddled Andalusians, pawing the ground in the morning, scenting battle.

Alfonso straightens in his stirrups. It is Rodrigo the Cid, emerging from the shadows as the Gate of the Snake in the curtain wall swings slowly open; he is rigid and erect astride the great war horse Babieca, his white cloak around his shoulders and his white banner floating wide above his head. Beside him ride his cousin, his right arm, Alvar Fañez on his right and the amir Moutamin on his left, watching the Cid closely. Only they, Alfonso and a handful of others know that the Cid is dead. As Rodrigo nears him, the king draws his sword and yells the battle cry so that all can hear it, 'For God, the Cid and Spain', and the roar is taken up along the lines, banners dancing, lances piercing the blue of the Andalusian sky.

The huge Moorish gates of the outer curtain wall of the city swing open and a shaft of sunlight bursts over the head of the Cid, framed in that moment like the icon he has become. Then we hear the organ thunder and a gravelly voice-over says, 'And thus the Cid rode out of the gates of history, into legend.'

For this is the Cid of Hollywood, of producer Samuel Bronston, screenplay writers Philip Yordan and Frederic Frank, director Anthony Mann and actor Charlton Heston. 'No one, ever,' wrote historian Harold Lamb in the introduction to the film's souvenir brochure in 1961, 'was quite like him.'[1] And that is precisely the problem for historians in search of the truth.

'He came out of the rugged lands beneath the Pyrenees nine hundred years ago to become the invincible champion of his people . . . Spain, the nation he helped create, made him into its hero. Europe wove into a deathless legend the story of this man, Rodrigo de Bivar.'[2] Rodrigo, like so many heroes of history, has become all things to all men. Such was his complexity that he was able to serve both Moorish amirs and Christian kings and go on to become the national hero of Spain. In fact, in contrast to the Hollywood version, Alfonso VI was not there when the Cid died. Neither was Alvar Fañez. And Moutamin, the amir of Zaragoza, had himself died years before.

Dead lies that good Cid
Rodrigo of Vivar.
Gil Diaz, his good servant,
Will do as he was bidden.
He will embalm his body,
And rigid and stiff it was left;
Its face is beautiful,
Of great beauty and well coloured,
Its two eyes equally open,
Its beard dressed with great care;
It does not appear to be dead,
But seems to be still alive,
And to make it stay upright
Gil Diaz used this cunning:
He set it in a saddle

With a board between its shoulders
And at its breast another,
And at the sides these joined together;
They went under the arms
And covered the back of the head.
This was behind and another
Came up as far as the beard,
Holding the body upright,
So that it leaned to no side.
Twelve days have passed
Since the Cid's life ended.
His followers armed themselves
To ride out to battle
Against that Moorish king Bucar
And the rabble he led.
When it was midnight
The body, thus as it was,
They placed upon Babieca
And onto the horse tied it.
Erect and upright it sits,
It looked as though it were living,
With breeches on its legs
Embroidered black and white,
Resembling the hose that he had worn
When he was alive.
They dressed it in garments
Displaying needlework,
And his shield, at the neck,
Swung with its device.
A helmet on its head
Of painted parchment
Looks as though it were iron,
So well was it fashioned.
In the right hand the sword Tizona
Was cunningly tied,
It is a wonder to watch it

Go forward in a raised hand.
On one side rode his bishop,
The famous Don Jerome,
On his other Gil Diaz,
Who guided Babieca.
Don Pedro Bermudez rode forth
With the Cid's banner raised.
With four hundred nobles
In his company:
Then went forth the main file
With as many again for escort;
The Cid's corpse rode forth
With a brave company.'³

This is the English poet Robert Southey's translation from the Cid ballads of the late Middle Ages, the fictionalized version copied closely by Hollywood, written four centuries earlier, yet focusing on the grisly mechanics of making a corpse appear alive so that a dead man could still win a battle. There is no Gil Diaz in the film version. There is no Pedro Bermudez. These verses are the fanciful creations of the myth-makers, the chroniclers of the fifteenth and sixteenth centuries, and they are further from the truth in their own way than the twentieth-century celluloid version.

Rodrigo died in Valencia in the month of July in the Era 1137.⁴ After his death, his sorrowing wife remained in Valencia with a great company of knights and footsoldiers. When news of his death spread all the Saracens who lived across the seas mustered a considerable army and marched against Valencia.⁵

This is the version closest to the Cid's passing in terms of chronology. It comes from an untitled, fragmentary document known today as the *Historia Roderici* (The Story of Rodrigo), which was written perhaps forty years after the man's death, and distinctly lacks the drama of the first two accounts we have read. There is no Alfonso, no Moutamin, no Alvar Fañez or Gil Diaz. Above all, there is no corpse strapped upright in the saddle, no apocalyptic battle won by a dead man. Instead, there is the grieving heroism of an unnamed wife.

This book examines the man who was Rodrigo Diaz of Vivar, called the Cid Campeador, placing him in the tangled context of the politics of eleventh-century Spain and attempting to understand how it is that some men become heroes. As the anonymous author of the *Historia Roderici* wrote, 'the flux of the years is vast and ceaseless'[6] and it is our job to stop that flow, if only for a moment, and, Hollywood-like, to freeze a frame for long enough for us to see him clearly.

George Macdonald Fraser categorized films that explore the Middle Ages as 'Hollywood's Second Age . . . a vague period in which history and legend co-exist and frequently mingle',[7] admitting that re-creators of this period are less at home with it than they are with the 'sword and sandal' epics of ancient Rome, perhaps because of the vividness of Roman writers in contrast to the wooden, overly pious chronicles of the Middle Ages which constitute their source material. The Romans, too, are more like us. We understand their greed, their jealousy, their ambitions and their failures. The bloodless, good characters of the chronicles – 'born in a happy hour' – are altogether more infuriating, because they are so one-dimensional.

Hollywood, says Fraser, 'has not been helped by the fact that men in armour are difficult to take seriously. They not only look clumsy and overdressed, clanking about and inviting ribaldries about spanners and tin openers, they seldom sound right either.'[8] In fact, Bronston's El Cid, though visually superb, told an eleventh-century tale with protagonists in thirteenth-century armour, brandishing two-handed swords that were unknown before the sixteenth century! Fraser accurately points out that Rodrigo of Vivar was virtually unknown outside his native Spain before the film's release in 1961, so the celluloid version is as important to our understanding of the legend as any of the written chronicles and personal relics that pre-date it.

In July 1960 Charlton Heston, one of Hollywood's most respected actors and already on his way to becoming 'Mr Epic', was wrestling with a script on El Cid and he was not happy about it: 'There's a hell of a lot more in the man than there is in the script, more than the bloodless ideal of medieval chivalry that the legend leaves us with. He seems . . . to have been nearly as often a bad man as a good one . . . I wish I could find more material on him. For one of the most outstanding men of the twelfth [*sic*] century, there's damn little contemporary comment.'[9]

What fascinated Heston, as it fascinates all of us, is that the image of the Cid has lasted for a thousand years and that takes some explaining. It was in the Spanish medieval epic poem of the fourteenth century *El Cantar de Mio Cid* (The Song of the Cid) that the actor found the soul of the man he was to play: 'Some modern historians, trying to clear the cloud of Arthurian legend that obscures him, have cast the Cid simply as a ruthless mercenary. . . . However politically correct that may be, I don't think it's a realistic view. . . . Even if we strip away a thousand years of mythic excess, history still gives us a battered, striving man, stubbornly loyal to the king who exiled him and imprisoned his wife and daughters. I came to see Rodrigo as a biblical Job figure, defiant and enduring.'[10]

Between filming on location in Spain, working with Italian actress Sophia Loren as his love and later wife Jimena, riding temperamental horses and exhausting himself with bone-crushing swordplay, Heston found time to meet Ramon Menendez Pidal, Spain's foremost Cid scholar of the twentieth century. He commented: 'Dr Pidal was exactly what I would have wished him to be. A trimmed white beard, clear black eyes and a blazingly vigorous mind.'[11]

Pidal was as impressed by Heston as the actor was by the historian. Heston was, Pidal said, 'a grand figure of our Cid'[12] although, as we shall see, Pidal had his own agenda in this context.

With Philip Yordan's screenplay and Anthony Mann's direction, Heston and the rest of Samuel Bronston's team spent months in Spain, finding the best location shots they could. Madrid's three central film studios – Chamartin, Sevilla and Cea – were co-opted to work on the project, rebuilding the eleventh-century church of St Gadea of Burgos, doubling the walled city of Pensicola for Valencia and spending staggering sums on costumes, armour, weapons and household objects ranging from crowns to crucifixes. The result? 'Nearly nine hundred years after El Cid rode in triumph, Samuel Bronston, Anthony Mann, Philip Yordan and their associates were ready to bring his epic portrait to the world.'[13]

And so are we: 'Here begin the deeds of Rodrigo the Campeador.'[14]

2

Castles in Spain

Rodrigo Diaz, the Cid Campeador or Lord Champion, was born in the little village of Vivar, 6 miles to the north of Burgos, probably in the year 1043. Today, in a land heavily reliant on tourism, it is known as Vivar del Cid and Burgos itself has capitalized on him, claiming to know the exact location of his town house and even the very spot on the banks of the River Arlanzon where he camped on the way to his first exile.

'They have very good houses [in Burgos] and live very comfortably,' wrote the Venetian traveller Andres Navagero in 1526, 'and they are the most courteous people I have come across in Spain.' He might also have mentioned the biting wind that whistles down from the mighty, snow-capped range of the Cordillera Cantabrica, giving substance to the famous local summation on the weather: 'neuve meses de invernio, tres meses de inferno' – 'nine months of winter, three months of hell'.

Not far away to the east, at Atapuerca, remains have been found of some of the oldest humans in Spain, the hominids known as Heidelberg Man, the cave-dwelling ancestors of the Neanderthals, who hunted elk, bear and mammoth some sixty thousand years before the Cid. From eighteen millennia before his time, the same caves of Cantabria and Asturias have yielded tools and weapons carved from bone and the primitive yet haunting art that reached its apogee across the Pyrenees mountains in Lascaux. Similar paintings in Altamira, further north towards the port of Santander, have been called 'the Sistine Chapel of the Quaternary Era', with wild horses, boar and deer painted in manganese oxide and iron carbonate mixed with charcoal and animal fat. Many centuries later an English traveller in Castillo, much further south, was treated to a snippet of wisdom he probably only partially appreciated when a local asked him, 'Do you know how long we have lived in these hills? Since the very sun was made. Since before kings and altars, or the Virgin herself was a mother. Since there were leopards in the caves. . . .'[1]

Northern Spain, a narrow frontier strip of Christianity in the days of Rodrigo, was home over the centuries to a bewildering and shadowy mix of races. Since the Romans called the area Iberia, most historians and ethnographers today use the generic term Iberians for these people, but their origins are obscure. Their language was not common to other early civilizations, yet it still survives among the fiercely independent Basques, who today occupy the central foothills of the Pyrenees. It may well be that they are derived from the oldest race of people in Spain, echoing one of their favourite sayings, that God made Adam from bones he found in a Basque graveyard! The Iberian settlements can still be traced today in the labyrinthine stone walls called castros, circular buildings huddled together like plasma cells under a microscope, like those near Oviedo.

But if the Basque influence is unique in northern Spain, that of the Celts was more universal. This Indo-European people, warriors, hunters, artists and poets, spread throughout modern Europe in the thousand years before Christ, taking their colourful culture wherever they went. It is no accident that one of the most popular musical instruments of Asturias and Galicia is the *gaita*, a simple bagpipe made of goatskin. The mountainous nature of the area, from the Pyrenees to the Cordillera Cantabrica, meant that pockets of people developed, settlements now Basque, now Celtiberian. Archaeologists have uncovered whole villages, like that at Monte Santa Tecla in Galicia, with typical round houses made of stone. On the coast to the east, where the county of Barcelona would flourish at the time of the Cid, Phoenician traders manned their bright-sailed ships, loading and unloading their fabulous cargoes, and men spoke Greek as they bartered at the quaysides. The Phoenicians imported tin at La Corunna and the Greeks had a trading post at Emporion on the Bay of Roses.

The rise of the great North African state of Carthage saw a colony established at Cartagena in the south. The Romans landed there in

211 BC and when the legions marched into Iberia they found a culture that was already well established and very far from primitive. To the Romans, however, anyone not from the city of the seven hills was a barbarian. Pliny spells out the motivation for the Romanization of the peninsula: 'Nearly the whole of Spain abounds in mines of lead, iron, copper, silver and gold . . . while in Baetica [the far south] there is cinnabar.'[2]

Carthage, Rome's great rival, had already discovered this mineral wealth. In the century before Christ a single mine in Cartagena produced some 300lb of silver a day and the region employed a staggering 40,000 miners.[3] In the north and north-west, the homeland of the Cid a thousand years later, gold, tin and copper were extensive. And long before the days of Toledo, Spanish swords were prized above all others. Justin[4] wrote 'nor was any weapon held in esteem by them [the Roman army] which has not been dipped either in Bilbilis or the Chalybs'.[5]

In the early years of Roman occupation trouble arose at every hand. The north was particularly difficult, with revolts among the tribes of the Turdentani, Lusitani and Celtiberi all over what is now Portugal and Castile. In high summer the warlike and nomadic Cimbri swarmed through the Pyrenees passes from Gaul to add to the unrest, and when Roman politics played itself out in the growing empire the rival factions of the generals Marius[6] and Sulla[7] fought each other everywhere in the peninsula. There was an action replay of this in the years shortly before Christ between the forces of Julius Caesar[8] and Gnaeus Pompeius[9] and as a result Spain, like Gaul, was divided into three, with Lusitania in the west, Baetica in the south and Tarraconensis sprawling over the centre and north of what today is Cervantes'[10] plain of La Mancha. Most Romans referred to these areas as Further and Hither [nearer] Spain.

Christianity came late to Iberia. The fierceness of the northern tribes meant that the Romans adopted an uneasy live and let live policy, and the geographer Strabo,[11] horrified, wrote that the Cantabrians grew their hair long like women and drank no wine – the depths of depravity to a cultured Roman! The Basques already worshipped a mother-earth figure whose name was Mari, so the arrival of the Virgin came relatively easily to them. The church of Santa Eulalia de Bóveda, with its underground shrine and baptismal pool adorned with frescoes of cured cripples, dates from the fourth century and is a remarkable survivor of this early Christian culture. But Christian Rome could not survive for ever. 'When the brightest light of the whole earth was extinguished', wrote St Jerome,[12] 'when the Roman Empire was deprived of its head . . . when the whole world perished in one city, then I was dumb with silence. I held my peace even from God and my sorrow was stirred.'

The man who sacked Rome and put out the light of civilization was Alaric, the elected king of a tribe called the Visigoths, who had immigrated from the Baltic, fighting Romans and other barbarians with an extraordinary degree of even-handedness. For six days in the summer of AD 410 the Visigoths burned and pillaged the city on the seven hills, but Alaric was a Christian and forbade his warriors to touch women or churches.

By 415 Alaric's people had turned north again into Gaul and then trickled south once more through the Pyrenees passes. Settling for a generation in Aquitaine, now the south of France, the Visigoths established a kingdom in what would become Spain eleven centuries later. It was of people like the Visigoths that historians of an earlier generation were writing when they coined the phrase the Dark Ages; much of their culture is shrouded in obscurity. Most of our contemporary written knowledge of them comes from the pen of Isidore,[13] Archbishop of Seville, one of the foremost scholars of the Middle Ages, who wrote a history of the Goths, the Vandals and the Suebi, who colonized today's Portugal in the decades before he was born.

It was not until the Visigoths were defeated by Clovis and his Franks at Vouille in 507 that the tribe migrated permanently south, their king, Alaric II, left dead on the field. They established the kingdom of Toledo in 554, a settlement that would feature centrally in the story of the Cid. Under their leaders Leovigild and Sisebut, the Visigoths destroyed the Suebian kingdom in Galicia and displaced the Byzantine colonists in the south. They became staunch Catholics in 587, abandoning their earlier Arian[14] creed, and the councils held subsequently at Toledo were among the most important of the early Church. The Jews were routinely persecuted, but a working relationship was established with the ever-rebellious Basques. The scattering of Visigothic churches in the north, with their curious blend of Germanic iconography and Roman styles, is a reminder of the two and a half centuries of their rule. The finest preserved Visigothic church today is the seventh-century building of terracotta-coloured stone at Quintanilla de las Vinas, south of Burgos. Its square blocks of stone are decorated with bold carved friezes of flowers, birds and geometric designs. Inside, symbols of the sun and moon are reminders of the people's pagan past. These churches, like the later monasteries of the high Middle Ages, were built in the peace of the countryside, away from the increasing bustle of the towns. They were, in St Augustine's words, *civitates deo*, cities of God.

The world of Rodrigo Diaz was shaped, as everyone's is, by all that had gone before, but of particular significance was the extraordinary invasion of Muslim fanatics from the south, known to history as the Moors. We shall consider them in detail in the next chapter, but we must remember that for the three centuries before the Cid's birth northern Spain was a narrow Christian frontier, desperately clinging on against the awesome power of Islam. It was because of this that the Visigothic epoch was remembered with nostalgia as something of a golden age long before Spain's *sieclo d'oro*[15] eclipsed it. Sisebut was something akin to a national hero before the Cid. He was a general of the first order, not only defeating the tribal lawlessness of Cantabria, but also removing the Byzantine influence from the south and, as a staunch Catholic, forcing Jews into Christianity, and he was also a scholar, writing a life of St Desiderius. His heir Wamba was another successful soldier-king, putting down revolts and destroying the fleet of a Muslim invasion force at Algeciras. The legendary scholarship of Isidore of Seville was augmented by Julian of Toledo; both men became saints.

The Muslim conquest which began so effectively in 711 saw refugees struggling north into Cantabria, bringing whatever they could carry along with their southern language and customs, their hopes and fears; and they spilled into and helped create three broad principalities whose frontiers often overlapped and thus were inevitably settings for conflict. Later ages would paint a clear-cut, black and white image of a united and embattled Christendom fighting back against the invasion of Islam, when crusade and *jihad* went head to head in the centuries-long duel for Jerusalem and later Byzantium. The reality, at least in early medieval Spain, was far more complicated. The Arab and Berber invaders reached the Pyrenees at one point, but withdrew to the River Duero, disenchanted with the bleakness of Cantabria: 'distant, mountainous, cold, wet, a wasteland where camels ailed and no dates grew'.[16] A visiting Englishman described the area nine hundred years later: 'And I'd come down at last to the rich plain of the Duero with its fields of copper earth, its violent outcrops of poppies running in bloodstained bandanas across acres of rasping wheat.'[17] Perhaps the rural economy of the region had improved by then. Certainly the Moors took a very dismal view of this harsh land:

The whole of the Christian north of Spain is flat [*sic*] and most of the land is covered in sand. [Christians'] foodstuffs are mainly millet and sorghum and their normal drinks are apple cider and bushka, which is a drink made from flour. The inhabitants are a treacherous people of depraved morals, who do not keep themselves clean and only wash once or twice a year in cold water. They do not wash their clothes once they have put them on until they fall to pieces on them, and assert that the filth that covers them thanks to their sweat is good for their bodies and keeps them healthy. Their clothes are very tight-fitting and have wide openings, through which most of their bodies show.[18]

In the north-west lay Galicia, a wild region conquered by the Germanic Suebi tribe, who settled in the valleys of the River Miño and its tributaries. Independent princes held pockets of land here until the ninth century when they were united with the neighbouring kingdom of Asturias.[19] Plagued by Norman raids in the years before

13

Duke William raided (and stayed put in) England, Galicia lost its political cohesion, but was still able to make life intolerable for the amir of Cordoba, al-Mansur, the Victorious, who attempted to take the region in 997. In the nineteenth century travelling Englishman George Borrow could still discern the essential *differentness* of the Galicians. He found them clownish but capable of extraordinary shrewdness. Although they had happily embraced Catholicism, the superstition typical of mountain peoples remained with them. Wizards and witches were real. And even Francisco Franco, Spain's Fascist dictator of the twentieth century, slept with a mummified hand and arm by his bedside. It was reputedly next to him on the operating table when he died.[20] The cause of death may officially have been 'endotoxic shock brought about by acute bacterial peritonitis, renal failure, bronchopneumonia, cardiac arrest, stomach ulcers, thrombophlebitis and Parkinson's Disease',[21] but somehow Franco was more at one with Spain's past than this scientific list allows. He occasionally, in the last hours, regained consciousness to whisper 'how hard it is to die',[22] echoing the passing of Fernando I of Castile, who lingered for at least a week before the saints came for him.

It was the little town of Compostela, 40 miles from the Coast of Death with its ancient tales of smuggling and shipwrecks, that put Galicia for ever on the Christian map. James, the son of Zebedee, so the Bible told Galicians and the rest of Christendom, was a fisherman from Galilee who gave up his nets to become one of the disciples of Jesus the Nazarene. Together with his brother John, he followed Christ during the brief period of his 'ministry' and may have preached as far afield as Spain in the years after Christ's crucifixion. Around AD 44 he died a martyr's death on the orders of the Judaean king, Herod Agrippa.[23] Eight centuries later a shepherd in Galicia is said to have received a similar visitation to that which attended Christ's birth, as angels and wandering stars[24] led him to a grave in a forest. Exactly how the local clergy decided this was the tomb of the apostle James is unknown. Medieval man needed no subtleties or probabilities. Every word of the Bible was gospel, God's word, and it was blasphemous and dangerous to doubt it. Our more cynical age can readily accept that beleaguered Galicia, at the mercy of Norman attacks from the north and Muslim attacks from the south, needed a saviour in an unhappy hour and that the grave in the woods handily became the shrine of Santiago at Compostela. When the dead saint was seen riding a white horse and slaughtering Muslims in the battle of Clavijo in 844, he became known as 'Iago Matamoros', the Moor-Slayer. The origin of James in Spain probably occurred in the first place because the actual site of his death, in Judaea, and the town that would later become Zaragoza, both carried the name Caesarea in the days of the Roman Empire. The concocted story is that James's Iberian followers brought his body back in a stone boat, kept afloat through the Pillars of Hercules[25] by the presence of the saint's body on deck. In rescuing a man from drowning in the treacherous waters of Finisterre, which, ominously, means the End of the World, James acquired the scallop shell as his symbol, carried for centuries by pilgrims to his shrine. By the time of the Cid, the pilgrims' road to Compostela was well established, and the shrine itself, after Rome and Jerusalem, perhaps the most venerated of the Middle Ages. The road was known as the Camino Francés, the French Way, because most of the early pilgrims crossed the Pyrenees from France,[26] and it ran through the Cid's own town of Burgos. Thirty years after the death of Rodrigo Diaz the French monk Aimeri Picaud wrote the *Liber Sancti Jacobi* (Book of St James), also called the *Codex Calixtinius* after Callistus II, pope between 1119 and 1124. In a way, this was the world's first travel guide, and it paints a very chauvinistic picture of the Spaniards who were the Cid's contemporaries. The Basques apparently were a mongrel people descended from the Scots, the Nubians and the inhabitants of Cornwall, who were widely held to have tails! The Navarrese on the other hand regularly had sex with their horses and mules and tied padlocks to the animals' tails so that no one else could have the pleasure!

If pilgrims successfully braved the Pyrenees, the appalling weather and the overt threat from hostile locals, then they would receive their Compostelana, a certificate proving they had reached the shrine itself. This, on their death, was enough to earn them a remission of their sins, so that they spent only half the allotted time in Purgatory.[27] If they reached Santiago in a Holy Year, when the saint's day, 25 July, fell on a Sunday, then their Purgatory was removed entirely and they would go straight to St Peter. Pilgrims too ill to complete the journey could still achieve absolution. Church bells rang in the foggy mountain passes to guide the lost, and at Puerto de Perdón and Villafranca del Bierzo there were 'pardon doors' that were the equivalent, to the genuinely sick, of reaching Santiago itself. At the true shrine the huge statue of St James and the gigantic swinging censer worked by eight monks were not put in place until the thirteenth century. At the time of the Cid, Compostela was more modest.

In political terms the most important town in Galicia was Oviedo, which was rebuilt by King Alfonso II[28] – the Chaste – as a new Toledo, since the old Christian city had long before fallen to the Moors. There was a monastery there as early as 761 on the hill called Ovetum (the place of the egg). Fruela, an earlier king of Asturias, built a palace and a church nearby. Alfonso was a visionary and spent money like water in creating a masterpiece of pre-Romanesque architecture, with its triple-arched churches, carved pillars and small windows, all adorned with palm-leaves and mythical monsters. Today's cathedral, with its Camara Santa (room of the saints), was part of Alfonso's palace in the ninth century and the jewelled Asturian cross that is its most sacred relic was a gift from the king to the church. The Cross of Angels, covered in gemstones, pearls and gold leaf, carries an ominous warning: 'May anyone who dares remove me from the spot where I have been willingly given be struck down by a divine lightning bolt.' Other relics in the museum – bread from the Last Supper, part of the True Cross, the robe worn by Jesus and the breast milk of the Virgin Mary – were probably acquired during the reign of Alfonso.

Oviedo too had its Cid-like hero in the centuries before Rodrigo. In 718 a local rebellion against the Moorish governor at Gijón on the north coast threw up a leader called Pelayo or Pelagius, who defeated the Muslims in the precipitous Picos de Europa mountains at Covadonga. Today this battle site lies at the centre of a national park, and it is considered by modern Spaniards as the symbolic birthplace of their country, in the heartlands of the *Reconquista* or reconquest of which Rodrigo Diaz was very much a part. Pelayo was outnumbered, so the story goes, and like the Scots king Robert the Bruce he took refuge in a cave which is now itself a shrine to the Virgin, whose miraculous appearance in 718 turned the tide of battle in Pelayo's favour. A modern statue to the man stands nearby, with sword in hand and a magical cross shining above his head. It was this victory that gave Galicia life and prevented it being swallowed up by Islam's relentless march from the south.

Details of life in the area are sparse. We know that the population was probably growing in the ninth and tenth centuries, especially because of the influx of refugees from the south. Most of them were so-called 'Mozarabs', Christians whose lifestyles had been changed for ever by regular contact with the Arabs or Berbers from North Africa. The result was increased trade, ever more exotic and adventurous building and probably a more structured pattern of farming, always the lifeblood of peasant communities. The Visigothic architecture of the north had already passed into a pre-Romanesque phase by the reign of Alfonso the Chaste. Mozarabic designs brought Moorish art to the equation of style, with its distinctive horseshoe arches. From the monastery at Burgos to the church of San Millan de Suso in Navarre, the cutting edge of architecture was to be found in buildings like these by the Cid's day. The church of Sant Ponçe in Corbera, north of Valencia, is a good example. Built in the lifetime of Rodrigo Diaz, its nave and aisles open on to a rectangular crossing with a dome above a square base. The external walls have blind arches and, most bizarrely, the roof has an external staircase that reaches to the belfry. Whether by accident or design, Sant Ponçe is built on high ground on a rocky promontory, and with its high, small windows it has more the look of a fortress than a church.

There is no doubt that kings like Alfonso II and his son Alfonso III[29] saw themselves as rulers on a grand scale. They introduced the panoply of the court with its hierarchies and protocols, held Toledo-style councils of the Church and sent ambassadors across the

Pyrenees to the fabulous court of the powerful Charlemagne[30] and his son Louis the Pious.[31] If the king of the Franks could style himself 'the Great', then so could the third Alfonso of Asturias. By the tenth century, however, the seat of power had slipped from Oviedo to Léon, which had fallen to the Moors in 716. Originally a Roman military base of the *Legio Septima Hispana* (hence Legionensis, the city of the Legion), Léon was won back in 850 and it became the established seat of the younger sons of Alfonso's successors. In 914 García I made it his capital. From that point on, all kings of Christian Spain styled themselves kings of Léon. The city's principal street patterns still reflect the fierce, rational geometry of its Roman military origins and sections of the Roman wall still stand. In 1063, when Rodrigo Diaz was reaching full manhood, the bones of St Isidore were brought here and the collection of calfskin-covered choir books, dating from before the Cid was born, have miraculously survived the passage of time near his tomb.

The second principality, which had a more unique racial history than anywhere else in the north, was the Basque country of Navarre, sandwiched between the Pyrenees and the Cordillera Cantabrica, the remoteness of the region offering a partial explanation of the separateness of its people. We know even less of the history of this area than of Galicia, Léon and Asturias. Roman finds here have been rare – just the occasional mosaic piece from one or two villages near Pamplona. Christianity came late; there was a bishop at Calahorra by 400, but some of the mountain villages may still have been pagan in the days of the Cid.[32]

One thing is certain – the Basques were just as anxious to see off their northern neighbours as they were the Moors to the south. The eighth century was a time of Frankish expansion, with kings such as Pepin the Short[33] and his more famous son Charlemagne busily extending the frontiers of their kingdom. It was while returning from just such an expansion into Spain that Charlemagne's rearguard was caught in a Basque ambush in 778. The action itself was insignificant, both in terms of what was achieved and probably in the small numbers involved. But the battle of Roncevalles passed into legend and Charlemagne's commanders Olivier and Roland

(Hruodlandus in Frankish), who both died that day, became immortalized as the epitome of chivalry two centuries before chivalry was invented! The anonymous *Chanson de Roland* (Song of Roland), written perhaps half a century before Rodrigo's birth, tells the tale of warrior knights sounding their horns, breaking their swords and dying in a hopeless but glamorized quest for immortality. So popular was this poem that it was translated into Norse with the title *Karla-Magnus Saga* (Story of Charlemagne) and legend has it that William of Normandy had a version of it read to his troops on the morning of 25 October 1066 as they watched Harold Godwinson's English *fyrd* form a shield wall on Senlac Hill.[34] The Song of Roland has enormous significance in the story of the Cid. It is highly likely that Rodrigo himself knew the tale and perhaps even read an early version in Cantabrian or Latin. Certainly later poets and chroniclers who wrote about the Cid saw him as a Roland-like figure, distorted and out of context, right down to Philip Yordan, who wrote the screenplay for the Charlton Heston film. And such is the lure of Roland, and such indeed is the tendency of later generations to misunderstand and oversimplify, that even works of relative scholarship assume that the hero died in battle with the Moors in true crusader tradition.[35]

The Visigoths had never quite conquered the Basques but an uneasy compromise had come into being by the ninth century. Sancho I[36] became Navarre's first king in the early tenth century, setting up his court at Pamplona and establishing an atmosphere in which the later wars called the *Reconquista* could take place. Sancho defeated the Moors at Viguera in 923, but the following year they struck back at his birthplace of Sanguesa: 'The Muslims fell on their enemies like ravening lions', wrote the Arab chronicler Ibn Hayan, a contemporary of the Cid, 'crossing the river and hurling upon them . . . they . . . continued the attack until they had put them to flight and made them fodder for swords and spears, pursuing them towards the steep slopes of a nearby hill which the Muslims sealed with Allah's help, killing many there and strewing the ground with corpses. . . .'[37]

Abd al-Rahman, the Moorish general, burned Pamplona to the ground before withdrawing south of the Duero. Five years later he took the title Caliph and became the most important ruler of Muslim Spain.

To the south and east of the kingdom of Navarre lay the Spanish Levante, the most 'civilized' area of northern Christian Spain and the earliest colonized by Phoenicians, Greeks and Romans. Under Frankish control as much of this was after 801, it was divided up into the counties of Barcelona, Gerona, Empuries, Andorra and Aragon. This was the land of the Catalans. The Visigoths had taken it in 418, but the Moorish occupation of 711 left the area with another unique culture, language and take on life. The establishment of the Frankish March of Spain by Louis the Pious gave Barcelona in particular the lead among the dozen or so counties and a nominal feudal link with France. The Count of Barcelona was in reality an important warlord, with the armies, power and prestige of a full-blown king elsewhere in Europe.

The earliest of these was Guifré el Pilós (Wilfred the Hairy), whose long-lasting dynasty was finally absorbed into Aragon half a millennium later. The Catalans spoke a language that was more than a simple mix of French and Castilian, and partially thanks to the Cid it is still spoken as far south as Valencia and the Balearic Islands. A later count, at the time of the Cid, introduced the *Ustages*, a series of laws drawn largely from Germanic sources that were used extensively across the Pyrenees as well as in Barcelona itself. This count was Rámon Berenguer, who was twice captured by the Cid during the course of their respective military careers, and a man who, in the peculiar world of eleventh-century Spain, was at once an arch-enemy and a relative by marriage!

It was in the central of the three principalities that Rodrigo Diaz would be born some time in the year of his lord 1043, in the land known as Castile. The name comes, unsurprisingly, from the fortresses (*castella*) that dotted this tough, uncompromising frontier kingdom. Modern Castile is divided into northern and southern regions and the guidebooks talk of a 'dry, harsh land of pious Inquisition-ravaged cities, ham, wine and bull-fighting. Visitors tend to love or hate the dusty *meseta* with its extremes of summer and winter temperatures; it's a bleak, almost desert landscape in parts.'[38] Old Castile (today's Castilla y Leon) is divided from New Castile by the River Tagus, but in the Cid's time there was also new Castile (now Castilla La Mancha) that was part of al-Andalus, the Moorish-occupied part of Spain that would become the battleground for the *Reconquista* for the next five hundred years.

The greatest city in southern Castile was undoubtedly Toledo, the Visigothic capital after AD 520. Its Catholic councils were legendary and it held political and economic primacy until its capture by the Moors. It was the largest city in northern Spain, with a roughly estimated population in the Cid's day of 30,000. It also boasted the grandest buildings. Its loss to the Muslims would only be eclipsed much later by the fall of Jerusalem itself and long after that, Byzantium. It would be over a hundred years before Christian kings took it back and Castile became 'whole' again. Until that day Castile was a tough and edgy border state, like the marches of Scotland and Wales to the Norman kings of England after 1066. In Spain, as in Britain, the fact that local nobility had to raise armies and castles for self-protection gave them an importance, a power-base and military experience, all of which established them as potential trouble-makers for their own rulers. Such men were often over-mighty subjects and it took strong kings to keep them in check.

Much of Castilian history is shrouded in legend. The area was believed to be governed after 842 by two judges, Nuño Resura and Laín Calvo, but the first known ruler was Rodrigo, who was made Count of Castile by Alfonso III of Asturias. The Cid-like hero of his own region was Fernán Gonzalez, a tenth-century count who described himself in charters in the royal style – 'by the grace of God count of all Castile'.[39] In fact, Gonzalez's career is remarkably similar to that of the Cid: he was a loyal champion of Alfonso against the Moors, but fell foul of the king and (unlike Rodrigo Diaz) served time in a royal dungeon. Local politics played neatly into his hands and he was able to play off his neighbours in Léon and Navarre, both of which had their own problems of instability, and created what was, in effect, a separate principality. All that

Gonzalez lacked was a crown. Here too, his career veers away from that of the Cid as Rodrigo took the crown of Valencia for himself in 1096.

Life in Castile in the time of the Cid was hard and development took time. 'We found the area abandoned,' wrote Abbot Vitulo in the year that Charlemagne was crowned Emperor of the West, 'we built churches there; we cultivated; we planted; we built there houses, cellars, granaries, wine-presses, mills. . . .'[40]

We know something of tenth-century Castile from the *fueros*, written charters that have survived. These documents were legal records of privileges granted to individuals or monasteries to encourage the resettlement of land that had recently been in Muslim hands. As the *Fuero Real*, it continued to be used in this way in Castile until the fourteenth century, although in Aragon it became synonymous with assemblies dealing with economic issues. Count Garcia Fernandez wrote in 974: 'We grant these good customs to the mounted soldiers, that they shall enjoy the status of noblemen . . . and let each man settle his land . . . and if anyone should kill a knight of Castrogeriz, let him pay compensation for him of 500 solidi. The men of Castrogeriz shall not pay tolls . . . and let the clergy have the same privileges as the knights . . . if a man shall be proved to have borne false witness let the council of Castrogeriz have his teeth.'[41]

Vestigial 'constitutions' like this were springing up all over western Europe in the years and centuries after the eclipse of the Roman Empire, mostly in the form of laws drawn up by kings. The structure of Spanish society in the century before the Cid was born is a confused patchwork of colours. The feudal system, most sharply defined north of the Pyrenees in Carolingian France, was still not fully developed when Rodrigo Diaz died. It is easiest to see it in operation in Norman England after 1066, when Duke William, now king and sole landowner in his newly conquered land, established it as his 'métier du roi'. In fact, elements of feudalism were already there as far back as the reign of the Viking king Cnut, but William formalized them. The knights who had ridden with William up the murderous slope of Senlac Hill were elevated to the rank of count (for the sake of harmony they were usually given the English title of earl) and were given a fief (the Latin variant *feudum* gave its name to the entire complex system) the size of an old English shire, now renamed as counties. These men were all vassals of the king, kneeling at William's coronation in London on Christmas Day 1066 to swear homage and fealty to him; they owed him their advice and military service. They were also his tenants-in-chief, who held (and in practice owned) vast swathes of countryside, including villages, manors, towns and even churches. They in turn leased their lands to the knights below them in the form of manors, in return for which the knights owed 'knight service' to their lord. Below them, freemen farmed their little plots and formed the spearmen, billmen and archers of the lord's army. In theory this army was obliged to stay in the field for forty days in any calendar year at the king's behest.

In practice, the system was rarely as neat as this and in Spain it was nowhere near as well structured. At the heart of Spanish feudalism was the *caballero*, the horseman. In the kingdom of the Franks he was *chevalier*, in the Italian states *cavaliere*, in the German territories *ritter*. In England he was the *cnight*, the household retainer. Yet all these language variants carried the same implication: the knight was a mounted warrior, the epitome of that section of society in all medieval states whose role was to fight – *pugnare*. And mounted warfare would dominate the battlefield for the next seven hundred years.

The length of feudal obligation varied hugely in northern Spain. Only in Catalonia, in the north-east, did the system come close to the 'purest' Frankish or Anglo-Norman form. The fiefs here were called *presimonia* or *honores*, and Aragonese records register anything from three days' to three months' service. Feudalism was slow to develop here because of the practice of paying vassals in cash, the so-called *fief-rente*, rather than with the use of land. The best examples come from England: two years after the death of the Cid, Henry I paid Count Robert of Flanders £500 a year to provide him with a thousand knights ready for service in England or Normandy. The Christian nobility of tenth- and eleventh-century

Spain raised armies because it proved their power and status, not because they owed allegiance to a lord. This selfish and semi-anarchic situation explains the Cid's apparently shifty and even duplicitous reputation. He did not always fight for his king (Charlton Heston's portrayal notwithstanding) because he was under no definite obligation to do so. Those who disparage Rodrigo Diaz because he was a mercenary and fought for pay have not understood the complexities of Spanish society at the time.

Interestingly, the different origins of the northern Christian principalities explain the diversity of names for the nobility. They are *barones* in Catalonia, *Ricoshombres* [rich men] and *hidalgos* in Castile, and *caballeros* or *infanzones* elsewhere.[42]

Cities were different. Unless they were royal, like Toledo or Léon, all able-bodied men (in practice between the ages of 12 and 50) were eligible to man the defences should the city be attacked. Long years of watching and waiting on the Moorish frontier had created something of a fortress mentality. In times of attack, even churchmen and Jews could be called on to buckle on a sword and man the ramparts.[43] In the half-century before the Cid's birth a new social group was developing: the *caballeros villanos* or town cavalry, who owned their own horses and armour and fought in exchange for land or exemption from taxation. Such men's status had risen dramatically by the thirteenth century, with their titles becoming hereditary, and many of them were on a par with the older *hidalgo* class. Reference is made to status elevation after successful campaigns in many of the Cid legends.

If feudalism was still in its infancy in Spain when Rodrigo Diaz was in his, the Catholic Church in Spain was firmly embedded. Since the decline of the Visigoths with their Arian beliefs, the Roman Church had established its power under a succession of popes who were God's vicars on earth. Across northern Spain the existence of the shrine of St James and the routes to it stressed the importance of pilgrimage to Christians of all ranks. This was particularly the obsession of the powerful and influential monks of Cluny, the abbey founded in Burgundy in 910 by the then Duke of Aquitaine, William the Pious. The grim Benedictine Order[44] was placed directly under the control of the pope and the abbey's influence spread all over France and the Italian states before reaching Spain. Twenty years before the birth of the Cid, Paternus, the abbot of the monastery of San Juan de la Peña, returned from his own pilgrimage to Cluny with a few monks who began to spread the Benedictine word. It would take until ten years after the Cid's death to accomplish it, but gradually the old Spanish liturgy was altered beyond recognition and canon law was introduced. No longer would the Spanish clergy wear their distinctive vestments or their congregations solemnly chant 'Amen' at the end of every line of the Lord's Prayer. Even the script in which Spanish churchmen wrote was swept away, with the alien Visigothic characters replaced by Frankish Latin – *francesa*. The story of the Cid is studded with references to local churches and monasteries that were affiliated to Cluny. Certainly the power and influence of the Catholic Church ran very deep in Spanish society, making the country the most fanatical of all states when Catholicism was challenged centuries later by the Reformation. An impartial Englishman, witnessing a church procession in Toro, near Zamora in the 1930s, was riveted by its power:

> The silence increased, and even the cries of the children began instinctively to smother themselves. Then the doors [of the church] were thrown open on to a sparkling darkness, like a cave full of summer fireflies, as several hundred candles streamed away from the altar and came fluttering towards the street.
>
> Slowly, to the sound of a drum and trumpet, the shuffling procession emerged, and the crush of spectators standing nearest the church fell to their knees as though they'd been sprayed with bullets. The dry beat of the drum and naked wail of the trumpet sounded as alien as I could wish, conjuring up in the glow of this semi-African twilight an extraordinary feeling of fear and magic. Was it the death of the saint they were so lugubriously celebrating with their black banners and dippling candles? . . . Clearly, to all eyes, she was the living Saint, Sister of the Virgin, Intimate of Christ, Eternal Mediator with the Ghost of God and Compassionate Mother of Toro.[45]

Beyond the walls of the churches and towns that littered the Cid's Spain, the lives of most men and women were regulated by the harsh reality of the seasons. England at the time of Rodrigo Diaz is very well documented, first by the Anglo-Saxon Chronicle[46] and second by the Domesday Book, collated when the Cid was in his 40s.[47] Nothing of this kind exists for eleventh-century Spain, but something of the life of ordinary people can be gleaned from the charters of the time. One from Castrogeriz in the 1020s makes it clear that lawlessness abounded and that the 'black economy' was based at least partially in cattle rustling: 'In those days there came Diego Pérez and seized our livestock and took himself off to Silos. We went after him and attacked his houses and estate and killed fifteen men and did a great deal of damage; and we brought our livestock back by force.'[48]

Much of this economy was animal husbandry, the high sierras tending to a life of transhumance in which the sheep-, goat- and cow-herds drove their animals into the lower pasture grounds of the *meseta* in the autumn and up into the high country as the world warmed with the coming of spring. The herdsmen had different names in their regions. In the Asturias they were *vaqueros*, in Cantabria *passiegos*. In both areas their descendants still exist, something akin to a lost tribe whose origins are shrouded in mystery. The muleteers who worked the treacherous paths of the mountains of Léon had a similar reputation. And they were still there nearly a millennium later:

The mule trains at that time [1930s] were the caravans of Castile, one of the threads of the country's life – teams of small, tasselled animals drawing high blue carts brightly painted with vines and flowers. As gaudy as barges or wedding floats, mounted on squealing five-foot wheels, they worked from city to city at three miles an hour – a rhythm unchanged since the days of Hannibal – carrying charcoal, firewood, wineskins, olives, oil, old iron and gossip. . . . They were the hereditary newsbearers of the Spanish plains, old as the wheel and separate in their ways as gypsies.[49]

Even today in the rugged Picos de Europa west of Bilbao, the long-horned *casinas* of Asturias and the *tudancos* of Cantabria graze on the *vegas* (pastures) before being shut up for the winter in slate-roofed, thick-walled barns. The local markets essentially sell beef, although without the advantages of modern stock-breeding it is unlikely that many of these cattle would have survived the harsh Cantabrian winters in the days of Rodrigo.

Spanish peasants lived in ramshackle houses made of timber and stone, propped up on stilt-like legs. Villages like Peñalba de Santiago in Léon looked much as they probably did in the Cid's time, although their tenth-century church frescoes are now whitewashed. All over northern Spain are eighteenth- and nineteenth-century examples of granaries of the type that must have stood, perhaps on the same spot, at the time of the Cid. Their styles vary from valley to valley, but most have thatch or slate roofs, are raised on stilts to deter rats and floodwater, and are tall enough to allow good ventilation for the grain. Nine centuries later villages like these probably looked very similar: 'At the end of the day, the doors and windows [of the hovels] admitted all the creatures of the family: father, son, daughter, cousin, the donkey, the pig, the hen, even the harvest mouse and the nesting swallow, bedded together at the fall of darkness. . . . The shadows of man and beast flickered huge like ancestral ghosts, which, since the days of the caves, have haunted the corners of fantasy. . . .'[50]

Today Rioja in the Basque country is most famous for its wine, but it was made in vineyards throughout Spain in the eleventh century, with the Pyrenean vintages being well known for their tar-like qualities.[51] The extensive apple orchards saw the production of local cider too, and it is likely that the drink was already being exported to Normandy by the time of Charlemagne. The charter of 978 drawn up by Garcia Fernández, Count of Castile, talks of 500 head of cattle, 1,600 sheep and 150 horses. His estates at Salinas de Añana, west of Burgos, had seven plots of arable land, four vineyards and six salt-pans, unworkable today but still eye-catching in the glittering sun.

Spain in the Cid's time was warmer than today, so the Christian frontier must have been more densely forested and the winds and snows perhaps a little less lethal. Even so, it was possible for a man to freeze to death in the Cordilleras at many times during the year and the summers were relatively short. Today's realization that our flora and fauna are precious means that breeds are checked and flocks of wild birds counted. Milkwort, rattle, vetch, sea purslane, adder's tongue spearwort and lady's tresses are among the flora noted by conservationists today. We have no way of knowing how widespread they were in the eleventh century although eagles certainly soared overhead as Rodrigo Diaz began his exile at the hands of King Alfonso VI and he rode Babieca through dangerous mountain passes that still teemed with wolves, brown bears and wild boar.

When the 20-year-old English writer Laurie Lee visited Spain in 1934, as the Cid's legend was about to be turned into propaganda for Franco's cause, he was actually attacked by animals he took to be wolves: 'They came slinking and snarling along the edge of my crater [he was sleeping rough], hackles bristling against the moon, and only by shouting, throwing stones and flashing my torch in their eyes was I able to keep them at bay. Not till early dawn did they finally leave me and run yelping away down the hillside, when I fell at last into a nightmare doze, feeling their hot yellow teeth in my bones.'[52]

But it was the castles that studded this wild, unpredictable landscape that were the true symbols of the age. In the Cid's time castles were *castella*, that is, fortified houses belonging to a king or a lord. Since the ninth century these fortresses, made first of local timber and then of quarried stone, were built on high ground so that an enemy could be seen approaching a day's march away to give the garrison time to prepare.[53] In rocky Castile they were often built on steep escarpments or rugged promontories, making the taking of them difficult. Laurie Lee slept in one of the many ruins that still dot the Castilian countryside: 'One night I took shelter in a ruined castle which I found piled on top of a crag – a gaunt, roofless fortress tufted with the nests of ravens and scattered with abandoned fires . . . I slept well enough in the tottering place, in spite of its audible darkness, the rustling in the walls, the squeaks and twitters, and the sighing of the mountain wind.'[54]

The earliest castles seem to have been built north of the Pyrenees in the Loire valley, at Doué-la-Fontaine and Langeais respectively. Before the end of the first millennium Doué had a stone keep and over the next fifty years, up to the time of Rodrigo Diaz's birth, outer earthwork defences completed the usual pattern of the motte (mound) and bailey (courtyard) type which the Normans imported into England in 1066. Similar castles were appearing in Italy, the Low Countries and central France, but there is no definitive record of them in Spain. It was not the Muslim invasion of 711 and its aftermath that led to extensive Spanish castle-building, but the bloody, internecine nature of Christian war and Christian politics. As historian Jim Bradbury points out: 'Castles have more to do with internal social struggle in the west than with defence against external invasion.'[55]

The Cid himself spent much of his military life laying siege to castles and the winning of them constituted a formidable rise in status. And it was a rather pious hope, perhaps, expressed by a character in the poem about Barbastro not far from Barcelona: 'No one should die in a castle or a city, but in hard battle against the infidel. This is how I want it to be for all time.'[56]

And for a time, this was how it was.

3

Al-Andalus

This country through which they first rode was Andalucia, the smiling, soft, orange-spiced southland. In the north, the brown soil would already have baked hard and almost grassless; but here the earth was green and gold where it was not splashed gaudy with flaming prismatic colours. Wild on the hills blazed hedges of geranium and clumps of pink and purple hepatica and flowers and trees as graceful or sharp or lovely as their names – tawny oleaster and crimson oleander, eucalyptus, wide beds of sea-blue iris and star-scatterings of asphodel, great crimson bloodstains of poppies, raw-white acacia . . .[1]

It is easy to be romantic about the Muslim-occupied south of Spain and to accept too rigidly the geographical, racial and intellectual differences from the north. It smacks of the apocryphal and allegorized tale from the Third Crusade of 1189[2] when the Christian leader, Richard the Lionheart,[3] smashed an anvil with his broadsword (almost certainly made in Spain, incidentally!) while his enemy Salah-ed-Din[4] slit open a floating silk handkerchief with his razor-sharp scimitar. Much of what we know about Moorish Spain – al-Andalus – relates, inevitably, to its rulers and their circles. Of the everyday people, our glimpses are few. But that is the nature of all history – the wealthiest, the most important are well documented; everyone else lives in obscurity.

Some 120 years ago the English historian and archaeologist Stanley Lane-Poole described the Muslim invasion of Spain: 'In 711, learning that Roderick[5] was busy in the north of his dominions, where there was a rising of the Basques, Musa[6] despatched one of his generals, the Moor Tarik,[7] with 7,000 troops, most of whom were also Moors, to make another raid upon Andalusia.'[8] But we need to go back to the Arabia of the sixth and seventh centuries to understand how all this came about. About 570 in the Christian calendar, a son was born to a merchant of the Quaraysh tribe, who were the hereditary guardians of the holy shrine of Mecca. The boy was called Mohammed and he followed in his father's profession, marrying the rich widow Khadija in the process. By 610 the merchant had undergone a spiritual conversion and his insistence that Allah, the one true god, had ordered the idols of the Mecca shrine to be destroyed and wealth redistributed among the poor, won him so many self-interested enemies that he was forced to leave his native town – the *Hejira* or flight – and take refuge with friends and supporters in nearby Yathrib, renamed Medina, the city of the prophet. From 623 Mohammed waged holy war – *jihad* – against the Meccans and by the time of his death nine years later all Arabia had gone over to him.

The word Islam means literally 'surrender to God's will', and that will can only be carried out by the faithful – Muslims. Crucial to its observance were the five so-called pillars of Islam – an unquestioning belief in Allah and Mohammed, his prophet; praying five times a day facing the holy city of Mecca; fasting during the month of Ramadan; going on pilgrimage to Mecca at least once in a lifetime; and the paying of *zakat* – alms and taxes.

Later centuries would see a head-to-head clash between Islam and Christendom in the period known as the crusades, but in essence this clash was avoidable. To Muslims, both Christians and Jews were 'the people of the Book' and their faiths were to be respected. The prophets of the Old Testament, most notably Moses, were revered by all three sects. Christians had an unquestioning belief in God and his son Jesus Christ and they were obliged to give to charity. Any number of religious shrines were springing up all over the known world – in Jerusalem itself, of course, but also, nearer to home for the Spaniards, at the tomb of St James at Compostela. And like death, no Christian could for ever evade taxes.

It was the sheer speed of the Muslim advance that astonished and terrified Christians and Jews alike. Under successive caliphs (the official title of the successors of the prophet) one-third of the Old

World fell under largely Arab influence. After a shaky start the aristocratic Ummayad[9] clan spread Mohammed's word north-west into Syria and north-east into Persia before moving due west across North Africa to the Straits of Gibraltar. Large numbers of different ethnic groups were swallowed up by Islam, but there is little evidence of wholesale conversion at sword-point. There is one clue to the success and astonishing rapidity of the Muslim advance – conquered peoples were invited to see the light of Islam for themselves and to accept it. Many thousands did, but there was normally respect and tolerance for those who did not. Tribal divisions and loyalties within Islam, however, remained and caused doctrinal differences, as in the Sunni[10] and Shi'ite[11] schism that still exists today.

The first tentative raids into southern Spain began shortly after the year 700. Islam was only two generations old and there was an urgency and fierceness about these warriors for which the Christian Visigoths were clearly ill-prepared. There was always a sense that southern Spain was more cultured than the barbaric north and its first well-documented inhabitants, called by the Greeks Tartessos, were accomplished miners, metalsmiths and sailors, trading across the Mediterranean a thousand years before Christ. Solomon's ships, the Bible tells us, 'went to Tarshish [Tartessos] with the servants of Hiram; once every three years came the ships of Tarshish bringing gold and silver, ivory and apes[12] and peacocks'.[13]

Seven hundred years later the Carthaginians extended their North African empire into southern Spain, which brought them into open conflict with equally emergent Rome and, as we have seen, the peninsula became a frequent battleground for the rivalries of various would-be emperors and dictators. One of the most famous reminders of Roman Spain is the Puente Romano, the Roman bridge that crosses the Guadalquivir at Cordoba. The Roman writer Livy would have had no problem, had he lived to see it, in explaining the relative ease with which the Visigoths streamed into southern Spain – the Andalusians, he said, were 'omnium hispanorum maxime imbelles' (of all the Spaniards, the least warlike).[14] We have noted already the powerful Visigothic kings like Wamba and Sisebut, but they were in the minority. Between 414 and the Muslim invasion of 711 there were thirty-three ruling kings, only nineteen of whom died natural deaths. There was an instability about Visigothic Spain which perhaps made it ripe for conquest.

The last of these kings was Roderic of Baetica, the province that would become Seville. Elected, as was the Visigothic custom, by his nobility in 710, he is portrayed in legend and folklore as a rash young hothead doomed to have his kingdom destroyed, either by breaking open a secret room in a tower in Toledo, his capital, or by seducing the daughter of one of his nobles. The eighth-century mind perhaps had need of such stories and such symbolism. The reality was that Roderic's kingdom was under repeated attack by Muslim raiding parties and he decided to do something about it.

All sources are agreed that the invading army was some 7,000 strong, led by the ex-slave Tariq ibn-Ziyad, who set up his tents on the slopes of Mount Calpe, ever afterwards to be called Jebel al Tariq, Tariq's mountain – Gibraltar. Like the fight at Senlac Hill in Sussex, England, two and a half centuries later, both sides risked everything on a single battle. Roderic's position was somewhere near modern Algeciras and he was probably, as decorum and the tactics of the time dictated, in the centre of his formation. After what seems to have been the defection of at least a portion of his army, Roderic was defeated and killed. From there, Tariq and his overlord, Musa ibn Nusayr, swept north to Toledo and Zaragoza, slaughtering indiscriminately as they went. Although Musa was recalled to Damascus, the holy city of the Ummayad dynasty, his son Abd al-Aziz continued Islam's northward spread to the Pyrenees.

Most of what we know about the early years of the Muslim invasion suffers from the same problem we have in understanding the life of the Cid; it is the embellished work of later generations. Only two documents survive, along with a scattering of archaeological evidence, to give us a strictly contemporary flavour. The *Chronicle* of 754 is the nearest Spain has to the extraordinary Anglo-Saxon Chronicle in England. Probably written by a churchman in the vitally important Christian centre of Toledo, it pours scorn on the luckless Roderic, but avoids the all-out propaganda of later generations. The author laments: 'Who could number these disasters? Human nature could not relate the ruin of Spain, nor the quantity and degree of her sufferings, not even if every bodily member were to be turned into the tongue.'[15] And in the 1270s, when King Alfonso X of Castile-Léon commissioned a history of Spain, its author wrote of the early eighth century:

> The whole realm was empty of inhabitants, full of blood, bathed in tears and loud with war cries; a host to foreigners, alienated from its natives, abandoned by its inhabitants, widowed and bereft of its children, plunged into confusion by the barbarians, weakened by wounds, lacking all sinew and strength, comfortless and without the support of its own people. . . . The Moors dashed babies at the breast against the walls, wounded the older boys and put young men to the sword; the older men died in the battles and all were destroyed by war; the cruelty of the Moors put to shame those who deserved honour at the end of their days.[16]

Similar lamentations were made in the Cid's time by scholarly Moors, appalled by the barbarism of Christians who were winning back territories that had once been theirs, tearing down mosques and building cathedrals in their place.

What the *Chronicle* tells us is that, within eight years of Roderic's defeat, the Muslims controlled (in a more or less peaceful state) all of Spain and the territory north of the Pyrenees in the Visigothic province called Septimania. Some historians argue (rather weakly) that the speed and ease with which the Muslims conquered Spain have a great deal to do with the very fact that the Romans had left a unified state there. Once Roderic's gambit on the battlefield failed, the collapse of the entire area was inevitable, or so the argument runs. This ignores the fact that Isaiah Berlin proved long ago that historical inevitability is a hugely controversial area, and certainly the fierce independence of the northern regions such as Catalonia, Galicia and Navarre, which we have already noted, hardly fits this flabby, complacent attitude of surrender. It is perhaps for this reason that the Muslims pulled back south to a frontier along the River

Duero by the mid-ninth century; endless battles with the Basques were not worth the candle.

Today we tend to think of al-Andalus as Arab and indeed its rulers were. The rank and file of its armies, however, were Moorish, Africans from the Maghrib, the area of North Africa conquered by Islam by 670. The name *barbarii* had been applied by the Romans to anyone outside the civilizing pale of their empire. Literally, the bearded ones, it specifically referred to those with no knowledge of Greek. Why the North Africans should have retained the variant Berber is unknown, but there was no denying their alien appearance and ways. They were a nomadic, pastoral people (as, up to a point, were the northern Spaniards), fiercely proud of their tribal and family groupings. Their religion was primitive and probably animistic, with no recognizable pantheon of gods. They had no towns in the European sense, just huddles of huts in the desert oases where they sheltered from the vicious sandstorms of the Sahara. They bartered without money and fought one another for slaves, water supplies, women and cattle, just as countless tribal peoples had done for centuries. Most of them were very dark-skinned, with broad Negroid features, unlike the smaller, more sallow Arabs.[17] It was a dangerous expedient, but one that seems to have worked, for the Ummayads to employ the Moors as mercenaries, giving them an outlet for their natural warlike qualities and happily telling them that the looting of cities was perfectly in accordance with the Shariah, Muslim law.

All these men, the Arab caliphs who pitched their tents and built their breathtaking mosques in Cordoba in the years after 711 and the black-skinned warriors who fought for them, were nominally under the authority of the Ummayads in Damascus, but Damascus was a long way away and the schism that saw Islam's capital shift to Baghdad further east led to ever greater autonomy in al-Andalus. In 750 the schism threatened Spain itself. In that year the Ummayads were overthrown by the Anassids, a Shi'ite sect determined to remove all Ummayad supporters and appointees throughout the Muslim world. One of these was Abd al-Rahman (the Refugee), who fled the Maghrib to Cordoba to begin what was an astonishing rule of thirty-two years. Centuries later the Moorish chronicler Ibn-Idhari described him as 'tall, fair, one-eyed, with sunken cheeks and a mole on his forehead, and wore his hair in long ringlets'.[18]

In Muslim tradition the mole was a sign of Allah's favourite, and if the fairness of his skin was unusual, it is a pointer to the fact that later caliphs of Cordoba were often sons of European Christian princesses, taken as slaves or in marriages arranged by their fathers. His grandson Mohammed's mother, was Iniga, a daughter of the King of Navarre, and Abd al-Rahman III had blue eyes and auburn hair. He spent a fortune on cosmetics to make himself look more Moorish. It was this Abd al-Rahman who first styled himself caliph,[19] along with other grand titles such as amir al-mu'mimin (prince of believers) and al-Nasir li-dini 'llah (champion of Allah's faith). Much of what we know about Abd al-Rahman comes from the uncorroborated pen of Ahmad ibn Muhammed al-Razi, and the earliest form of his work dates from two hundred years later. Even so, allowing for the sycophancy of court historians and their natural penchant for exaggeration, the court of Cordoba was clearly something special by the tenth century, as all who saw it testified.

'The biggest city in Spain is Cordova,' wrote the traveller Ibn Hawqual about fifty years before the birth of the Cid, 'which has no equal in the Maghrib and hardly in Egypt, Syria or Mesopotamia, for the size of its population, its extent, the space occupied by its markets, the cleanliness of its streets, the architecture of its mosques, the number of its baths and caravanserais.'[20] A little of Cordoba in its heyday can still be glimpsed today in the rabbit warren of streets of the Jewish quarter, where leather-workers, jewellers, smiths, armourers, tailors, dyers and weavers once jostled elbow to elbow in the largest city by far in western Europe. 'Cordoba', wrote another traveller, 'is the Bride of Andalusia. . . . Her long line of Sultans form her crown of glory; her necklace is strung with the pearls which her poets have gathered from the ocean of language; her dress is of the banners of learning, well knit together by her men of science; and the masters of every art and industry are the hem of her garments.'[21]

Abd al-Rahman I began the Mezquita, the Great Mosque, in 784. It cost him a reputed 80,000 gold pieces, looted from all over Visigothic Spain. Its first phase was completed by his son Hisham from the spoils taken from the sacked city of Narbonne in modern France in 793. Today the mosque is a museum charging an entrance fee. Inside it was built a comparatively nasty little cathedral, a visible symbol of the *Reconquista* as it had developed by 1236, when the Christian army of Alfonso X reconquered the city. In its heyday the Great Mosque had nineteen marble arcades from east to west and thirty-one from north to south. There were twenty-one doors, all faced with polished brass, and the roof was supported by 1,293 columns, inlaid with lapis lazuli. The pulpit was carved of ivory and exotic timber, and consisted of some 36,000 panels, some encrusted with precious stones and nailed with gold. Four fountains played continuously in the cool, dark interior for the faithful to wash before prayer. At night it was lit by hundreds of brass lanterns, made from the looted bells of Christian churches, and during Ramadan a huge wax candle weighing 50lb burned day and night. Ambergris and aloes burned in the censers. And it was all to the glory of Allah.

More impressive still was the palace called Madinet al-Zahra, built by Abd al-Rahman III on the Hill of the Bride overlooking the city. Work began on this magnificent symbol of Islamic power in 936. An estimated 12,000 builders were employed on it, using 15,000 mules and 4,000 camels (the Arabs did not use wheeled transport) to carry the dressed stone, lime, bricks and gravel. Architects and craftsmen from as far away as Byzantium came to add their particular skills. Recent archaeological work has revealed that the palace was built on three levels: at the bottom was a mosque, with above it exotic gardens and finally the palace itself. This 'City of the Fairest' was designed to overawe. An estimated 13,000 male slaves worked within its walls and legendary accounts still exist of how much it cost to feed them all. The palace's female complement, including Abd al-Rahman's wives and the handmaidens of the harem, added up to a further 6,500 people. According to various eye-witnesses of the tenth century, this slave/attendant army received a daily menu of fish, roast fowl, partridges, loaves of bread and black pulses.

One such visitor was the mystic Ibn al-Arabi, who noted with astonishment the 3 miles of crimson carpet that stretched from the palace to the gates of Cordoba. A double-ranked guard of Berber soldiers lined the route, their scimitars crossed in an arc of shining steel over the heads of important guests. Ibn al-Arabi described what he saw:

> The Caliph [Abd al-Rahman] had the ground [inside] covered with brocades. At regular intervals he placed dignitaries whom [visitors] took for kings, for they were seated on splendid chairs and arrayed in brocades and silk. Each time the ambassadors saw one of these . . . they prostrated themselves before him, imagining him to be the Caliph, whereupon they were told, 'Raise up your heads! This is but a slave of his slaves.' At last they entered a courtyard strewn with sand. At the centre was the Caliph. His clothes were coarse and short – what he was wearing was not worth four dirhams. He was seated on the ground, his head bent. In front of him was the Koran, a sword and fire. 'Behold the ruler.'[22]

Like all great empires, the caliphate of Cordoba acted as a magnet for astonishing culture and learning and much of it found its expression in the appearance of the city itself. Abd al-Rahman I had sent his people all over the known world in search of exotic plants, fruits and flowers. He imported a date tree from Syria to remind him of his home. Pomegranates (which were to become one of the many heraldic symbols of Spain's golden century), followed later, as did watermelons, spinach, artichokes, aubergines, sugar cane, oranges, lemons, limes and rice. By the time of the Cid figs grown in Malaga were being exported to Baghdad, from where fig seedlings had been stolen in the first place!

For these pioneering horticultural works to succeed, irrigation was vital and the Moorish conquest provided scientists and engineers who were well up to the challenge. Using a system of water-wheels and baskets known as a noria, an idea known for centuries in Syria, the gardens of Cordoba were watered into magnificence. Along the banks of the Guadalquivir an estimated 5,000 water-wheels were in use by the end of the tenth century, creating the Garden of the Waterwheel and the Meadow of Murmuring Waters at Madinat al-Zhara. Cordoba at its height boasted more than 50,000 lavish houses (*munya*) of the aristocracy and bureaucracy, a chancery, a mint, barracks and a prison, not to mention the markets, bazaars and workshops, and it was also home to an estimated 900 public baths. Stanley Lane-Poole rather overstated the case in 1886 – 'While the medieval Christians forbade washing as a heathen custom and the monks and nuns boasted of their filthiness, inasmuch that a lady saint recorded with pride the fact that up to the age of 60 she had never washed any part of her body . . . the Moslems were careful in the most minute particulars of cleanliness and dared not approach their God until their bodies were purified'[23] – but his words were based in truth. Certainly the baths were an important feature of Cordoba's magnificence.

One of the most famous acolytes at the court of Cordoba was the Persian musician Ziryab, who, legend tells us, knew more than a thousand songs by heart and introduced to Spain a new lute with a fifth string. He would entertain the caliph for hours, and apparently had rather bizarre ways of putting would-be singers through their paces, by tying straps round their diaphragms or forcing wooden blocks into their mouths to stretch their jaws. He established himself as an arbiter of fashion, drinking from glass goblets rather than pewter, directing the court's dress sense and even using a type of toothpaste. Neither the Cid's Burgos, to the far north, nor King Alfonso's court at Léon had anything like this.

Scholarship in the Arab world was far advanced. The love poems written by Arabs at the time of the Cid were the forerunners of the troubadour tradition of western Europe and its extraordinary culmination in the 'Court of Love' of the fourteenth century.[24] Arab translators in the two centuries before Rodrigo was born were busy copying ancient Greek texts into Arabic, continuing the philosophical, architectural and above all medical traditions of the ancient world into the new. Chief among the physicians at Cordoba was Hasday ibn Shaprut, who worked on the important botanical treatises of the Greek scholar Dioscorides.[25] Not only did this man bridge the cultural and religious divide by treating the Christian king Sancho the Great of Léon for obesity, he was widely respected throughout Europe as a key figure in the Jewish community, as a patron of poets and a political adviser to the caliph himself.

Al-Hakem, Abd al-Rahman's son, though a competent ruler, was never happier than when surrounded by the estimated 400,000 volumes in his library. The catalogue for these alone ran to forty-four volumes. Al-Hakem employed a personal staff of copyists, including a female poetess called Lubna, whose sole job was to reproduce books for others. Lesser mortals in their *munya* built up more modest libraries a century before the time of the Cid.

By the tenth century Cordoba had acquired an awesome reputation for learning. The principal astronomer of his day was Maslama al-Madjriti, from the then tiny town of Madrid to the south, who wrote technical books on the astrolabe,[26] a device that would revolutionize navigation in the years to come. He also translated the geographer Ptolemy's[27] works on the planets and wrote what is probably the first mathematical treatise in the world intended for everyday commerce. But it would be wrong to assume that the enlightenment of tenth-century al-Andalus was confined to Cordoba only. The metallurgy of the Muslims revived the mines of the Roman period and the introduction of new crops and irrigation systems to water them meant a longer life and a healthier one for all the area's inhabitants. It says a great deal for the rule from Cordoba that the Muslim conquest took a bare two years to achieve, but the reconquest by Christian Spain took nearly seven hundred. Large numbers of people must have seen the advantages of living under Moorish domination, not just because of improved technology and material comforts, but also because of the relatively tolerant approach of the conquerors to manners, customs and religion. This is even apparent in architecture, where the horseshoe arch of the Visigoths was perfected by the Muslims and became the dominant feature of mosque and palace alike. Religious conversion did take place, after the first wave of terrified Christians fled north in the early eighth century, but it is difficult to quantify. Historian Richard W. Bulliet has tracked the conversion by meticulously cross-referencing the family trees compiled by Cordoban scholars in the tenth century. By plotting the change of name from Christian/Visigothic to Muslim/Moorish, he is able to chart a steady but steep curve towards Islam from the middle of the eighth century to the end of the thirteenth, when the process could be said to be complete (and by which time al-Andalus was shrinking to the kingdoms of Seville and Granada as the *Reconquista* reached its zenith). At the time of the Cid Bulliet estimates that between 70 and 80 per cent of the inhabitants of Spain were Muslim.

It would also be wrong to believe that al-Andalus was a place of peace and enlightenment between 720 and the end of the tenth century. The very fact that Abd al-Rahman III kept a huge bowl of quicksilver (mercury) in his new palace hall was testimony to his love of theatricality and his dazzling sense of interior décor, but he used it as a device to terrify potential enemies and insubordinates. At a signal from him, a slave would rock the huge bowl and the sun's rays glancing off the mercury's surface sent shafts of light whizzing around the room like lightning bolts. Not even the prophet Moses could perform miracles like this.

Abd al-Rahman crossed the Pyrenees in 732 and was trounced by Charles Martel, the Hammer, between Tours and Poitiers. Although the battle itself and the Frankish nobleman's role in it have been exaggerated, this was the last Christian–Muslim battle on French soil and it marked a check to Islamic expansion. Both Martel and Charlemagne who followed him were ranked with the Cid as Christian heroes fighting against what was seen in the later Middle Ages as a tidal wave of havoc, slaughter and invasion.

Nor was the Christian/Frankish presence to the north the only worry to befall al-Andalus. The racial tensions between the Arab overlords and the Moorish Berbers of the Maghrib boiled over in 739–40, causing a nasty situation of in-house fighting, cattle-rustling and raiding that often lapsed into total anarchy. By the year 800, when Charlemagne was crowned Emperor of the West, al-Andalus had retreated to an east–west axis parallel to but north of the River Duero, skirting Pamplona in Navarre and Barcelona on the Frankish-held Spanish March. To the south of this the *tierras desplobadas*, the disputed territories, where tensions were at their height, extended to the Duero itself in the west but climbed significantly north of Zaragoza and the Elno to the east. A century later the frontiers had begun to change significantly. In the east there was little difference, but the Christian kingdoms had fought their way to the Duero and the *tierras desplobadas* extended as far south-east as the River Tagus.

If Visigothic Spain was rendered a soft target for Muslim invasion by its very centralization, then al-Andalus fell into a similar trap for the beginnings of the *Reconquista*. In the early years the Moors were nomadic, tribal warriors constantly on the move, and many of them are likely to have been inspired by the Koran and the fundamentalism associated with *jihad*, holy war. By the years before the birth of the Cid they had become settled, urban, soft. They were content with their lot, smug that Cordoba had broken so successfully with Baghdad – to the extent that although only Christians made and sold alcohol in al-Andalus, it was widely drunk by Muslims at all levels of society. And that society, preferring a life of peace and prosperity, increasingly hired mercenaries to stem the rising tide of reconquest from the north. It was a pattern that would repeat itself in the days of Rodrigo Diaz.

There was, before the Cid's time, one last Islamic warrior-hero in Spain – Abu Amir Mohammed ibn Abi Amir al-Ma'afari, known as al-Mansur, the Victorious. An ambitious politician, al-Mansur made himself indispensable at Cordoba by becoming vizier to the caliph (the unimpressive Hisham, grandson of Abd al-Rahman III) and controlling the royal mint. In a bitter civil war against Ghalib, Hisham's ancient commander, al-Mansur earned his sobriquet 'the Victorious'. The old man died in battle at San Vincente in July 981 and his head and right hand were brought to al-Mansur on the battlefield. Until his death twenty years later al-Mansur was de facto caliph, with Hisham effectively a prisoner in his own palace at Madinat. A soldier by inclination, he led an astonishing fifty-seven campaigns against the Christian north, capturing at various times Barcelona, Coimbra, Zamora and Léon. He crowned it all in 997 by sailing in his impressive fleet to Oporto and sacking the very heart of Christian Spain, the shrine of St James at Compostela. Christian captives stumbled back by the overland route, chained together and dragging the giant doors of the cathedral and its huge bells to decorate the Great Mosque at Cordoba. Only the shrine itself remained intact: al-Mansur was only victor *bi'allah*, with God's help. He was not a barbarian.

4

The House of the Seed

At that moment a frail little thing came forth, looking almost like an aborted foetus, except that it was born at term. It looked like a most miserable being and the only reason for rejoicing was that the mother had been saved.[1]

The French monk Guibert de Nogent was a contemporary of Rodrigo Diaz, born some twenty years after the man who was to become Spain's national hero. He is here describing his own birth and it was a difficult one, because de Nogent 'turned round in [his mother's] womb, with my head upwards'. Breech births like this were always difficult and often led to the deaths of both mother and child, even if a panicky Caesarean operation was carried out.

'If it is obvious', wrote de Nogent, 'and irrefutable that one's merits cannot precede the day of one's birth, they can, nevertheless, precede the day of one's death; but if one's life is spent without doing good, then I think it makes no difference whether the day of one's birth, or death, was glorious or not.'[2]

It was not until two hundred years after the birth of the Cid that we begin to find instructions for midwives that have a modern feel to them. Arnold of Villanova, an Italian doctor, in the thirteenth-century *De Regimine Sanitatis* suggested that the mother's lying-in chamber (and baby's birthplace) should be as close to conditions in the womb as possible, with soft candlelight, blankets and quietness. If the baby was born in the daytime, the shutters of the window must be closed.

Difficult births, such as de Nogent's, could be speeded up by tying a bunch of herb agrimony to the mother's thigh to make her sneeze and expel the baby more quickly. A whole variety of incantations, some of them originally pagan, were used by midwives and mothers in labour in the eleventh century. Childbirth was exclusively a female matter and Rodrigo's father would not have been allowed into the chamber, even assuming, as is unlikely, he wanted to be there. Perhaps Rodrigo's mother wore an amulet or a birth girdle, with an eaglestone around her right leg to ward off the evil eye, both from herself and her child.

Little Rodrigo would have been taken from his mother and bathed in warm water before being wrapped in tight swaddling bands of linen. The end of the umbilical cord, once cut, would be rubbed with saliva, cumin and cicely to aid healing. Possibly, since this appears to have been a Mediterranean custom generally, Rodrigo's mouth would have been rubbed with a mixture of honey and hot water so that he would be able to speak properly in the years ahead. His ears were pressed back against his head and his arms and legs wrapped with swaddling to straighten them. Only when all this was done would little Rodrigo be placed in his mother's arms. His father would be told the joyous news and the bells of the church of Vivar would ring out their clanging message of welcome.

We do not know the exact year in which Rodrigo Diaz was born, still less the month, but historians today generally agree on 1043. In that year Edward the Atheling, son of Ethelred Unraed, was crowned King of England, George Maniaces took the famed city of Byzantium by force from Emperor Constantine IX, and the German Emperor Henry III declared a Day of Indulgence on 8 August when all his enemies were pardoned and his subjects urged to love one another in the true Christian tradition. There is no manor house in Vivar now, but Rodrigo was almost certainly born in one of these heavily fortified dwellings that had sprung up to house the nobility along the frontier line of the *tierras desplobladas*. Later generations would give the family a town house to add to the birthplace, but this seems pointless to a family not engaged in the trade of the market place.

In the various texts that we have from the medieval period on the Cid, the oldest of which is the Song of the Campeador (*Carmen*

Campi Doctoris) written in the 1080s, his lineage is referred to either in disparaging terms or defensively. So the *Poema de Mio Cid* of the fourteenth century has the villain Assur Gonzalez taunting Rodrigo with his humble origins:

> Ah, knights, whoever has seen such evil?
> Since when might we receive honour from my Cid of Vivar?
> Let him be off to the River Ubierna to dress his millstones
> And take his miller's tolls in flour, as he used to do![3]

Traditionally millers were greedy, uncouth louts – the Miller's Tale from Chaucer's fourteenth-century *Canterbury Tales* is pornographic – and Gonzalez clearly was casting a slur on Rodrigo's family. In the Song of the Campeador, the anonymous author wrote (in Latin) 'He is sprung from a more noble family, there is none older than it in Castile'[4] as though there was a need to establish the Cid's pedigree against doubters. This is not snobbery. Status in the Spanish Christian world was everything; it defined the day-to-day rituals of society and reflected God's plans for the world. The Song of the Campeador was written at a time when Rodrigo had established himself as the foremost general of his age, if not yet Lord of Valencia, and this alone had made him enemies. North of the Pyrenees three centuries later the ancient aristocratic families of France similarly looked down their noses at Bertrand du Guesclin,[5] who was busy scoring important victories against the English when they were not.

It is probably correct to place Rodrigo's family among the *hidalgos* or *caballeros*, the lesser nobility. The anonymous author of another Cid text, the *Historia Roderici* (Rodrigo's History) produces a genealogical table from Lain Calvo, a legendary ruler of ninth-century Castile. Similar genealogical nonsense was being produced by scholars and heralds throughout the Middle Ages, linking all sorts of unlikely people with King Arthur, the Romano-British leader, and even Aeneas, escaping from the destruction of Troy. The eleventh century was not a meritocracy in the remotest sense; lineage was everything and it set a precedent that lasts, in some senses, to the present day.

Rodrigo's grandfather was Lain Nuñez, a landowner of some standing in Castile, whose name appears on the royal charters of King Fernando I when Rodrigo was a small boy. His father was Diego Lainez, who had fought successfully in the internecine warfare of the 1030s, taking back estates at Ubierna, La Piedra and Urgel from Fernando's brother Garcia of Navarre.[6] We do not even know the name of Rodrigo's mother, but the likelihood is that her family was higher up the Castilian social ladder than that of Diego; perhaps his exploits in war had won her hand. Her father, Rodrigo Alvarez, after whom the future Cid was probably named, was present at the coronation of Fernando at Léon in 1038 and her uncle Niño held the castle of Amaya, north of Burgos. Between them, these brothers controlled at least six regions of Castile and that made them important to the king at a time when territorial squabbles were endemic and al-Andalus as a political entity was falling apart.

We do not know if Rodrigo's anonymous mother breast-fed him herself, but if a wet nurse was employed there were strict regulations as to how she should behave. In thirteenth-century Italy (and eleventh-century Spain was probably very similar) she would feed the baby in the early morning. Her own breakfast should avoid sharp-tasting food, salt and especially garlic. Her job was to act as a nanny to older children, repeating words to them – 'breathing on the child's tongue' – so that they picked up her vocabulary, bathing them and putting them to sleep with lullabies. When little Rodrigo was old enough to take solids, the wet nurse/nanny would chew meat into bite-sized pieces the boy could handle. Such was the relative slowness of change in domestic circles that it is likely that Rodrigo's own children were brought up in this way in their turn.

The boy's baptism would have been his first meeting with the Church, which dominated all men's lives in the medieval period. The ceremony would have been held either in the church at Vivar or in the more sumptuous surroundings of Burgos cathedral, dedicated to St Gadea. In an age that believed implicitly in original sin, it was important that 'churching' took place quickly. On the forty-first day after Rodrigo's birth, his mother underwent a cleansing ceremony to remove the impurity within her. Seven days after the birth, the little infant, accompanied by his parents, three godparents (two male and one female) and family attendants and friends, underwent the first public ceremony of his life. The priest, in alb and surplice (perhaps the Bishop of Burgos himself), placed a pinch of salt in little Rodrigo's mouth and rubbed his back and chest before immersing him fully in the cold water at the font. No doubt he cried from the rough handling and sudden shock, but now he would have a full life, safe from drowning or being eaten by the wolves of the *meseta* and, should he be taken to Jesus's bosom ahead of time, he could legitimately be buried in a church. It is unlikely that Rodrigo was an only child, although there is no record of siblings. Various followers in the later chronicle are referred to as 'cousin' and 'nephew', but these are imprecise terms often simply meaning close friend or godson. Infant mortality was, of course, a major factor in determining family size.

The education young Rodrigo received is almost a blank page, but not quite. In his 'book of the film' novelist Robert Krepps conjectures that the boy was taught by an Arab scholar in keeping with the reputation that still clung to Cordoba in the 1040s. In contrast historian Richard Fletcher agrees that he could understand and perhaps even read Arabic, but suggests that he acquired this knowledge from his time in exile as an adult in Moorish-held Zaragoza. We know that Rodrigo could read – astonishingly, we have an example of his handwriting, in the charter that begins 'Ego Ruderici . . .'. And we know from his adult life that he was conversant with the complexities of Visigothic law. A tutor would have been more likely than the existence of any school in Burgos and that tutor would almost certainly have been a Christian and a churchman.

Most of our knowledge of the training of boys of Rodrigo's class comes from a much later period. In the high Middle Ages manners, politesse, playing the lute, composing poetry, carving joints of meat and serving at tables were all considered to be the social accomplishments of a knight – Chaucer's squire, with his carefully pressed hair, is a case in point from the England of the late fourteenth century. The Cid's upbringing was probably rather rougher, but central to the training of a boy whose father and grandfather were landowners and warriors was skill at arms.

In the thirteenth century the encyclopaedist Bartholomew, an Englishman, probably spoke for the Cid's father two centuries earlier: 'when he is especially loved [a son] does not appear to be loved, because he is even more stricken by scoldings and beatings, lest he become insolent'.[7] Any number of home-made toys would have been available to the boy – balls, rattles, blocks, bones, hoops, kites, spinning tops, whistles, cymbals and drums could all have occupied his relaxation time in the house at Vivar. It is not true that children in the Cid's day were expected to behave like miniature adults. Giraldus Cambrensis, writing of his childhood in Wales fifty years before the Cid's death, tells us that he and his brothers and sisters played on the beaches, building sandcastles.[8]

From about the age of 7 Rodrigo would be expected to be an accomplished horseman. Spanish horses had already earned a Europe-wide reputation in the Cid's day; William of Normandy allegedly rode a Galician destrier at Senlac in October 1066. The destrier (from the Latin *dextrarius*, right-handed) was the warhorse *par excellence* of the Middle Ages, but it was too heavy and slow for a good battle animal. William's cavalry probably used about 3,000 of them at Senlac; they were riding uphill, but even so it took them an estimated eight hours to break through the English shield wall, partly because their lack of speed reduced momentum. For everyday use, on campaign, in battle and in the hunt, a lighter horse of about 13 or 14 hands called a genet was normally used and boys like Rodrigo almost certainly learned to ride one of these first. There is still huge controversy over the availability of Arab stock in eleventh-century Spain. The Arabs have always taken their horses seriously:

Then Allah took a handful of the South Wind and he breathed thereon, creating the horse and saying 'Thy name shall be Arabian and virtue bound into the hair of thy forelock and plunder on thy back. I have preferred thee above all beasts of burden, inasmuch as I have made thy master thy friend. I have given thee the power of flight without wings, be it in onslaught or retreat. I will set men on thy back that shall honour and praise me and sing Hallelujah to My name.'[9]

Such horses were the 'drinkers of the wind' and there may have been some pure Arabians among the estimated 12,000 horses brought across the Straits by Tariq in 711. Most of them, however, were probably Barbs (the name deriving again from the *barbarii* of the Roman period), which went on to become the nucleus of the Andalusian breed. It is probable that the Cid's famous Babieca was one of these.

Rodrigo would have learned to hunt, riding through the Cantabrian forests in search of wild boar, wolf or even bear. He would be taught to use a bow from the saddle and a spear for skewering game to the ground. He would wear his stirrup leathers long so that he could straddle his genet with nearly straight legs, standing in the stirrups to balance shield and lance. On the ground he would build his muscles by hurling ever heavier stones, leaping obstacles in gymnastics, wrestling with boys slightly older and stronger than he was and endlessly practising combat skills, first with a wooden sword, then with an iron one.

The sword was the weapon of choice of the medieval knight, and it was worn as a status symbol long after it had disappeared from the battlefield.[10] Weighing between 2lb and 3lb, the Spanish *caballero*'s sword of the eleventh century was about 3 feet long, with a broad, slightly tapering blade that was sharp on both edges. It differed little from the Viking types that had been seen all over northern Europe and the Mediterranean for nearly three hundred years. The pommel was usually walnut-shaped and the quillons (the cross-piece below the grip) straight. The sword associated with the Cid, the *Tizona* preserved in Museo del Ejército in Madrid, would seem to be of a much later pattern, dating from the last quarter of the thirteenth century.[11] Two magnificent royal swords have survived from Spain and are of the type the Cid would have carried, but even these are of later manufacture. The weapon found in the coffin of Fernando de la Cerda, a son of Alfonso X, has been dated to about 1270. The dead prince's hand has turned the bronze pommel black, but both the buckskin covering of the scabbard and the red and yellow silk cords of the hilt are still clearly visible. The sword from the tomb of Sancho IV – el Bravo – of Castile dates from the next generation and is more elaborate, the hilt decorated with three glass discs painted with the arms of Castile and Léon. The hieroglyphics on the quillons and pommel have so far defied translation, except, curiously for a king so forceful in the *Reconquista*, the word 'Allah' can be made out.

How much of these rough sports, swordplay and horsemanship Rodrigo learned at his father's elbow at Vivar and how much at the court of Prince Sancho at Léon is impossible to know. Most commentators estimate that at the age of 14 the future Campeador learned the ways of his world for real.

Fernando, King of Castile and Léon, was typical of his age. He cannot have been much older than 18 when his father, Sancho the Great of Navarre, helped himself to the county of Castile. Six years later, when the old king died, Fernando received it as his share of the kingdom. This habit of dividing territory among siblings was always problematic and sometimes fatal. It would be repeated in the Cid's generation, leading directly to the murder of Rodrigo's patron. By June 1038 when Fernando was crowned at Léon, he had defeated his brother-in-law Bermudo III of Léon at the battle of Tamaron and was lord of most of northern Spain, which he held until his death in 1065. Irritatingly the surviving sources for Fernando's reign are few. The fact that he reigned for so long when other rulers came and went in a few years, or even in as little as a few months in some cases, indicates a powerful and successful man. He assumed the title of emperor with its associations of the long-dead Charlemagne and probably exiled or executed internal opponents. He also curried support by providing loyal vassals with loot and territory – most of which came from al-Andalus.

The death of al-Mansur, the Victorious, signalled the beginning of the end for al-Andalus, at least as a coherent political unit run from Cordoba. In the previous chapter we looked at the glories of the city in the reigns of the three Abd al-Rahmans, but these men were outstanding and before them, between them and after them came many caliphs who were not. Medieval society throughout Europe and beyond was dominated above all by ruthless politicians and hard-nosed generals. Before the creation of parliaments, bureaucracy and all the panoply of the complex nation-state, the quality of the individual ruler was all. Between 1008 and 1031 a series of weak caliphs became, in effect, puppet rulers, the real power passing to rivals and contenders who did not stop at murder to achieve their goals. The career of one of these will make the point. Sulayman was a descendant of Abd al-Rahman III and he marched against the Caliph Mohammed II at Cordoba in November 1009. Interestingly in the context of the story of the Cid, with him rode Sancho Garcia, Count of Castile, and several thousand Christian troops. The world had not yet hardened into a black and white, Christian versus Muslim mindset. Mohammed abandoned Cordoba and ran north to Toledo, where he engaged the services of two more Christian warlords, the Counts of Barcelona and of Urgel. So much damage was done in the north-east of Spain that in Moorish chronicles the year 1010 is called 'the year of the Catalans'. Sulayman laid siege to Cordoba for nearly three years, with its beleaguered inhabitants suffering from plague, hideous overcrowding of terrified refugees and even, as if to confirm God's wrath against them, appalling flooding of the Guadalquivir to a depth that no man remembered. The fact that the city could hold out for so long is eloquent testimony to the defensive power of its walls and fortifications.

When the city finally fell, Hakem's magnificent library, already partly sold to buy mercenary help, was scattered all over al-Andalus and beyond. And Sulayman's Berber troops, out of control and no doubt letting off steam after such a long siege, hacked down hundreds of Cordobans cowering under market stalls and in the dark corners of mosques. One of the greatest scholars of the eleventh century, Ibn Hazan, lists sixty great men – poets, historians and mathematicians – who were butchered in those dark days. As is so often the case, the sword is, in fact, mightier than the pen.

The fall of Cordoba cannot be ranked alongside the destruction, say, of Constantinople (Byzantium) in 1453. The city and its splendours struggled on for many years. But what happened was that al-Andalus became fragmented, descending into a series of between fifty and sixty tiny states called in Arabic *taifa*, which means faction. This has been a general trend with the collapse of empires throughout time – a once great power, creaking and infirm, cracks and gives way to the petty, personal ambitions of lesser men. What we have in al-Andalus after 1031 is a series of 'colonels' revolts', where military might, thuggery, deceit and medieval *realpolitik* combined to create a dangerous climate of social Darwinism. Some of these rulers were generals, men (like Rodrigo of Vivar in the next generation) who could command armies through sheer personality and military success. Others were bureaucrats, skilled in the ways of organization. A surprising number were ex-slaves, many of them foreigners from other parts of Islam. Some were already de facto rulers of provinces, and they used the implosion at Cordoba to underline the fact.

By the time Rodrigo was born, the *taifa* states had been amalgamated and reshuffled, finding a natural level of co-existence in the form of the most powerful six. In the far south, which would remain Moorish for another five hundred years, stood Seville and Granada. Seville itself had been a cultural Cordoba in the Visigothic era, a centre of learning personified by St Isidore. In 1031 the Abbasid clan became its rulers, beginning with Abu al-Kasim Mohammed Ibn Abbad, who had been the *qadi* (a combination of judge and mayor) for several years before this. His son, Abbad al-Mutadid, was a poet and patron of the arts to rival the Abd al-Rahmans of Cordoba itself. He conquered a swathe of territory south of Seville, including Huelva, while Rodrigo was learning the rudiments of swordsmanship, and Algeciras in the year before Rodrigo was sent to the court of Prince Sancho to complete his education. By the time Rodrigo was knighted, Mutadid had taken Rond, Arcos and Moron and almost certainly ordered the suffocation of those states' rulers in his private baths while they were his guests on what was supposedly a mission of peace and goodwill.

Granada, at the foot of the majestic Sierra Nevada, had been a summer retreat for the Ummayad dynasty of Cordoba. Some of its eleventh-century buildings, though much added to and reinforced, still stand today – the Albaicin was the ruler's palace until it was eclipsed by the more famous Alhambra, today easily the most impressive Moorish palace in the world. At the time of the Cid the palace compound contained thirty mosques and was the scene of a hustling, bustling market of potters' wheels and weavers' looms. Its *aljibes*, public wells, were still in use forty years ago and the houses beyond the palace walls had walled gardens shaded with orange and eucalyptus trees. The baths, built where the River Darro disappears underground, have recently been restored to recapture some of their eleventh-century brilliance. There is no better example in all Spain to illustrate the deeply amicable relationship which existed between the Muslim and Jewish communities. Every major city had its Jews, but the name Granada is derived from Garnatha, the Visigothic word for the city of the Jews. From 1038 until his death in the year Rodrigo Diaz joined Sancho's court, the effective 'chancellor' of Granada was Samuel Ibn Naghrila. Like the Muslim rulers of many of the *taifa* states, Naghrila was a Renaissance Man, born ahead of his time. Warrior, statesman, rabbi and scholar, he also wrote poetry which has relevant echoes for the life of the Cid:

> War at first is like a young girl
> With whom every man desires to flirt
> And at the last it is an old woman;
> All who meet her feel grieved and hurt.[12]

Perhaps the Jews of Granada overreached themselves and the Muslims needed to remind them who was boss. In the same year that William of Normandy invaded England, the Muslim Abu Ishaq initiated violence against them and untold numbers were hacked to death in the city square. Pogroms like this would punctuate the history of the Jews throughout time.

In the broad central plain of Spain the dominant *taifa* states were Valencia, Toledo and Badajoz. Valencia has become forever linked with the Cid, for it was here that the Campeador died in the summer of 1099. In 1031 it was ruled by a grandson of al-Mansur, who surrounded it with what were reputedly the finest walls in al-Andalus. Toledo, as we have seen, had been an important Christian centre in the days of the Visigoths and it was to reach new heights in the thirteenth century. As one of the *taifa* states closest to the Christian north, it was always vulnerable and was a prime target for the aggrandizement of Fernando I in the days of the Cid's youth. Badajoz, which would be for ever linked with the British army under Wellington in the Peninsular War (1808–14),[13] was ruled by Sabur al-Sqlabi, an ex-slave. His tombstone still stands.

The most northerly of the *taifa* states was Zaragoza in the northeast, right on the Christian frontier. Because of this, it is likely that Christians in the province were better treated here than they were further south. Most of the evidence on this point is that by and large in the tenth and eleventh centuries Muslim and Christian ignored each other and certainly made no real attempt to understand each other's faiths or outlook. This live-and-let-live attitude is in stark contrast to the crusading centuries that followed the Cid, which makes it more difficult for us to understand the man himself. Zaragoza was known as al-Baida, the white city, for its gleaming mosques and walls. It was here that the Virgin appeared to St James seven years after the crucifixion of Christ and a church was built on the site. The *al-jaferia* was the Moorish palace built to the west of the old town. Today it is the parliament building, but it still contains the horseshoe-arched courtyard of the Arab architects and a prayer niche that points towards Mecca.

When Rodrigo Diaz rode to Léon to the palace of Sancho, the prince's father Fernando was busy making himself rich and powerful by means of the *paria* system. A number of historians have tried to make the past more accessible to modern readers by making shaky parallels. Richard Fletcher's casual translation of El Cid as 'the Boss' is a case in point. So is his explanation of *parias* as 'protection racket'. Equating medieval kings with gangsters and mafia godfathers of the twentieth century has its attractions, but it is not accurate.[14] Such a tribute system was certainly hard-headed but it was an example of *realpolitik* and in any case was not new. In early eleventh-century England Aethelred II was paying a fortune to Swein

Forkbeard and his son Cnut, the Viking invaders, to go away. This was the infamous Danegeld and it signally failed in its purpose as the Vikings stayed.

In Spain Fernando's demand for tribute was met with gratitude by the rulers of Zaragoza, Badajoz and Valencia because they could ill afford protracted warfare with the Christian north. Such behaviour today is viewed as appeasement and is taken to be a sign of weakness, but in the uneasy eleventh century it was a perfectly workable system. Fernando easily doubled the contents of his coffers and the legendary wealth of the man encouraged adventurers of all shapes and sizes to come to Spain to try their luck. Typical of frontier states throughout history, Fernando's Castile offered untold riches to men with the ambition and guts to grab what they could. Such a man was Rodrigo of Vivar.

'Do not claw at your head or back', advised a fifteenth-century expert to young squires, 'as if you were after a flea. Retch not, nor spit too far, nor laugh nor speak too loud. Beware of making faces or scowling; and be no liar with your mouth. Do not lick your lips or dribble . . . do not lick a dish with your tongue to get at the last crumbs.'[15] Similar advice may well have been given to the 14-year-old boy from Vivar, who would be expected to crawl along walls and mind his manners while learning all he could of the ways of the court.

Unfortunately our knowledge of Fernando I's court comes to us from one of the most corrupted texts of the period. It is called the *Historia Silense*, which on first reading suggests it was written in the monastery of Silos in Castile. Various scholars have doubted this, however. Like many documents from the eleventh century, the *Historia* has only come down to us from the late fifteenth century and there may be who knows how many versions between that and the original. In Chapter 7, the anonymous author wrote: 'I, then, submitted my neck to the yoke of Christ from the very flower of youth and received the monastic habit at the monastery called Domus Seminis.'[16] 'Domus Seminis' means literally the house of the seed. Silos has been equated with this because of a note in the margin of the text at that point. But the note was probably added about 1500, so it must be conjecture. It is tedious to argue the pros and cons, but it is likely that 'seminis' in the original was probably written *sci ihris* – 'of St John' – which would place it in the monastery of the same name in Léon, at the heart of Fernando's kingdom. The monastery had been founded in 966, as a house for monks and nuns, by Sancho I. It was badly damaged by the raids of al-Mansur but restored under Alfonso V, whose daughter Sancha married Fernando of Castile.

If the likelihood is that the *Historia* was written in Léon, then it is set in the city where Rodrigo of Vivar arrived in about 1057. Various throwaway lines in the chronicle make it clear that the work was written between 1109 and 1118, in other words only a few years after the death of the Cid and perhaps immediately after the death of his on-and-off patron, Alfonso VI. The early chapters are a rambling attempt at the history of Spain, but there appear to be later (sometimes irrelevant) inserts and much 'lifting' of phrases from the Bible and classical authors like Sallust.[17] The prejudice of the Catholic Christian north is evident throughout: 'But then, over-whelmed by the strength of the barbarians, study and teaching died away.'[18] The Muslims ('barbarians') would, of course, have argued the opposite – that not until they arrived in 712 did study and teaching really begin!

Ironically, the purpose of the *Historia* was to chronicle the life of Alfonso, 'the orthodox emperor of Spain',[19] as 'his more noble deeds seem worthy to be remembered'.[20] I say ironically because either this was never carried out or the text has not survived. A 'biography' of Alfonso, even in the biased and corrupted style of the medieval chroniclers, would have been hugely revealing about the life of Rodrigo Diaz.

Fernando and Sancha were probably married in 1032, but because of the corruption of the text in the *Historia* it is not until Chapter 81 that we learn of the births of their children. Sancho was the eldest and a daughter, Elvira, followed. Alfonso was next and the last son was Garcia. Then 'the parents bore Urraca, a girl of the utmost nobility in comeliness and behaviour, before they attained the fullness of the kingdom'.[21] The chronicler singles out this daughter because she was a lavish patroness of the monastery of St John – indeed, a silver-gilt cup known as the Chalice of Doña Urraca is preserved there to this day. If 'the fullness of the kingdom' refers to the year of Fernando's coronation, 1038, then Sancha had borne five children who survived (and perhaps carried others who did not) in six years. This was her duty. She was a daughter of the *Reconquista* and Léon-Castile needed kings in those troubled times. There was also little alternative. The only known form of contraception was coitus interruptus and the aptly named mother church frowned on that. The children's education would have echoed that of Rodrigo, born perhaps five years after Urraca, but the *Historia* is infuriatingly vague about what form it took: 'that, first, they should be instructed in the liberal disciplines to which he himself had given study'.[22] The next stage is clearer: 'he had his sons learn to ride after the manner of the Spaniards, to practise the use of weapons and to hunt'.[23]

Spanish techniques in riding were to become famous in the centuries ahead, with the seventeenth century producing the caracole and other dressage techniques, culminating in the Spanish riding school at Vienna dating from the days of the Holy Roman Empire. It may be that a rudimentary form of this already existed in Fernando's day or it might simply mean in the Christian style, as opposed to the 'barbarian' variant in al-Andalus. Mail-clad knights rode, as we have seen, with their stirrup-leathers long. The Moors, with shorter stirrup-leathers, rode as today, with the knee bent. Elvira and Urraca 'lest [they] should languish in idleness, he ordered them to be taught every womanly skill'.[24]

The next chapters of the *Historia Silense* deal with Fernando's strained relations with his younger brother Garcia, King of Navarre. The chronicler spares no blushes on this internecine period, although the implication is that Garcia was in the wrong, being consumed with envy, whereas Fernando 'showed himself in all things mild and devout'.[25] Matters came to a head on 15 September 1054 'in the middle of the valley of Atapuerca, when King Fernando's troops took possession by night of the hillside which rose above'.[26] Atapuerca, with its ancient caves, is only 12 miles to the east of Burgos, a day's march from Vivar, where the 11-year-old Rodrigo was beginning his long training for the wars that would shape his life. Did his father, perhaps, ride down that valley, stirrup to stirrup with his lord Fernando? A body of knights, determined to avenge the death of Bermudo III, their lord and master, charged, hacking their way through the enemy centre, making for Garcia's banners: 'They fell upon King Garcia, transfixed him and hurled his lifeless body from his horse onto the ground.'[27] The large Moorish contingent with the Navarrese tried to run (again, the Christian prejudice) but most of them were taken prisoner. Then, says the *Historia*, 'King Garcia's body was taken for burial to the church of Santa Maria de Najera, which he himself had devoutly raised from its foundations and had splendidly embellished with silver and gold and silken textiles.'[28] With his back secure, Fernando turned to the lure of the south, ordaining 'that the remaining time be given over to campaigning against the barbarians and strengthening the churches of Christ'.[29] We must remember that when the *Historia* was written, Jerusalem had fallen in the First Crusade and the East versus West conflict had assumed a harder polarization. Its author sees nothing wrong with portraying the Muslims in al-Andalus as 'belching forth profanities'.

We have no information about Sancho's involvement in his father's wars, but it was certain he was central to them. As the eldest son, the prince would inherit the lion's share of his father's territories, though not all, because of Alfonso and Garcia. Sancho would have been about 16 when his father won at Atapuerca, old enough to command a division.[30] Two years later he would have been old enough to 'live of his own', with his own household and retainers in what was effectively an off-shoot of his father's court. Whether this was a physically separate building from the royal palace in Léon we do not know. It may simply have been a wing of Fernando's apartments. Either way it was here that Rodrigo of Vivar arrived about 1057. He would have made his way through the wild, high *meseta* of Castile, crossing imperceptibly into Léon, always with the snow-capped Cordillera Cantabrica to his right, following the pilgrims' road to Compostela.

As the crow flies the distance is about 90 miles. If young Rodrigo rode by mule or pony, with at least one attendant from his father's home in Vivar, he could have travelled the entire distance in three days. Perhaps on the first night he sought sanctuary in the Benedictine monastery of San Zoilo on the bridge at Carrion de los Condes. Later legends of the Cid, particularly the *Poema*, have his daughters marrying the counts of this region. He may have reached the red-brick churches of Sahagun by the second night. There was no Franciscan monastery of La Peregrina then, but San Tuiso with its horseshoe arches of the Mozarabic style may already have been standing. Beds, food and wine were not difficult to obtain on the pilgrims' road.[31] In the Cid's time the town was much larger than today and was still called after its saint, Sanctus Facundus. Perhaps Rodrigo rode over the field 'where, it is said, in olden times the splendid lances which the victorious warriors thrust into the ground in the Glory of God's holy name, sprouted leaves again'.[32]

Then Rodrigo came to Léon. Was he riding Babieca? Great heroes have great horses. They have names and an undying heroism of their own. Alexander had Bucephalus, Charlemagne rode Tencendur. But Babieca means 'idiot' or 'booby', which is so homely that the story may just be true. Later Cid legends from the fifteenth century have Rodrigo, still 'of tender years', begging a colt from his godfather, Peyre Pringos. The man knew his horseflesh and was appalled at the boy's lack of knowledge, shouting 'Babieca!' at him. And the name stuck. If Babieca was an Andalusian destrier, he would have grown from the scrawny colt Rodrigo chose into a powerful warhorse perhaps 16 hands high. Most of the Cid stories refer to Babieca as a stallion and the assumption is that he was white – all heroes ride white horses! Many of the animals shown on the Bayeux tapestry woven in England about 1070 show obviously male horses, but they may be geldings, castrated as foals to make them more reliable in battle and on campaign. It is even more likely that Babieca was actually a mare, as these were considered the most reliable of all in the terrifying atmosphere of a battlefield. If the story of Rodrigo's acquisition of Babieca as a boy is true and the date of the horse's death is accurate, the animal would have been 50 years old when it died.

For the next six years Rodrigo of Vivar would finish his knightly training, riding at a canter against the quintain, an upright post with outstretched arms that swung on a pivot when the shield buckled to the left arm was struck. Ride too slowly and the iron mace in the right hand spun to catch the rider in the back. Ride too fast and there was a serious chance of missing the shield altogether; a live opponent would not make the same mistake. He would have used his broadsword to hack at the pel, a wooden stake that stood in for an armed enemy. And he would endlessly have practised, from the rising to the setting of the sun, with Prince Sancho, nine years his senior or perhaps with a master swordsman the prince had selected for the purpose. No one alive today knows how tiring this must have been. When Charlton Heston, one of the most athletic and physically tough of Hollywood actors, faced such an expert, he found it exhausting: 'Enzo's[33] record as an Olympic fencer and his experience training actors for make-believe combats was awesome. He was a quiet man of modest demeanour, but with the legs of a leopard and a forged steel wrist. Parrying his sword thrust was like deflecting a train.'[34] But, unlike Heston, the real Cid's make-believe combats were intended for one thing – survival on the battlefield. He was probably only 19 when he experienced real combat for the first time.

5

Song of the Campeador

The year 1063 was a remarkable one in the affairs of Léon, Asturias and Castile. It saw the 'translation' of a man who was already a saint and it saw the birth of a legend. Kings like Fernando were anxious to hold and extend their realms here on earth, but their eyes increasingly turned to heaven as they grew older. Not only had Fernando let Queen Sancha talk him into building a sumptuous tomb for themselves in Léon rather than the traditional burial-place for the Kings of Castile at the church of San Pedro at Arlanza, south of Burgos, but he sent an embassy under the aged Bishop Alvito of Léon to collect the bones of 'the most blessed virgin'[1] St Justa from Seville, where she was martyred for her Christian beliefs in 287.

To our modern, cynical minds it seems as if Fernando was buying his place in paradise by doing this, but we have to accept that belief in a heaven somewhere above the clouds was a very real concept to medieval man, as was the paradoxical belief in a horrific, fire-scorched hell far below the earth. The removal (translation) of a saint's body not only found favour with God, but blessed the city, church or monastery that newly housed the remains. Conversely, of course, the city, church or monastery that 'lost' their saint believed itself cursed. In the event, the Moorish amir of Seville, Ibn Abbad, whom the *Historia Silense* calls Banhabet, could not find the woman's tomb. No doubt a great deal of Islamic building had gone on in the half millennium that separated St Justa from Fernando. While Bishop Alvito spent three days trying to decide what to do, God showed him the way in a vision. An old man appeared to him, saying 'I am Isidore, Doctor of the Spains and bishop of this very city',[2] and he offered his remains instead. 'When it was uncovered,' the chronicler of the *Historia Silense* wrote, 'so powerful a fragrance

61

was emitted that it drenched the hairs of the head and beard of all who stood by as if with a rinse of nectar or the dew of balsam. The blessed body was enclosed in a wooden coffin made of juniper.'³ A week later, Bishop Alvito was dead.

All this fits a familiar medieval pattern and we are not obliged to believe a word of it. The 'odour of sanctity' which clung to saints for years or centuries after their deaths was widely accepted as evidence of their holiness and of God's power. Alvito expected to die as St Isidore of the vision had told him he would. The Bishop of Léon was an old man. We can attribute his death on 3 September 1063 to worldly ill-health, perhaps contracted from the germs probably present in Isidore's tomb, or perhaps from the strain of crossing most of Spain in a scorching August to make difficult demands from a powerful Muslim ruler.

When the funeral procession returned to Léon, Fernando had Isidore's remains, draped in a silk brocade placed there by Ibn Abbad, reburied on 21 December 1063 with all solemnity in the church of St John, which was duly renamed Basilica de San Isidoro. The saint's bones lie there still.

'On that festive occasion', wrote the author of the *Historia Silense*, 'the most glorious king is said to have been assiduous in humility, with such great devotedness out of reverence for the holy bishop, that when the time came for the feast he laid aside his royal pride, and, in the place of the servants, with his own hands served the elaborate dishes to some of these men of religion. Queen Sancha also, with her sons and daughters, humbly waited upon the remainder of the company. . . .'⁴

Among them must have been Rodrigo of Vivar. And it is not stretching credulity too far to posit the theory that this may have been the occasion of Rodrigo's knighthood.

In the previous spring Fernando's remaining brother, Ramiro of Aragon, had gone to war with al-Muqtadir, the amir of Zaragoza, perhaps with a view to winning over the whole *taifa* state and wrenching it, in effect, from Fernando and Castile. The first phase of Ramiro's operation was the capture of the town of Graus, north of Lake Embalse de Barasona and about 30 miles south of the French border.

Fernando sent his eldest son Sancho to get it back. Technically the prince was responding to a call for aid from al-Muqtadir, but in reality he was looking out for his own. Sancho was probably 28 that year, a king-in-waiting, and he acquitted himself well in the battle that was fought below the town on 8 May. It was the future Cid's first battle but we know very little about it. One of the Cid sources, the *Historia Roderici*, says merely 'When King [*sic*] Sancho went to Zaragoza and fought with the Aragonese king Ramiro at Graus, whom he defeated and killed there, he took Rodrigo Diaz with him; Rodrigo was a part of the army which fought in the victorious battle.'[5] We are given no details of the battle. Much of the warfare in eleventh-century Spain, indeed in the *Reconquista* generally, was based on manoeuvre and siege. Pitched battles were rare but were fought essentially on the Roman plan, with a central body of footsoldiers (spearmen and slingers) and a screen of archers to the front. The flanks were protected by cavalry.

The *Historia Roderici* from which the above quotation is taken is something of a first. Most medieval chroniclers wrote about saints or kings, but Rodrigo Diaz was not quite either, despite attempts by others to make him both. To judge by a highly critical comment on the Cid's attack on the Rioja in 1092, it seems likely that the anonymous author came from there, or perhaps had family or friends who did. Scholars are divided – when are scholars not? – over the date of publication. Comments in the text give us the wide parameters of 1102 to 1238 (years in which the Cid's Valencia was in the hands of the Muslims), but the weight of probability is that the *Historia Roderici* was written before about 1150, the expert Richard Fletcher throwing his cap into the ring with a conjectural date of before 1125. Such decisions are important, because the further away from Rodrigo Diaz the book was in time, the greater was the temptation of the author(s) to embellish and invent. This book needs to find the Cid as he was, as well as the Cid as he came to be.

I believe that Sancho made Rodrigo a knight for his services at Graus. Men did not have to fight battles to receive the accolade, but it was often a precursor. Edward, the Black Prince, a 16-year-old boy and heir to the throne of England, 'won his spurs' after his impressive command of a wing of the English army at Crecy in

1346.[6] And, in an example much closer to Rodrigo, so too did Harold Godwinson. In 1064, according to the Bayeux Tapestry and other sources, Harold, the heir to the English throne, found himself shipwrecked on the Normandy coast. As the 'guest' of Duke William, the Saxon accompanied his host on a raid into Ponthieu, a nearby province. For his prowess there – Harold is shown in the tapestry apparently saving men from drowning – William made him a knight. The needlework quite clearly shows William placing a helmet on Harold's head, and the likelihood is that a lance with a fluttering cloth pennant was part of this bestowal of arms too. The scene is often cited to prove that knighthood in this sense did not yet exist in England and that the Normans introduced it in 1066.

Perhaps Rodrigo underwent a similar ceremony on the battlefield at Graus, although Sancho was, after all, only a prince at this stage. What could be more natural than that Rodrigo's dubbing be made formally by the king himself, and when better than at Christmas after the translation of St Isidore's bones? By the thirteenth century the ceremony of knighthood was very elaborate. The squire was washed by servants to purify his body and dressed in robes of red and white (as it happened, the colours of Castile). He then knelt before an altar to keep vigil for ten hours, praying for strength to guide him to the right. On the altar before him lay his sword and shield. At dawn a Mass was sung and the squire was presented to his lord by two sponsors who vouched for him. In Rodrigo's case, if this was carried out in the basilica soon to be renamed San Isidoro, the sponsors may well have been Sancho and his younger brother Alfonso, who were both older than Rodrigo, and the lord, of course, was Fernando himself. Attendants buckled on the sword-belt and slung the shield's baldric (retaining strap) over the squire's shoulder. The idea of the sword blade touching the new knight's shoulder was a much later modification and it is likely that in 1063 Fernando lightly struck the acolyte's cheek with the flat of his hand or even with the blade of his sword. From then on, if any other man struck him, it was the knight's duty to return the compliment – a concept that was curiously at odds with Christ's teaching in the New Testament. This was one blow the new knight could never return.

Rodrigo would have knelt and sworn homage and fealty to Fernando, his liege lord, and to Sancho, whose man he was.[7] He was now Don Rodrigo, but he had yet to become the Campeador.

Two years after Rodrigo Diaz received his knighthood, there was an event of a kind that would plague Spain for years: the death of a king and the division of his kingdom. According to the *Historia Silense*, which is the fullest version we have of the reign of Fernando, the king was raiding as far south-east as Valencia on the coast when he became ill. The campaigning season throughout the whole of the Middle Ages was May to September, the hottest months of the year in Mediterranean Spain, and a foraging army could expect to fall prey to any number of diseases as an occupational hazard. Not only that, but Fernando was nearly 50, a good age for a man who, almost by definition, lived on his nerves. His men carried him back, probably on a litter, to Léon, where he lingered until shortly after Christmas 1065.

The *Historia Silense* gives us a sad farewell to the old man. He still had the strength, on Christmas Eve, to kneel in the crypt of St Isidore in the Basilica, and he joined the monks in their Mozarabic version of the Christmas services, in the 'Toledan manner' that would disappear for ever in 1080. 'Advenit nobis,' intoned the bishop and the clergy, and the dying king replied 'Endemini omnes qui indicates terram'[8] – 'Let him come to us' and 'Be instructed, you judges of the earth' – from the Psalms. Fernando then took communion, 'the body and blood of Christ',[9] before being led to his bed.

The following day he assembled his clergy and they carried him to the church 'clad in his royal apparel with his crown upon his head'.[10] Kneeling before the bones of Isidore and other saints he had brought to Léon, he offered up his last prayer: 'Behold, I render back to thee the kingdom which I received as thy gift and which I have ruled for as long as it freely pleased thy will. Only, I pray, receive my soul in peace, snatched from the whirlpool of this world.'[11]

It is unlikely that these were his exact words, but we should not doubt his sincerity. Heaven and hell were physically real places and kings had no more right of entry to heaven than other men. Like all military commanders in the 'whirlpool of the world', Fernando had the blood of the innocent on his hands. He took off his velvet cloak, placed the gem-encrusted crown of Léon and Castile on the stones and lay sobbing on the ground, begging God for forgiveness. His bishops placed him in a state of penance, hauling a rough hair-shirt, crawling with lice, over his scarred old body, and they scattered ashes over his head. So he lingered for two more days, slipping deeper into a coma until on 'Tuesday, at the sixth hour of the day on which the feast of St John the Evangelist is celebrated [27 December], he rendered his soul to heaven between the hands of his bishops'.[12] He was buried in the tomb that Queen Sancha had insisted upon, years before, on 2 January 1066.[13]

'He lived in peace and reigned for 18 years,' wrote Bishop Pelayo of Oviedo. He was wrong on both counts, but then Pelayo is known today as el Fabulador, the fantasist, and much of his *Chronicon Regum Legionensum* (Chronicle of the Kings of Léon) is pure fabrication. He was writing in the 1120s, when the Cid had been dead for two decades and the world had moved on. Most of Pelayo's concern is with the see of Oviedo and puffing up its importance. Of politics and war he knew or cared little. Even so, his summation of the ordering of Fernando's kingdom after his death is sound enough:

he gave Sancho all of Castile as far as the River Pisuerga, Najera and Pamplona, with all the royal rights pertaining to them; he gave Alfonso Léon as far as the River Pisuerga and all the Asturias de Trasmeira as far as the River Eo, Astorga, Campos, Zamora, Campo de Toro and the Bierzo as far as the town of La Uz on Monte Cebrero; he gave Garcia all of Galicia, together with the whole of Portugal.[14]

The royal sons also inherited the *parias* that went with Fernando's demesnes. Sancho gained the tribute from Zaragoza, Alfonso that from Toledo and Garcia that from Badajoz. The decision seems foolhardy in the extreme, especially bearing in mind that Fernando had spent a great deal of time, effort and money subduing his own brothers throughout his reign. The *Historia Silense*, always more forthcoming than the *Chronicon*, sheds more light on this struggle for superiority: 'Although while yet alive their father had divided the kingdom equally among them, nevertheless for eight entire years they waged internecine war without result.'[15] Determined to avoid similar warfare among his own sons, Fernando had made this momentous decision years earlier and it was ratified at a great council he called at Léon early in 1064, when 'he chose to partition his kingdom among his sons in order that after his death they might – should this be possible – live at peace among themselves'.[16]

Primogeniture – the seniority of the firstborn – was not yet fully established anywhere in Europe. In England, the German states and most of northern Europe there was even an electoral element about kingship. The author of the *Historia Silense* tells us that Alfonso was the old king's favourite and that 'upon his daughters [Elvira and Urraca] he bestowed all the monasteries of his whole kingdom, in which they might live to their lives' end without the bond of a husband'.[17]

This was a sort of fail-safe idea. To give territory with castles and frontiers to daughters was asking for trouble in the eleventh century. There were redoubtable women at this time – Cnut's wife Emma Aelfgifu for instance – but they survived (if they did) because they played a man's game and obtained male support if at all possible. If Elvira and Urraca were to marry, their husbands would have claims to their territory and the very trouble Fernando wanted to avoid would have become more likely. Royal daughters often ended their days, if not as actual brides of Christ, at least as honoured guests in a nunnery.

Despite Fernando's efforts, civil war broke out after his death and Rodrigo of Vivar was obliged to take sides. Unlike the wise gravitas which later chroniclers invented and which Charlton Heston brought to the role in the film of *El Cid*, where he is depicted as a mentor to the squabbling boys, already clashing daggers over the barely cold body of their father, the real Rodrigo was younger than all the royal brothers and probably still at this stage had fought only one campaign. Moreover, he was Sancho's man and, however distasteful he found it, it was his duty to ride at Sancho's side.

If we take the three major accounts of the late 1060s together, the *Historia Silense*, the *Historia Roderici* and the *Chronicon*, we can piece together most of what was happening. The first reported clash came at

Llantadilla on 19 July 1068. Since we know Fernando was buried in January 1066, that means some eighteen months had passed before there was any serious fighting. We can rule out the treacherous winter months, however, when snow lay thick on the Cordillera Cantabrica and the Spanish days were short. The delay might also be explained by the fact that the boys' mother, Queen Sancha, did not die until 7 November 1067, when she was buried alongside her much-missed husband. Perhaps once she was gone, the gloves were really off.

Rodrigo would certainly have fought at Llantadilla, perhaps his second battle, but again we have no details about it except that Sancho won and Alfonso went back to Léon with nothing permanent achieved. A battle like this was not fought as part of an ongoing campaign, with enemy armies hunting one another down in alien territory. Sancho's envoys would have agreed a time and a place with Alfonso's and, for whatever reason, Llantadilla was chosen.

The next clash of arms was at Golpejera, 30 miles west of the Pisuerga river. Unusually, this battle was fought in January 1072, a rare winter campaign for which there is no explanation. Some three and a half years had passed since Llantadilla; perhaps there were other skirmishes and posturings between the royal brothers that the chroniclers were unaware of, although in the meantime a kind of truce had been set up. With the treachery so typical of feuding royals in the Middle Ages,[18] Sancho and Alfonso buried the hatchet for long enough to turn on their little brother Garcia, and they defeated him in May 1071. Garcia's Galicia was to be divided between the victors, but this proved impossible and chaos ensued in north-west Spain. Garcia went into exile in Seville, far to the south, where it was safe.

At Golpejera Alfonso lost the battle and was captured and taken in chains to Burgos. Sancho was now effectively master of Léon as well as Castile, and he had done exactly what his father had done back in the old days at Atapuerta by defeating his brother Garcia. Two things resulted: Sancho staged a coronation ceremony in Léon on 12 January 1073, the symbolism of which was crucial, and Alfonso went into exile in Toledo. Rodrigo would have been at Sancho's side during the ceremony; perhaps, as we shall see, he was the first knight to swear fealty to his king.

Pelayo's phrase in the *Chronicon* may be more than just a figure of speech: 'Then King Sancho seized the kingdom of his brother King Alfonso and crowned himself in Léon.'[19] The days of self-made rulers dispensing with religious support lay far in the future. When Napoleon Bonaparte became Emperor of the French in 1804, he famously placed the laurel crown on his own head, even though the pope was in attendance. No eleventh-century king would carry out such a gesture – he would have feared his God too much. It is possible, however, that Pedro, Bishop of Léon, refused to perform the task out of loyalty to Alfonso and that Sancho had to find some other priest who was more obliging.

The deposed king was accepted without a qualm by the amir of Toledo, who doubtless had his own agenda. A Christian king as his 'guest' was worth a great deal, either as a military ally or as a potential source of ransom. And since the man to whom the yearly tribute was paid was now in no position to demand it, the amir may have hoped for a financial respite, at least until Sancho came knocking. The *Historia Silense* calls him Halmemon; Pelayo uses Alimemone. He was in fact al-Ma'mun, and he had been ruling in Toledo since 1044.

The fact that two of the three Christian kings of northern Spain could take up residence so easily in different *taifa* states speaks volumes for the complexity of relationships in the country as a whole in the eleventh century. The author of the *Historia Silense* saw all this, at least on Alfonso's part, as a cunning ruse to spy in Toledo, but this assumes that Alfonso in 1072 knew he was going to attack the city in 1085. What is more interesting is that 'he was hugely esteemed by those very same Saracens [Muslims] as a great king'.[20]

None of the chroniclers is very clear as to exactly what going into exile meant. Later in his career Rodrigo the Cid was forced into exile twice by Alfonso. Here, it seems to mean seeking asylum rather than actual banishment at the command of the king. Later generations, including our own, have a different take on exile. To the earlier Vikings it was literally a punishment worse than death, since their homeland was so sacred to them. Spain in the Cid's time enjoyed a flexibility of relationships between Christian and Muslim which would become unthinkable even a generation later. This has led to a serious miscalculation of the kind of man Rodrigo Diaz really was.

But what of Rodrigo in these years? The *Historia Silense* and the *Chronicon* do not mention him at all, but the *Historia Roderici* fills in some details: 'King Sancho valued Rodrigo Diaz so highly, with great esteem and affection, that he made him commander of his whole military following.'[21] Some historians today doubt that the future Cid was given so much power. Why, they argue, would Sancho risk so much on a younger man who had, at most, fought two battles? There are many, much later, parallels. Napoleon Bonaparte was given command of the French Army of Italy in 1796 when he had no experience of leading a campaign. William Pitt (more or less Rodrigo's age at the time) was made Prime Minister of England purely on the strength of his dead father's reputation. The answer to Rodrigo's status depends on what the chroniclers do *not* tell us, and most of them concede they do not know all Rodrigo's exploits. It also depends on what Rodrigo actually *did* in those battles. If his advice yielded positive results, if an attack delivered by him drove the enemy from the field, then why should Sancho not put his army in the man's hands?

From 1065 Rodrigo's fortunes rose. First, Sancho was now a king and thus the status of his followers would have risen automatically. From documents we know that Rodrigo was not just muscle for the new king; he witnessed a number of royal charters up to the time of Sancho's death, proving his worth as a supporter of the king in a civil and legal context. But it was as a military authority that Rodrigo excelled. He became in fact *armiger* to the king. Such a post is notoriously difficult to define, if only because nothing like it exists today. It means literally 'armour-bearer' and on ceremonial occasions that was exactly what Rodrigo did, standing at Sancho's elbow with his helmet, sword and shield, especially on parade days when the king needed to impress. The role was extended in a much more dangerous manner on the battlefield: 'In every battle which King Sancho fought with King Alfonso,' wrote the author of the *Historia Roderici*, 'at Llatada [*sic*] and Golpejera . . . Rodrigo bore the king's royal standard and distinguished himself among all the warriors of the king's army and bettered himself thereby.'[22]

For centuries it had been regarded as the highest honour for men to carry a king's personal standard in battle. The standard itself was sacred, blessed by priests before it was taken to war. At Senlac in southern England two years before Rodrigo fought at Llantadilla, William's Norman army took comfort from the fact that the pope's banner, the gonfalon, fluttered at their head. It was as though God Himself rode with them. Today the colours of the British army, faded and riddled with shot from long-forgotten battlefields, still hang in English churches.

The job of standard-bearer was notoriously difficult and dangerous. The flag was not a weapon, so Rodrigo would have found it difficult to defend himself in the crush. It was also a target. Formal heraldry, with brightly painted shields and embroidered horse-bards, had not yet made an appearance on European battle-fields, but by definition a standard could be seen from hundreds of yards away. When Richard III of England was trying to find Henry Tudor on the slope of Ambion Hill at Bosworth in 1485, he recognized him by his red dragon standard. Its bearer, William Brandon, was hacked to death as the king thundered past him.

But the role was much more than just a flag carrier. Rodrigo would have been expected to advise Sancho, almost in the role of a modern staff officer, on what line to take against any potential enemy. He may, for instance, have selected Llantadilla and Golpejera as suitable battlegrounds. Both were about a day's ride from Burgos and Rodrigo may have known the ground well, realizing its advantages to Sancho's troops. He was also responsible for recruiting the army, paying the mercenaries that the king employed and using any amount of diplomacy to keep them out of trouble. He would check and select horseflesh, something in which he was clearly an expert, and he would put soldiers and knights alike through their paces in readiness for the field. There is no post today that covers all this. But there was at the time and it is contained in the earliest references we have to the Cid – the Song of the Campeador (*Carmen Campi Doctoris*).

The phrase literally means 'field trainer' and military writers like Vegetius[23] had used it in the fourth century, long before the Cid's time; however, the term had since fallen into disuse and no one has satisfactorily explained why it reappeared in the *Carmen* and is always attributed to the Cid. The poem, in fairly rough Latin, exists in a seventeenth-century copy, but we know there was an earlier version copied at the monastic library at Ripoll in Catalonia about 1200. The poem itself was never finished and we have no idea who wrote it, although the author had clearly read both the Bible and Latin poets like Virgil.[24] It is likely that the Song of the Campeador was written soon after 1082, as it ends in mid-verse before the battle of Almenar was joined and there is no mention of what was probably Rodrigo's greatest exploit, the taking of Valencia.

> Gesta bellorum possumus referre,
> Paris et Pyrri necnon et Eneane,
> Multi poete plurima in laude
> Que conscripsere.

So reads the first verse, extolling the ancient heroes written about by many poets. Paris was the Trojan prince in Greek and Roman mythology who kidnapped Helen, the wife of Menelaus of Sparta; Priam was his father. Aeneas was another Trojan hero, who, unlike the others, survived and went on, according to legend, to found Rome. Given these classical allusions, we must ask who wrote the *Carmen* and at what audience it was aimed. At first sight, the answer is likely to be a monk. But the copying at Ripoll could be a colossal red herring. Most medieval chronicles compiled by churchmen have an obvious bias – they refer to ecclesiastical events and church people or they offer a moral lecture. There is only one direct reference in the *Carmen* to God and it occurs in the unfinished last line: 'tunc deprecatur . . .' – 'then, he prays . . .'.

In answering the second question, we may find our answer to the first. Verse V says:

> Village people, listen to this poem of the Campeador.
> Especially those who have fought with him; come here![25]

This is a doubly fascinating verse, because if the audience were a crowd of villagers, then the writer was not likely to be a churchman. It also means that the history of the poem is likely to be accurate because it was being presented to men who knew the facts, soldiers who had ridden with the Campeador. Thus our poet, who was writing about Rodrigo Diaz in his own lifetime, is likely to have been a troubadour.

We have already discussed the general *gesta*, epic poems, the most famous of which is the Chanson de Roland. The *Carmen Campi Doctoris* is another in the same genre. It is at once entertainment and living history for a society that was only partially literate. The singer was literally that and the *Carmen* would have been recited to a repetitive melody line, perhaps one or two phrases, to the accompaniment of lyre, lute or harp. The troubadour, trouvere or jongleur was a travelling minstrel, working for money and usually performing at a royal court, perhaps that of Sancho or Alfonso, the brothers who were successive Kings of Castile and Léon. Unfortunately for us, the troubadours, although they recited verses that were well known (like the 'greatest hits' of rock singers today), were also expected to ad lib depending on the circumstances of their performance. The claim in Verse V, however, makes it seem that most of what followed was factually correct in the way that the later Cid chronicles certainly were not.

A possible crossover link between the monastery of Ripoll and the violently secular theme of the *Carmen* exists in the *goliards* or travelling scholars, usually students who had taken minor orders in the church but nevertheless sang songs of love, war and drinking. The earliest of these dates from the ninth century.

The *Carmen* agrees broadly with the *Historia Roderici*, which is the most detailed early account of the life of the Cid. Rodrigo's first battle, Verse VII tells us, took place when he was very young – 'cum adolescens' – against a knight of Navarre. The *Historia Roderici* refers to such an encounter and it is clearly a single duel, though whether as part of a skirmish, battle or campaign is unclear. It was because of this, the *Carmen* contends, that Rodrigo was called the Campeador by those in power. With a degree of hindsight, Verse VIII says:

> That first battle,
> was a forecast of what else he would overcome,
>   As he fights against Counts with his swords and gains
>   more power.

We will return to the *Carmen* later, to set it alongside other commentaries, but in essence it is our most important text because it is clearly contemporary and open to the scrutiny of the men who knew the Cid; it is even written in the present tense, giving it a sense of urgency and current affairs. One fascinating possibility exists about its author. The Homeric references of the first verse tell us that he was a cultured man and he clearly knew his politics, the double-dealing of the court of Alfonso VI. There is a curious tradition in the early Middle Ages of a titled singer-poet. William IX, Duke of Aquitaine, was a contemporary of Rodrigo Diaz and eleven songs of his written in the langue d'oc of the south of France still survive. Years later, another such was Bernard de Ventadour, a minor nobleman at the court of Eleanor of Aquitaine, the mother of the crusader king, Richard the Lionheart. Thibaut of Champagne, who became King of Navarre, was the composer of some seventy-six songs.

The exact sequence of events for Rodrigo in the 1060s is vague. If the *Carmen* is right about the duel with the Navarrese champion, then this may be a different fight that is not alluded to in the *Historia Roderici*. On the other hand, the *Historia* tells us, '*Afterwards* [my italics] he fought with Jimeno Garcés, one of the most distinguished men of Pamplona and defeated him.'[26] The 'afterwards' refers not only to the battles of Llantadilla and Golpejera, but to Sancho's siege of Zamora, which did not happen until 1072, by which time the Cid was hardly 'adolescens' but nearly 30 years old. I believe the *Carmen* is likely to be right here. Rodrigo's elders would surely only have hailed him champion if he had dazzled them in single combat. The brilliant scene in the Heston film, though wrong in so many ways historically, catches at least Rodrigo's inexperience at this point. Perhaps it was 1063 or 1064 and he had only recently received his accolade. He was untried, a risk, but he not only delivered, but delivered handsomely.

The tournament of the type we associate with medieval chivalry had yet to develop. Properly speaking, the tournament was actually a contest involving many men, either singly or in the free-for-all mêlée version developed by the fourteenth century. Single combat was the joust, though we have no way of knowing whether

Rodrigo's duels were fought on horseback or on foot. Certainly the tilt, where two men rode towards each other at the gallop, with only a barricade between them, belongs to a much later period. It is likely that when Rodrigo fought Jimeno Garcés, both men advanced on foot. We have no accurate way of knowing what sort of armour they wore, because the battle-gear of northern Spain was influenced by both the Norman-Frankish styles from beyond the Pyrenees and the Arab technology of al-Andalus to the south.

In the 1060s it is likely that duels like this were fought in armour very like that portrayed on the Bayeux Tapestry. Not only did the Normans invade England successfully, they also took Sicily and their influence in Godfrey de Bouillon's First Crusade, as the Cid lay dying, was enormous. Over a shirt of linen Rodrigo and his opponent would have worn the hauberk, a knee-length mail tunic with three-quarter sleeves, which weighed about 30lb. It was slit at front and back for ease of riding. Documentary evidence from the eleventh century talks of 'double' and 'triple' mail, but this, if taken literally, would make the hauberk impossibly heavy. More likely, the terms refer to the size of the iron links or to the riveting method. Hauberks were expensive and much prized, some, like swords and horses, even earning names. A contemporary of Rodrigo Diaz, Harald Hardrada of Norway, who was killed at Stamford Bridge near York in September 1066, had a hauberk called Emma! A few of the Norman knights on the Bayeux Tapestry wear mail leggings too, but this seems to have been reserved for the leaders only – William himself and his half-brother Robert, as well as Bishop Odo of Bayeux.

Rodrigo's head would have been protected by a coif or hood of mail worn over an arming cap of leather. The great helm with the crest of Castile used in the film of *El Cid* dates from the late thirteenth century. In the 1060s the iron headpiece was crucial to deflect sword-blows, with a nasal that extended to cover the tip of the nose. This is the type of helmet described in the *Carmen*, though its elaboration and ornament date it to the 1080s. Verse XXX reads:

> He also puts on his helmet.
> It has silver lines

– probably damascened in the Moorish style.[27] The face seems to have been curiously exposed, hence the invention of the great helm in the next century.

For foot combat, Rodrigo would have chosen a light circular shield of a type that was common in al-Andalus. It was easier to use than the kite-shaped Norman variant, which was essentially a horseman's defence to protect the left leg while in the stirrup.

We have talked about Rodrigo's sword before. The Tizona as it exists today is a thirteenth-century creation, and the Colada a version of a sixteenth-century German or English broadsword. In the duels of the 1060s Rodrigo's weapon of choice would have been a cruciform-hilted, double-edged sword, about 3 feet long and perhaps weighing 3lb.

No fighting manuals have survived from this period. By the fifteenth century such books were being printed on the new presses, especially in Italy and France where two different styles of fencing were developing. In the 1060s Rodrigo and Jimeno Garcés would simply have stood toe to toe and hacked at each other, blocking blows with sword and shield until one of them found an opening. Garcés was lucky: Rodrigo seems to have spared his life. In the other duel recorded in the *Historia Roderici* his opponent did not fare so well: 'He fought with equal success against a Saracen [Moor] at Medinaceli, whom he not only defeated but also killed.'[28] Medinaceli is described in the *Historia Roderici* as a great city, and it was also the scene of the death of al-Mansur on 11 August 1002. The anonymous author was convinced that 'Almanzor was snatched away by the Devil (who had taken possession of him during his lifetime) . . . and buried in Hell.'[29]

This is Rodrigo's first clash with the Muslim world but it almost certainly happened in the reign of Alfonso and a defining moment in the Cid's life had to happen first. The ever-succinct Pelayo sums it up for us in the *Chronicon*: '[Sancho] was a very handsome man and a valiant soldier. He travelled throughout the Asturias, Galicia and Portugal. He reigned for six years and was killed by treachery by a soldier named Vellito Ariulfo outside the walls of Zamora which he had besieged.'[30] The *Carmen* is infuriatingly vague about the death of Sancho; proof, if it were needed, that this work was meant to be performed in public and was subject to the medieval equivalent of the slander laws. Verse X translates:

> Rodrigo did not accept the power
> That Sancho was willing to give him,
> But Sancho died unexpectedly.

The city of Zamora had been in the thick of fighting for centuries, having been consecutively a Celtic, a Carthaginian and a Roman settlement. Its place on the northern frontier of al-Andalus ensured that it became a trysting-place in the *Reconquista* too. There is still a local saying, 'A Zamora, no se ganó en una hora' (Zamora wasn't taken in an hour). It stands on the rocky banks above the Duero at the edge of the *tierras desplobladas* and its castle and much of the old city walls are still preserved. It boasts twelve Romanesque churches, some of which would have been standing when Sancho laid siege to the place.

We do not know why the king was there in the late summer and early autumn of 1072, but there are many possibilities. The Zamorans may have revolted against him; such revolts were frequent in all states throughout the Middle Ages. The city was in Leonese hands and lay only a day's march from Portugal, which until the previous year had been Sancho's brother Garcia's demesne. The Muslim *taifa* states of Badajoz and Toledo must have known about the squabbles among the royal brothers and may have inspired a revolt to take advantage of the fact. Equally likely is that Alfonso was behind whatever was going on. It is possible that he was present there, but even if he was not he could still have directed operations from his exile in Toledo. The only time we see Sancho take the field in person is when he is fighting against a fellow king – Alfonso (twice) and Garcia. A later, twelfth-century, source credits the king's sister Urraca with involvement too. Decidedly feistier than Elvira, Urraca may well have owned ecclesiastical estates near Zamora. Medieval law was never going to let her be queen in her own right, but she may have played one brother off against the other in a deadly extension of some never-forgotten nursery feud. The implication in the Heston film that Urraca and Alfonso had some sort of incestuous relationship seems to have no basis in fact. The nearest we come is the *Historia Silense*, whose author is clearly pro-Urraca. After Sancho's death, Alfonso went to Zamora, perhaps to pray at the site of his brother's murder[31] and Urraca joined him there. 'This Urraca,' says the *Silense*, 'indeed had loved Alfonso from childhood more than the other brothers with the warmest sisterly love; and since she was the elder, she chose for herself and took on the place of a mother.'[32]

Alfonso's man in Zamora was Pedro Ansurez, a senior official at the king's court, who had been created count by 1071. He would become a friend of Rodrigo's in the years ahead, but his role in what happened to Sancho is unknown.

Bizarrely the *Historia Roderici* glosses over Sancho's death, merely reminding us that the king 'maintained [Rodrigo] and loved him well'.[33] Everybody else was talking about murder, including the anonymous author of the *Historia Silense*:

> Meanwhile, King Sancho assembled an army and laid siege to Zamora. . . . The Zamorans, however, remained unmoved by this development. Fortified by the assistance of King Alfonso . . . the Zamorans despatched a knight of great courage and killed King Sancho by treachery while he was besieging them.[34]

Immediately we are in the curiously twilight world of the medieval chronicler. Surely a knight of great courage would have challenged Sancho to mortal combat, man to man (and almost certainly would have faced Rodrigo instead), and not resorted to treachery. Perhaps, though, the assassin Ariulfo had seen the Campeador in action under Zamora's walls and so chose the more furtive option. The *Historia Roderici* tells us 'it happened that Rodrigo Diaz fought alone with fifteen enemy soldiers; seven of them were in mail; one of these he killed, two he wounded and unhorsed and the remainder he put to flight by his spirited courage.'[35] Historian Richard Fletcher, as anxious to play down the future Cid's heroism as Menendez Pidal was to play it up, believes this to be a typical war story, embellished with each retelling. To me it is highly plausible. The chronicler does not say Rodrigo killed all fifteen of his opponents and he even hints that some of them were not very well armed. Certainly something spectacular must have led men to call him the Campeador. In the event, Ariulfo played the assassin: 'The king was transfixed with a spear by him, unexpectedly, from behind and shed his life together with his blood.'[36]

The Castilian army seems to have fallen apart when the news spread through the camp like wildfire. It was 7 October 1072 and the campaigning season should already have ended. According to the author of the *Historia Silense*, the soldiers panicked and fled, leaving most of their possessions behind. This is certainly odd, but we must remember that wars were fought at the behest of kings; the soldiers were only camped outside Zamora because Sancho had ordered it. Now he was gone, there was little point in carrying on. Even so, 'a squadron of the bravest knights of Castile, mindful of their birth and of their deeds of old under arms, carried off the lifeless body of their lord with such honours as they could'.[37] Foremost among them would have been the Campeador, Sancho's right-hand man. In the Heston film, Rodrigo arrives just too late to save Sancho's life in a cowardly night attack, but he pins the killer to Zamora's city walls with his sword and we all sit easier in our cinema seats as justice is done. In reality, we have no idea what happened to Ariulfo; none of the chronicles mentions him again.

'They laid [Sancho] in his tomb with the trappings of a royal funeral, with great honour as was fitting, at the monastery of Ona.'[38] It was here that Count Sancho of Castile had built the monastery and nunnery that were designed to be the burial-place of all rulers of Castile until Fernando chose to be buried in the Basilica of San Isidoro in Léon, at his wife's suggestion. Unlike his father, who had weeks to put his house in order and time to say goodbye to his family, Sancho died quickly, perhaps alone in the dark, unshriven. Priests said Masses for his soul, and men grieved in the face of an uncertain future. Sancho was dead. Garcia was in exile far to the south. Urraca and Elvira could not inherit. That left Alfonso, Fernando's and Urraca's favourite, in his exile in Toledo.

The king was dead; long live the king.

6

The Story of Rodrigo

One of the most striking scenes in the Heston *El Cid* depicts a windswept town square outside the church of St Gadea in Burgos. The new king, Alfonso VI by the grace of God, is publicly swearing to the assembled townsfolk that he had no hand in the murder of his brother Sancho. All kneel and pay him homage accordingly. All, that is, except one – Rodrigo Diaz of Vivar, the late king's champion. The Cid forces the issue, pinning Alfonso's hand down on an open Bible and making him swear again. Only then does Rodrigo kneel to kiss the king's hand and the petulant Alfonso, furious, snatches it away and exiles the man.

The exile certainly happened, but the events in Burgos are fictional, deriving from a thirteenth-century legend. We could leave it there, except that the Cid's most famous biographer, Ramon Menendez Pidal, believed the story in the 1920s, when he wrote what many still regard as the definitive biography. Indeed, he seems to have accepted the tale as fact.

The historical record tells a different story, however. The reality of Spanish politics at the time meant that Alfonso was the only practical successor to Sancho and he wasted no time in getting to his throne. Only six weeks after Sancho's death Alfonso was issuing charters in Léon. And on 8 December 1072, almost exactly two months after his brother's murder, Alfonso was granting land to the monastery of Cardena, near Burgos. This was the monastery of San Pedro (St Peter), which would loom large in the story of the Cid in the years and centuries ahead. A Benedictine foundation established in 899, it was a natural watering place on the pilgrims' road to Compostela but quite early in its existence it had become a scene of slaughter when two hundred monks were beheaded in a Moorish raid. There are still people who come to Cardena to witness the statue of the Virgin shedding tears in memory of those who died. The important point here is that one of the charter's signatories was Rodrigo Diaz. Where, in those eight short weeks, was there time for the head-to-head confrontation between Rodrigo and his king, for exile and for reconciliation? It clearly never happened. The author of the *Historia Roderici* was probably more accurate: 'After the death of his lord King Sancho, King Alfonso received him with honour as his vassal and kept him in his entourage with very respectful affection.'[1]

These were triumphant but difficult days for Alfonso. He was a king in his own right, but essentially of Léon, not of Castile, and whispers of his involvement in Sancho's murder must have taken months, possibly years, to die down. In the meantime he had to deal not only with Sancho's loyal followers – like Rodrigo – but also with the potential ongoing rivalry of his remaining brother Garcia. The Menendez Pidal image of the Cid, borrowed heavily from the later legends, shows a man of deep honour whose loyalty, once given, was absolute and unshakeable. The real Rodrigo Diaz was far more complicated and far more flesh-and-blood than that. He swore fealty to Alfonso because he knew, like all eleventh-century Europeans, that a powerful patron was a meal-ticket for life. Alfonso, on the other hand, needed men like Rodrigo Diaz. His brother's campeador had defeated him twice and Alfonso's ambitions would require generals of such ability. Perhaps it was with Rodrigo's help that he resolved the problem of Garcia, even as a test to check the man's loyalty.

Pelayo in his *Chronicon* implies that all this happened quickly: 'After a few days [of regaining his own throne and taking Sancho's] [Alfonso] resolved to seize the kingdom of his brother Garcia and by a cunning trick King Garcia was captured without a fight and was kept in chains for twenty years or more.'[2]

The chronicles do not help us with the whirlwind events of those weeks. We last heard of Garcia exiled to Seville in 1071, but Seville was nine or ten days' journey from Léon. Had he returned to Galicia after Sancho's death to reclaim his throne, assuming he could sweet-talk Alfonso or beat him in battle? It all depends on the speed of communication – and in the Middle Ages that came down to hard men riding fast horses. Were there men who backed Garcia because he was, after all, their rightful king? Or did they realize that their futures actually lay with Alfonso?

Whether Rodrigo was involved in the arrest of Garcia we do not know, but we do have evidence of what he was doing. In April 1073 he was hearing a law-suit over grazing rights between the monastery of Cardena – there it is again – and local farmers in the Orbaneja valley nearby, both sites a stone's throw from Burgos and adjacent in terms of territory. Such disputes were the stuff of medieval local government. A world away from the clash of arms, vestigial chivalry and the rumblings of crusade, life went on, as petty, selfish and small-minded as it usually is. Rodrigo represented the Church on this occasion, along with Ciprian, the governor of Burgos, and won the case. He must therefore have been conversant with the law, which was essentially still Visigothic,[3] and was no doubt fluent in Latin, the language of the courts.

Early in 1075 he was in the Asturias on Alfonso's business. All medieval kings were peripatetic, travelling with large and noisy entourages from castle to castle, bestowing largesse, putting down the odd revolt and settling legal disputes. But they could not be everywhere and when the need arose trusted nobles were sent in their stead where appropriate. In England Henry II formalized all this by establishing his *justicii in iter*, travelling judges with a fixed circuit to hear cases in the king's absence. This time, Rodrigo's case was about inheritance. Count Gondemar Piniolez had left the monastery of Tol, near the River Eo, to his daughter Gnutroda (the odd Visigothic name was still in use at this time) during her lifetime. She died in February and the monastery should have reverted to the Church, namely into the hands of the Bishop of Oviedo. The dead count's great-nephews contested this, however. Monasteries were rich prizes, with an income from sheep, fish and vines, not to mention any largesse a passing king or wealthy pilgrim might bestow. For the hearing Rodrigo was part of a four-man panel; the others were Tuxmaris (who seems to have been a legal expert); Bernard, Bishop of Palencia; and Sismondo Davidez, who held estates at Corimba. Rodrigo's role, as the only non-local, was clearly to speak for Alfonso. Again the result went Rodrigo's way.

In fact Alfonso was probably on his way to Oviedo while the Cid sat in judgment. On Friday 13 March a mysterious chest was opened there and it is almost certain that Rodrigo was present at the time, having ridden across the open country at the behest of his king. The chest was one of several relics belonging to the cathedral of San Salvador, housed in the *Camara Santa*, the Room of the Saints. As we have seen, this sacred shrine held many of the precious objects rescued from the Moorish conquest of Toledo three centuries earlier. Legend has it that an earlier Bishop of Oviedo had tried to open the chest, but had been blinded by the brilliance of the light that flooded out from under the lid. There seems to have been no such problem in March 1075 and the chest was found to contain fragments of the cross on which Christ was crucified, a crust of bread from the Last Supper, the blood of Christ and the milk of Mary, as well as bits and pieces of assorted less prestigious and more local saints. No one in the awestruck entourage would have doubted the genuineness of these objects, and it is part of the fascinating legacy of the past that men like Alfonso and Rodrigo could kneel in wonder at this organized charlatanry on the part of the Church, yet think nothing of destroying towns and villages of Muslims and fellow Christians alike.

The contents of the chest were duly written down, signed by Rodrigo as a witness, and reburied in a beautiful silver casket that is still on display in the cathedral. It was perhaps later that year or in the following year that 'the king gave [Rodrigo] one of his relatives to wife, the lady Jimena, daughter of Count Diego of Oviedo. She bore him sons and daughters.'[4]

Astonishingly, their marriage contract, known as a *carta de arras*, has survived. It is a sort of eleventh-century 'pre-nup' and implies that the Cid's wedding was a financial arrangement as well as a dynastic alliance, as so many marriages of couples of this social status were. It tells us nothing of course about the nature of the relationship, where and how the pair met or even anything concrete about Jimena. Later legends, which became enshrined in the Heston film, have a tortuous love–hate relationship between them. Rodrigo kills Jimena's father,

Count Gomez de Gormaz, in a duel of honour. Jimena is obliged to avenge her father's death even though she is betrothed to Rodrigo. For a third of the film, she wears black in mourning for her father and wills death and destruction on her lover. Because the king (Fernando) wishes it, she even reluctantly goes through a marriage ceremony with Rodrigo, although clearly 'bed' is out of the question.

Since none of this is based on fact, it remains unhelpful. There is no historical record of a Count Gomez de Gormaz nor of a Count Diego of Oviedo, and the efforts of Menendez Pidal to establish Count Gondemar Piniolez of Tol as Jimena's grandfather is stretching the flimsy, dubious records we have to breaking point. It is likely that Jimena came from Asturias and that Alfonso arranged the marriage. If she was indeed related to the king, then it meant that Rodrigo's marriage would further elevate him, perhaps as his own father's marriage had done in the previous generation, and indicated that Alfonso trusted the man implicitly. The *arras* tells us that Rodrigo gave various scattered estates to Jimena 'according to Leonese custom', or in other words up to half his possessions. These were hers for life, even if, as actually happened, she outlived him. We know from the *arras* that he owned estates at Grajera and Yudego, and that his friends who witnessed the document were Pedro Ansurez, who had been on the other side of the wall from Rodrigo when he laid siege to Zamora, and Garcia Ordoñez, who by 1075 was *armiger* to Alfonso, the pivotal role that Rodrigo had held under Sancho. The king himself, his sisters Elvira and Urraca and a number of courtiers also put their seals or signatures to the vellum. Oddly, the *arras* has the wrong date, but this is almost certainly a case of careless copying. 'July 1074' may actually be 'May 1076'.

If the latter date is correct, Rodrigo would have been 33 and at the pinnacle of his success, though not yet of his fame. How old Jimena was we do not know. The usual age of consent throughout Europe in the Middle Ages was 14 for a boy and 12 for a girl. We believe that Jimena died in 1116, but we do not know the cause of her death, so that does not help us either. Since she bore Rodrigo two daughters and a son who survived (and perhaps others who did not) it is reasonable to assume that she was considerably his junior, perhaps in her late teens when they married. This was certainly the assumption by the time the fifteenth-century legends appeared.

We have no information that is at all reliable about the marriage of Jimena and Rodrigo. The neo-contemporary chroniclers whose works we have used so far were writing in a genre known as *chansons de geste*, the *geste* meaning deeds or actions. Building churches, endowing monasteries, fighting battles, besieging castles – this was the stuff of the *geste*, not the trivia of daily domestic life. After the Cid's wedding he disappears for a time, in the words of James Fitzmaurice-Kelly 'into the dense obscurity of domestic bliss'.[5]

We know that the Cid owned many estates. He had no doubt been richly rewarded by Sancho in his role as Campeador and Alfonso seems to have continued the favours. It is likely, however, that the Cid's principal home would have been his father's castle in Vivar. We have no idea when Diego Lainez died, but it is a strong probability that he had by the 1070s. We have no idea either of the size of Rodrigo's household, but it would have been overseen by a chamberlain or seneschal, precursor to the roles of butler and bailiff in nineteenth-century aristocratic houses. An anonymous English manuscript of the Cid's time explains the man's duties: 'the seneschal of lands ought to be prudent and faithful and profitable, and he ought to know the law of the realm to protect his lord's business'.[6] Below him came the chancellor, often a priest who looked after the daily services and handled most of the paperwork. The bailiff oversaw the running of the estate, ensuring that the flocks and herds were tended, the ploughing done properly and the vines watered and pruned. In the yards at Vivar blacksmiths hammered Rodrigo's iron, farriers shod his horses, bakers baked his bread, vintners stored his wines and perhaps his cider, and cooks prepared his food. He would have had a regular garrison, men who had served with him at Graus, at Llantadilla and Golpejera. Almost certainly they were commanded by Alvar Fanez Minaya, described variously as Rodrigo's friend, cousin or nephew. The later chroniclers refer to him as the Cid's *diestro braco*, his right arm, although whether he was with him to the end at Valencia is unlikely. Perhaps he had with him another nephew, Felez Muñoz, and his own *armiger*, the standard-bearer

Pedro Bermudez. These are the names of the Campeador's company in the most famous of his legends, the Poem of the Cid. A man whose fortunes wavered as much as the Cid's would have had a fluctuating following. Such was his commanding personality, however, that it is likely that a loyal cohort of men stayed faithful to him, even in exile. The size of the entourage, no doubt exaggerated by the later chroniclers to seven thousand, would depend on practicalities – the size of Rodrigo's castle at Vivar, for instance, and his ability to feed them all.

Rodrigo rose with the dawn, along with the entire household. A drum or horn would be the early morning alarm call. Lying-in was for pregnant women and most of a lord's work could be done before midday. Jimena and Rodrigo slept naked – nearly all the medieval artwork depicting couples in bed shows this – and attendants would be on hand to wash them both. The water was cold, scented with oils and flower petals, and they used soap from Castile, the finest soap in all Europe, it was said, made with olive oil. Then they were dressed.

In terms of historical costume, the Cid's lifetime falls within the Romanesque period. What we think of as medieval costume is mostly shaped by films and especially by Hollywood. The problem is that the medieval period lasted for half a millennium and change, though at a slower pace than today, was constant. Wool and linen were the usual materials, although in Spain, with al-Andalus a few miles to the south, it would be unusual if the ex-Campeador and his wife did not wear silk as well. Rodrigo probably dressed himself, with undergarments of wool and perhaps, though it was still a rarity, a shirt. Over that would come a calf-length tunic, em-broidered at the cuffs and hem, probably with three-quarter length sleeves. His hose, described by much later chroniclers as black and white, fitted like modern stockings and his shoes and boots were made of local leather, or perhaps came from Cordoba to the south.[7]

Jimena's dress was of a much older style and had changed little in shape from that of the late Roman empire. An undergarment made of linen reached the ground and had long, narrow sleeves. An outer garment was looser fitting and the sleeves ended at the elbow. As a married woman and a Catholic, she would be expected to wear a headdress or veil in public and her hair would be tied in a simple, single plait or allowed to flow loose over her shoulders. It was in the 1080s that tailors' guilds began to appear in parts of Europe and such was the trade with the East that all sorts of exotic fabrics, including damask and cloth-of-gold, may have been available to the couple. Lists of booty acquired by the Cid and his contemporaries often refer to valuable materials and rich hangings. Spanish dress differed from that in the rest of Europe by its passion for horizontal stripes woven into various garments.[8]

Rodrigo and Jimena would then have prayed, either in their bedroom or in the castle chapel, lying face down on the rushes on the floor with their arms outstretched. Not for another century would the now-familiar kneeling position be adopted. On saints' days (and there were many of these in medieval Spain) the couple probably attended a full-blown Mass, again either in the castle or in the church at Vivar, or perhaps even in the great church of St Gadea at Burgos.

The first meal of the day comprised bread and meat and a goblet or two of wine. Then it was down to business. The lord of several estates had a great deal to organize and Rodrigo's seneschal and bailiff would spend hours each week closeted with him discussing all the issues that concerned them – the harvest, the floods, the snow, the frozen ground, the drought. No one, not even a legend in the making, could escape the weather for long.

The midday meal, universally referred to as dinner throughout Europe, was the largest of the day. Rodrigo and Jimena were expected to eat this in the public setting of the great hall. If guests were arriving, this was the meal they came for. A horn would 'sound the water' and they would assemble in an ante-room to wash their hands. Visiting clergy came first, then a strict hierarchy of lay guests. The tables were covered in cloths and the Campeador, his family and guests ate off silver or pewter plates. Everybody else used platters made of wood or horn. Pages and servants scurried in and out carrying food and wine. In most castles the kitchen was actually some way from the great hall and so food was, at best, warm rather than hot. The room was strewn with scented flowers, lavender, jasmine and wild mint. Just as Rodrigo had been brought up in the household of Prince Sancho as part of his squire's role, it is not unreasonable to assume that a number of young hopefuls fulfilled this role in Vivar too. These lads served Rodrigo and Jimena, carving joints of meat and serving wine from the Rioja or further south.

In later years Rodrigo's table would groan with cups and chalices that were the spoils of war. Perhaps he owned some of these already. He and his guests chatted, slicing pieces of meat with their daggers, wiping their fingers on the tablecloth. It would be another two centuries before a Spaniard saw a fork. Most of what we know about the food served at these meals comes from a later period.[9] Fourteenth-century French dinners were often fifteen courses long, and might include venison served with pepper, wild boar and even stuffed bear. Swans and peacocks were a favourite delicacy, followed by capons, geese, hare and rabbit, crane, heron and duck. The fish course was usually the tenth and consisted of trout, salmon, mullet or eel, depending on what swam in local rivers. The sweets were figs, apples and tarts, and all of it was washed down with astonishing quantities of wine. Much of the above was already available in eleventh-century Spain, although how much of this was usual fare in the household of the Campeador we shall never know.

The afternoon usually saw Rodrigo and Jimena part company. He had a heavy meal to ride off and he might do it by putting his troops through their paces, overseeing his crossbowmen at the butts or checking the swordplay of his squires. The crossbow was a more popular weapon in Spain than the short bow because its range and accuracy were greater. The squires would have counted themselves doubly lucky to be taught by a man with the Campeador's reputation. Alternatively he might hunt, no doubt with his guests and Alvar Fañez and the others of his retinue. We know that wild boar roamed the *meseta* and boar-hunting was enormously popular everywhere in Europe. Riding fast coursers, Rodrigo's company would wait for the beaters to scare the wild pigs into the open. They are shy animals, but noise frightens them and their instinct is to run. The challenge was to skewer the boar with a spear while riding at the gallop through wooded or rutted country. A cornered boar was dangerous. An adult male could weigh up to 200kg (440lb) and could bring down a genet at full tilt, goring horse and rider with its deadly tusks.

Falconry was an altogether more aristocratic sport and Rodrigo would doubtless have had mews at Vivar where his hunting birds were kept and a falconer whose job it was to train and tend them. A century after his time Frederic II, the Holy Roman Emperor, wrote the first known book on the subject, *De Arte Venandi cum Avibis* (The Art of Hunting with Birds). The work is based on Frederic's Arab falconers and it is likely that the Christians of Spain learned the sport from al-Andalus, certainly by the late eighth century. Various falcons were used by the early thirteenth century – the gerfalcon, saker, peregrine, gentle and lanner – of differing sizes and colours. The chicks were taken from the nest between June and September, and this in itself was a job for an expert. Nests were difficult to reach and in the fierce heat of Spain an unprotected chick could easily die. Rodrigo's mews had to be quiet and secluded and the fourth moult (*mue* in Norman-French) was the right time to train the birds. The falconer slept with them. The birds were fed with fresh meat, preferably wild and still warm. If that was not available, then cheese or scrambled egg would do.

The training of a hawk was complicated, involving getting the bird used to a cover, ultimately an elaborate hood, and to waiting on a perch carried by the falconer. Robert Krepps's novel *El Cid* has King Alfonso carrying such a bird with him at the battle of Sagrajas in October 1086, and that is entirely plausible. The bird had to be turned to the wind and kept away from a man's face as human eyes upset it. Some falconers trained their birds to respond to their voices, others to their whistles. Rodrigo and his company would ride the *meseta* north and west of Vivar, searching the rolling hills for pigeons, plovers, snipe and other game birds, the flapping of wings and the jingling of falconers' bells ringing in the Castilian afternoon.

In the castle Jimena would spend the time with her ladies. From time to time she would join her husband on the hunt with hawks, but never for boar, which was considered exclusively a man's work. She would embroider, gossip and spend time with the children as they came along. Many women took their roles as ladies of estates very seriously and one who could hold the city of Valencia for nearly three years after her husband's death must have had a great deal of nerve and determination. Even so, Jimena is largely a closed book to us. The later chroniclers portray her as a beautiful and loving wife, totally loyal to her husband, the peerless Christian knight, and we have to draw inferences from a wide range of eleventh-century sources to provide any kind of picture of her. A woman was offered natural respect because all men had been born to one. The cult of the Virgin Mary, prevalent all over Catholic Europe and gathering ground in Rodrigo's day, placed women on a pedestal. On the other hand, women also carried the stain of Eve, the first woman, who was directly responsible for man's fall and the expulsion from Eden. Many churchmen adopted this misogynistic view. The Greek doctor Galen had taught that whereas male seed was precious, female seed was toxic. Menstruation was the periodic reduction of this poison. Failure to menstruate meant either pregnancy or 'uterine suffocation', which would lead to fits and madness. Menstrual blood, the Roman Pliny had written, destroyed crops and soured wine; dogs became rabid if touched by it. A child conceived during the menstrual cycle would have red hair and probably leprosy. Menstruating women could blunt swords by their mere gaze.[10]

When his horse clattered into the courtyard in Vivar at the end of the day's hunting, Rodrigo would bathe sitting on a stool in a wooden tub in his chamber. Perhaps Jimena would wash his back as they talked over the day. The Arab custom of public baths had not caught on in Christendom, but the Muslim jibe that Christians were unwashed applied only to peasants. Dressed in their finest, the couple went down to supper as the horn sounded again to preside over a lighter meal and the evening's entertainment. The minstrels or jongleurs were already making their appearance in royal courts and noblemen's castles by Rodrigo's day. The *chansons de geste* such as the Song of Roland were popular and designed to be sung. One wonders whether the *Carmen Campi Doctoris* was sung to the couple in their later years, rather as the Skaldic poets of King Cnut sang to him of his own successes in his court at Winchester, England.

Some lords had jesters, professional comedians like the curious dwarf Turold, shown holding Norman horses on the Bayeux Tapestry. Musicians, playing in a gallery perhaps at the far end of the hall, entertained the company with castanets, bagpipes, trumpets, tambourines and lutes. The wine flowed and stories were told. These were the days of peace and plenty.

The festivities ended when Rodrigo and Jimena went to bed. Helped out of their clothes, they lay in the great bed made of local wood and linen and feathers, and the candles burned all night in the room. Rodrigo would be given the keys of the castle by his seneschal and the horns would sound as the drawbridge was raised for the night. The hawks fluttered briefly on their perches in the darkened mews. The dogs curled before the dying fire embers in the great hall, still now and nearly dark. Babieca lowered her head to munch the hay in her stable with Rodrigo's other horses. Was it like that, in the quiet days of the Campeador and his lady? Probably, but we have no hard evidence at all.

'She bore him sons and daughters',[11] wrote the author of the *Historia Roderici* – but we do not know when. If Rodrigo and Jimena married in 1074 or even 1076, it is likely that all of the children were born within five years. There was no effective birth control in their generation, any more than there had been in their parents', and the rather risky suggestion by a cardinal a century later that men stick a hemlock poultice on their testicles prior to intercourse probably had little effect! The surviving children (and we do not know of any who did not survive) were Cristina, Maria and Diego. The tradition that the girls were twins comes from a later version of the Cid story, but there is no intrinsic reason why it could not be true.

Jimena would have borne her pregnancies with the usual stoicism expected of eleventh-century women, despite the (all-too-realistic) horror stories in treatises like *Holy Maidenhood*:

Your rosy face will grow thin and turn as green as grass; your eyes will grow dull and shadowed underneath and because of your dizziness your head will ache cruelly. Inside, in your belly, a swelling in your womb which bulges you out like a waterskin, discomfort in your bowels and stitches in your side and often painful backache; heaviness in every limb; the dragging weight of your two breasts and the streams of milk that run from them . . .[12]

Knowledge of pregnancy and childbirth in Jimena's day were a mixture of local folklore and classical medieval knowledge, translated from the Greek, ironically, by the Arabs. A mother who walked slowly on her heels would give birth to a boy, and one who walked quickly on her toes, a girl. So much for folklore!

Jimena's girls would have been brought up by her. Isidore of Seville had laid down in the seventh century that children were infants until the age of 7 and parents and godparents must watch over them – but we have no record of who these godparents were. Cristina and Maria would have been wrapped in swaddling clothes and wet-nursed, as was the usual custom. Bartholomaus Anglicus (Bartholomew the Englishman) quoted Isidore five centuries after his time: 'Like a mother, the nurse is happy when the child is happy and suffers when the child suffers. She lifts him up if he falls, gives him suck when he cries, kisses him if he is sick. . . .'[13]

We do not know if Jimena could read and if so whether, like her contemporary Queen Margaret of Scotland, who would become the patron saint of childbirth in the thirteenth century, she read to her children. The girls were taught to sing and dance, to ride and to play the lute and castanets. They learned to sew and embroider. Everything else would be done for them, all their lives. They would become the tragic heroines of bad marriages according to the Poem of the Cid, but in the reality of history we know nothing about the marriages they actually made.

For Diego the path was different. He was taught, as his father had been, to read, to wrestle, to ride. For him, the son of the Campeador, the road was never going to be as easy. Yet only one chronicler mentions him and then only in connection with the boy's death, grown to manhood in a violent age.

And in the meantime, the idyll was shattered. A man of Rodrigo's ability and reputation was not likely to be left to his children and his dogs and his hawks for long. His king had need of him.

7

Exile

It was probably in 1079 that Alfonso VI of Castile, of Léon and of the Asturias sent Rodrigo of Vivar to the rulers of Seville and Cordoba. The plural term is rather odd in the *Historia Roderici*, because both of these *taifa* states were ruled by the same man, al-Mutamid, who had been ruling in Seville for ten years and in Cordoba for perhaps three.

We have met al-Mutamid before. Like his father, he was a serious poet whose poetry has survived. Like his father, he was ambitious and bent on power. So was his great rival al-Ma'mun, called Abenabut in the *Chronicon*, who ruled Toledo during Alfonso's period of exile there. The collapse of al-Andalus as a single state centred on Cordoba had led to years of tension and power struggles between the various amirs, as we have seen, which merely encouraged the *Reconquista*. The duel between al-Mutamid and al-Ma'mun was merely one episode in the long suicide of al-Andalus.

First, al-Ma'mun had taken advantage of the death of Fernando to grab Valencia. He was now the 'possessor of dual glory'[1] in the poetry of the time, lord of Valencia and Toledo, but he was not content with that. Cordoba, as the once-great heart of al-Andalus, was the obvious prize and for all its decline by the Cid's time, it was still an extraordinary city and the most impressive in Spain. By February 1075 Cordoba was in al-Ma'mun's hands too, so that three of the greatest *taifa* states were now under one man's control and it must have appeared that the threat of Islam was growing again. We do not know enough about the intelligence services of the eleventh century or the speed and power of rumour. Perhaps Christians believed that al-Andalus was an archaic concept and posed no real threat at all. Perhaps, by the 1070s, they had already heard echoes of the distant drums from Africa, where fundament-alism was about to flex its muscles.

Four months later al-Ma'mun was dead, perhaps by poison, and his successor was not the man his grandfather was. Al-Qadir, 'the powerful', was anything but. He may have been feeble-minded; he was certainly something of a joke at a time when any sign of weakness, mental or physical, was seized upon as an opportunity for self-seeking and regime change. In Valencia Abu Bakr, whose father Abd al-Aziz had once ruled the city, staged a popular revolution; al-Qadir was ignored completely and the place reverted to its former status quo. But what was happening in Toledo was worse. In August 1075 the vizier Ibn al-Hadidi, chief adviser to al-Ma'mun, was murdered, almost certainly on the orders of al-Qadir. The reasons for this are unknown, but jealousies abounded in royal courts, be they Christian or Muslim, and if al-Qadir was genuinely unstable, then we need look no further for an explanation. Ibn al-Hadidi was hugely popular and there must have been many who yearned nostalgically for the days of al-Qadir's grandfather. The result was anarchy. The city of Toledo was a dangerous place to be that August and the new amir feared for his life. In desperation, he turned for protection to the most unlikely of saviours, Alfonso of Castile-Léon.

In the culture of the time, this actually made good sense. Alfonso's father and Alfonso himself had exacted the *paria* tribute from Toledo. This was only part of the contract, however. Like the Christian feudal system itself, only now gaining credence in the north, the quid pro quo was protection. This was in fact Alfonso's duty. He had also spent nine months in Toledo recently and knew the place like the back of his hand. For Alfonso, of course, the opportunity was heaven-sent; he got the *paria* back without a single crossbow bolt being fired and began to style himself in his official correspondence *imperator totius Hispaniae* – Emperor of All Spain. It is this phraseology, incorrect and designed to build up Alfonso's standing, which has led to the element of the Cid legend that credits him with forging a united nation south of the Pyrenees.

Al-Qadir, now having to raise taxes to pay the *paria* to Alfonso, became even more unpopular and got out while he could, fleeing

north to Cuenca and safety. In the autumn of 1079, as Rodrigo of
Vivar was on his way to another Castilian-Léonese satellite state, the
impossibly laid-back Umar al-Mutawakkil became amir of Toledo,
invited in by al-Qadir's opponents. This man also governed Badajoz,
but his chief interests were eating and poetry. Legend has it that he
served his guests from dishes floating on a stream that ran through his
palace and that he wrote his best poetry, as the mood took him,
on cabbage leaves! He was hardly the type to resist a hard-bitten
Castilian-Léonese army led by a warrior king who had with him the
finest general in all Spain, and Alfonso was most assuredly on his way.
In the campaigning season of 1080 the Castilian drove al-Mutawakkil
back to Badajoz and reinstated al-Qadir on the throne of Toledo.

Technically Rodrigo was not with his king on this campaign. The
weather was changing in the Cordillera Cantabrica and the Lord of
Vivar would have left his wife and young family in the care of his
seneschal and attendants and above all the local church and saddled
Babieca for the ride south. 'At the time,' the *Historia Roderici* tells
us, 'al-Mutamid, king of Seville, and Abd Allah, king of Granada,
were enemies'[2] – and the Campeador was riding right into a war. We
know a great deal about Abd Allah, because, alone among the amirs
of al-Andalus in this period, he wrote an autobiography.[3] The work
is, as would be expected, highly critical, even bitchy, about his
enemies, but he is also critical of his own father and grandfather and
their excessive drinking habits. He was also a great believer in
horoscopes, even risking an accusation of heresy by declaring
'Astrology is a form of worship'.[4]

Abd Allah was no stranger to Alfonso of Castile. In 1074 he had
concluded a treaty with him which is the equivalent of a non-
aggression pact today. It cost the amir 10,000 dinars a year, as well
as quantities of silver, carpets and silk. This was the kind of
'protection-racket' that had served Alfonso's father so well and
Alfonso was carrying on the tradition.

Abd Allah was no stranger to other Christian warlords either. At
his side, says the *Historia Roderici* were 'Garcia Ordoñez and
Fortun Sanchez, the son-in-law of King Garcia of Pamplona, and
Lope Sanchez the brother of Fortun Sanchez and Diego Perez, one of

the magnates of Castile. Each of these men with his following of warriors came first against the king of Seville.'⁵ Once again, we have ample evidence of the nature of Spanish warfare in the Campeador's day and the reason why we should not count the *Reconquista*, at least in its early stages, as a true crusade. Most historians today do not accept the *Reconquista*, at least until 1099, as part of the true crusading movement because there were no quasi military-religious orders in Spain at the time and no overt 'mission statement' on behalf of the Christian community. This seems a little narrow. All crusaders, from 1099 until 1571 (or whenever we accept the notion of crusade came to an end), mixed other motives with their religious zeal. Grabbing a kingdom in the Middle East would increase a man's power and prestige enormously, whether he did it in the name of God or not. Rodrigo was riding to the aid of a Moor, al-Mutamid of Seville, and against the Christian – indeed, Castilian – supporters of another Moor, Abd Allah of Granada. Later generations might see this as treason and heresy of the most damnable sort.

There was an exchange of letters. We have no idea of the scale of events or the time-frame, but it seems likely that whatever forces Rodrigo had with him reached Seville before Abd Allah's. This gave time for diplomacy in which the Campeador contacted Abd Allah, asking that Garcia Ordoñez 'and . . . the Christians who were with him . . . for the love of their lord King Alfonso not to come against the king of Seville nor to enter his kingdom'.⁶

We know something of the men Rodrigo faced. He knew Garcia Ordoñez well. The fact that the pair may have been friends was seen as no barrier to facing each other across a battlefield if the stakes were high enough. Ordoñez had acted as guarantor to Rodrigo's marriage settlement and was Alfonso's *armiger* in 1074. Like Rodrigo a loyal servant to Sancho, he had switched allegiance to Alfonso and been made Count of Najera before marrying Alfonso's sister, the Infanta Urraca (so much for her father's apparent wish that she be married to Christ). Historian Richard Fletcher implies that Rodrigo was jealous of Ordoñez, who now had a more honourable title and a more high-born wife, but the whole thrust of Fletcher's work on the future Cid is to belittle and put in context, as if the notion of a hero on a white horse is somehow wrong for the twenty-first century. So battles, to Fletcher, become skirmishes, while the *Historia Roderici* is important for what it does not tell us!

What it does tell us is that Ordoñez, or 'Crooked Mouth' as he was known, ignored Rodrigo's warning and began plundering towns and villages in the vicinity of the castle of Cabra. The fortress itself was not important, but it stood near the wealthy Jewish stronghold of Lucena and it may be that this was a target for Abd Allah's armies. Almost inevitably, 'When Rodrigo Diaz heard and checked the truth of this [plundering in the countryside] he at once went out with his army to confront them.'[7]

Pitched battles on a massive scale were unusual in the eleventh century, when raids and sieges were the norm, but the *Historia Roderici* makes a point of the great size of Abd Allah's army so perhaps what followed was exceptional. We know the battle near Cabra was hard-fought and lasted 'from the third hour of the day until the sixth'[8] – which means it was probably dark by the time Fortun Sanchez dragged himself away with whatever surviving retinue he could muster.

There would have been little to tell the two sides apart. Before the advent of true heraldry in the twelfth century, knights were largely indistinguishable from one another, their faces partially obscured by broad nasals and mail aventails. Their shields, kite-shaped or circular, may have been painted, but the symbols on them were still totemic, artistic and personal rather than heraldic. Banners may well have been carried and we have various references to but no accurate descriptions of the banners of the Campeador. Most of these are from later chroniclers to whom heraldry was not only an everyday event but an exact science. The exception is the *Carmen* of the 1080s. Verse XXIX reads:

> He also takes his shield with his left arm.
> The shield has a shiny gold dragon painted on it.[9]

and possibly resembled the Dragon of Wessex banner carried by Harold Godwinson at Hastings in 1066. Senior commanders, like

Rodrigo on the one hand and Ordoñez on the other, probably wore scarlet cloaks as a mark of their rank, but these were removed before battle. They rode powerful destriers like Babieca and would probably be found in the centre of any formation with wings of light cavalry and archers.

What is most confusing – and we have no information about it at all – is that both armies were composed of Christian and Muslim forces with their conflicting styles of fighting and weaponry. We do not know how the forces were deployed or whether it was al-Mutamid and Abd Allah or their hatchet men, Rodrigo and Ordoñez, who gave commands on the field. It is tempting to assume the latter – after all, this sort of expertise was what the *paria* was being paid for – and to speculate that the Castilians and Navarrese formed the centre while the Arabs/Moors on their fast horses and in their leather or horn armour formed the wings.

This can only be an assumption, as can the order of events. Short-bow arrows hissed through the Granadan air, and crossbow bolts, heavier, shorter, deadlier, thumped into shields and bodies. Infantrymen crowded together, thrusting against each other with spears and shields, locked in mortal struggles while grunting curses to God or to Allah. The cavalry of Abd Allah and al-Mutamid pranced past each other, exchanging glancing blows with their curved or straight swords, before wheeling back in tight circles to renew the attack. Rodrigo and Ordoñez rammed home their prick-spurs, drawing blood from their horses' bellies, hooking their lances under their right arms and cantering for the thick of the press. Men went down before them, skewered on lance points or reeling, bloody and senseless, from sword and axe blade. 'Eventually,' writes the author of the *Historia Roderici* grimly, 'defeated and disordered, all fled from the face of Rodrigo Diaz. There were captured in that battle Count Garcia Ordoñez and Lope Sanchez and Diego Perez and others of their fighting men. . . . The army of the king of Granada, both Saracens and Christians, suffered very great carnage and casualties.'[10]

Both armies would have benefited from Arab medicine, which was far ahead of Christian throughout the Middle Ages. The works of

al-Razi, the Persian philosopher of the early tenth century, would not
be translated into Latin until the century after the Campeador, but it
is likely that his ideas had reached both Granada and Seville. Even
better known was Abn Ali al-Hussayn Ibn Sinna, who would become
known in the west as the Latinized Avicenna. He died perhaps six
years before Rodrigo was born and his work *The Laws of Medicine*
was already a prescribed manual in Muslim and Jewish circles by the
time of the battle near Cabra. Surgery was a last resort, although
Moorish doctors carried a wide variety of saws and scalpels.
Dissection was forbidden in the Koran, just as it was abhorrent to
Christians. Wounds were stitched, bandages wrapped around cuts
and if possible open gashes were cauterized with iron heated over
coals to seal stumps and stop bleeding. Following the social
hierarchy, the nobility and knights were treated first, then the rest,
the rank and file. *Te Deum*s were sung for the dead and their bodies
were thrown into communal graves, except those of gentle birth who
were given individual burials. Similar services must have been held
for each of the Muslim dead, the imams calling and chanting into the
night air. Camp followers and local women hovered around any
corpses that remained, looting and pillaging by flickering torchlight.
If bodies remained by morning, the ravens would swoop in to begin
the scavenging again, going first for the eyes and the soft issue.

It is possible that it was the victory at Cabra that earned Rodrigo
Diaz the title of El Cid. Its original version al-Sayyid, the Lord, is of
course Arabic and Cabra represents the first known time that he was
in battle against al-Andalus. The fact that Moors fought with him as
well makes the title more likely – he must have impressed his allies
as much as his enemies. The *Carmen*, written soon after this,
contends that it was this victory that gave Rodrigo the title of 'Lord
of the [battle]field'.

The Cid kept his prisoners with him for three days. Whether the
victorious army kept the field, staying camped where they were, or
rode in triumph into Seville is not recorded. Garcia Ordoñez, as we
have seen, was a man of wealth and substance. So was Fortun
Sanchez. A high-ranking Basque, *armiger* at the court of Sancho IV
of Navarre, he had joined Alfonso's service in 1076. As the brother-

in-law of Ordoñez, he was part of the powerful clique of inter-married families who were in the ascendancy in the Christian north. Rodrigo took their titles away from them, seized the booty they had plundered from the Sevillean and Granadan countryside and 'set them free to go their way'. It might have been better if he had had them executed. At last he collected the *paria* from a grateful al-Mutamid and returned home to Castile laden with gifts for Alfonso. The fact that the chroniclers specifically mention Castile as opposed to Léon may imply that Alfonso had taken his court, at least occasionally, to Burgos by 1080. Sadly, the conquering hero would not enjoy the fruits of victory for long: 'In return for this success and victory granted him by God, many men, both acquaintances and strangers, became jealous and accused him before the king of many false and untrue things.'[11]

The Song of the Campeador, written in this decade and reporting news that was virtually still current, is more blunt:

> Alfonso was so keen and loved Rodrigo so much that he gave him anything he wanted. All the other members of the aristocracy are very envious about the situation.
>
> The members of the aristocracy say 'What are you doing? You are creating your own enemy by giving him anything he asks you. Be aware he will never love you, as he was a member of your brother's court, and will always be up to something.'[12]

We can assume that Garcia Ordoñez was a prime mover against the Cid, but Alfonso surely cannot have held Ordoñez in quite the exalted position he had beforehand. If Ordoñez had been sent to Granada on the same sort of cash-collecting mission that Rodrigo had been sent to Seville, then why did Ordoñez not agree to bury the hatchet with Rodrigo as the Cid had asked in his letters? In Ordoñez, Alfonso had an over-mighty subject every bit as difficult to handle as the Cid himself.

The situation came to a head in the summer of 1081. The *Historia Roderici* says that there was a rebellion 'in a land of the Saracens', which seems to have been the border country of the *tierras desplobladas* along the Duero, specifically the castle of Gormaz. Like the Krak des Chevaliers in the Holy Land, Gormaz was an impressive fortress with a reputation for impregnability. One of the 'front teeth' of al-Andalus, it was built by the Muslims about 950. Its walls are nearly a mile in circumference and the castle today still boasts the Caliph's gate with its distinctive horseshoe arch. Fernando, the old king, took the castle as part of his southward push of the *Reconquista*. We do not know who took Gormaz in 1081 or who held it previously. The Cid was ill in Vivar, with what complaint we do not know, but because news of the attack seems to have affected Rodrigo personally (the chapter is one of the few in the *Historia Roderici* where the author gives him dialogue) it is possible the castle or at least the lands around it were his.

Rodrigo's speech – 'I shall go after these robbers and with any luck I shall take them'[13] – makes it clear that this was not an amir-backed thrust to reverse the *Reconquista*, but a lawless rabble, possibly from Toledo, who were trying their luck, perhaps knowing that Rodrigo was ill and thus unlikely to take the field against them. This presupposes a high degree of intelligence-gathering in al-Andalus, but it is not impossible, and in fact they may have been very wide of the mark if the assumption was that the Cid was dead or dying.

The *Historia Roderici* talks of Rodrigo's army and 'all his well-armed knights'[14] laying waste the area around Toledo. There is no actual mention of the castle of Gormaz being retaken, but the raid rounded up seven thousand captives whom Rodrigo brought back to Burgos. This was precisely the excuse that the Cid's enemies needed. Even assuming that the figure of seven thousand was an exaggeration[15] and the real number did not cause a food shortage in Burgos, Alfonso now found himself petitioned by Christians living in Toledo and along the Duero who feared reprisals. Rodrigo's raid had not been sanctioned by the king and it would look to outsiders as if Alfonso could not control his own subjects. As the *Carmen* has it – 'Alfonso is afraid of losing his power and his throne.'[16] Certainly there is some sense of a private army about the men the Cid took to the Duero with him. In the previous year the weak amir al-Qadir had granted various castles (Zorita, Canales and Brihnegra) to Alfonso by treaty; the Cid's recklessness now was threatening to damage a precarious equilibrium, which Alfonso had probably worked hard to create. 'The king was unjustly impressed,' wrote the author of the *Historia Roderici*, 'and angered by his wicked and envious accusation [that the Cid had engineered the situation deliberately to put Toledan Christians' lives in jeopardy] . . . he expelled Rodrigo from his kingdom.'[17] As the author of the *Carmen* put it:

> All his love becomes hate,
> and Alfonso tries to confront Rodrigo more and more.

Exile was almost a way of life for Spanish royalty and aristocracy in this period. Alfonso himself had spent nine months in Toledo, and his brother Garcia would die in exile in Seville. It meant different things in different countries and at different times. Banishment, or 'abjuration of the realm' as it was known in England by the fourteenth century, was a heavy and serious punishment. It usually meant that the exile must leave alone (faithfully shown in the Heston film) and that no one within the king's realm could offer shelter, food, water or even talk to the exile.[18] It also meant that all property of the exile was forfeited to the crown. Given that Alfonso coolly walked back to Léon to claim his own kingdom and that of his murdered brother, it was clearly not quite so harsh (or permanent) in the Cid's Spain. Rodrigo himself, of course, would be pardoned – and exiled again – later in Alfonso's reign.

The *Historia Roderici* tells us that the Cid left his 'sorrowing friends' behind, but makes no mention of his family. In 1081 Rodrigo's children would still have been little, the girls perhaps 6 or 7, Diego 4 or 5. At the very least Rodrigo's future was uncertain and he probably left them either with Jimena's family in Asturias (a document of 1083 would seem to confirm this) or with the monastery of San Pedro at Cardena where the Cid and his wife would lie buried years later.

His first port of call was Barcelona. He would presumably have offered to hire out his sword to the count, Ramon Berenguer, but for whatever reason he was turned down. This is not recorded in the chronicles, but some historians today think it probable. Given that Berenguer and the Cid became arch-enemies in the years ahead, perhaps it was hatred at first sight in 1081. The exile wandered on to Zaragoza. The amir here was still al-Muqtadir, who was paying a *paria* of 12,000 gold dinars to King Sancho IV of Navarre. He was an old man by this time, having ruled in Zaragoza since Rodrigo was a small boy, but he had recently been cashing in on the squabbles of the Christian north by conquering the kingdom of Denia in the Levante, probably buying off Alfonso of Castile and eliminating his jealous brother Yusuf by poisoning him in his castle of Rueda. One of al-Muqtadir's sumptuous palaces, the Aljaferia, still stands.

Within a year of the Cid's arrival, al-Muqtadir died, leaving Zaragoza to his son Yusuf al-Mutamin and Denia, Tortosa and Lerida to his other son Mundhir al-Hayib. As with the Christian kingdoms, sibling rivalry and the constant splitting of legacies led first to tension, then to open warfare. The author of the *Historia Roderici* says: 'This al-Mutamin was very fond of Rodrigo and set him over and exalted him above all his kingdom and all his land, relying on his counsel in all things.'[19] Again, Richard Fletcher pours scorn on this. Rodrigo, he contends, was just one of several Christian knights in al-Mutamin's service, simply a mercenary. This may be so, but we have no way of knowing what sort of personality al-Mutamin had. In the Heston film, he is wise and dignified, played with gravitas by Douglas Wilmer; it is he who first gives Rodrigo the title al-sayyid, the Lord. If this is correct and al-Mutamin recognized a 'soul-brother', then why should the friendship not have blossomed? We have already established that the Christian/Muslim divide engendered by the crusades belonged to a later generation, and perhaps never fully to Spain. Again, if al-Mutamin were an indecisive figure (he is unlikely to have had Rodrigo's military expertise), then why should he not come to rely heavily on the Cid? We simply do not know enough about either man or the exact temper of the times.

What we do know is that the exile was caught up in a war again, exactly as he had been in Seville three years earlier. Verse XVII of the *Carmen* sees this as a turning-point:

It is then when Rodrigo starts and fights against the Moors
And conquers the regions where the Moors are in power.

Al-Hayib, the younger brother, described by Abd-Allah of Granada
in his memoirs as 'reckless', had enlisted the aid of Sancho of
Navarre and Ramon Berenguer, the Count of Barcelona. Both men's
interests would be served by moving south into the Levante and
Sancho, at least, had an old score to settle: his father Ramiro had
been killed at Graus in Rodrigo's first battle. When word filtered
through to Pamplona that the Cid was with al-Mutamin in
Zaragoza, it must have seemed like a heaven-sent opportunity.

The initial moves of the campaign were a masterpiece of outman-
oeuvre. One of the key strongholds was not Zaragoza city itself but
nearby Monzon, guarding the mountain passes to the north. Rodrigo
seems to have let the news reach Sancho that this was his goal,
presumably goading the Navarrese into fighting him. He reached a
village called Peralta after a day's forced march at the head of the
largely Moorish army of al-Mutamin. It may be that the Cid was
facing the classic Napoleonic problem of two opponents simul-
taneously. Peralta was 'within eyesight of his enemies; the whole army
of al-Hayib'[20] – but no battle was given. The next day he reached
Monzon itself, 'under the eyes of King Sancho'.[21] The text of the
Historia Roderici is defective at this point and the Cid's best known
biographer, Ramon Menendez Pidal, added a section gleaned from
other sources. He could, of course, have been wrong, but he says
Rodrigo left Monzon and went on to Tamarite, only 6 miles away. He
had left the River Ebro behind him and was facing the giant sweep of
the Sierra de Montsec. It was here that the first attack came from
Sancho's Aragonese but the Cid dashed them aside in his usual style:
'He left the town with ten knights and encountered nearly a hundred
and fifty knights of King Sancho; and he defeated them all and
captured seven knights with their horses and the rest fled.'[22] Again,
modern historians have doubted this, finding the numbers laughable.
But the Cid had a reputation. It is likely that within months of the
clash at Tamarite, the first literature about him, the *Carmen Campi
Doctoris* (Song of the Campeador) was written. Verse XXII reads:

> After this battle [Rodrigo] was well known in all Spain
> and was feared by all kings.[23]

The author of the *Historia Roderici* says that Sancho did not attack Rodrigo at Monzon because he 'did not care to come against him'.[24] We know that the Cid consistently took on large odds and won. Again, we only have seven knights taken (by Rodrigo's total of eleven, including himself) before the others ran. Medieval armies had a habit of doing that. In what seems to have been a lull in this war of manoeuvre, the Cid and al-Mutamin occupied the castle of Almenar and refortified it, no doubt with local stone, the labour of locals and the expertise of al-Mutamin's engineers and architects.

One thing Almenar seems to have lacked was its own water supply, or at least one that could be relied upon. In what may have been an exceptionally dry summer, Ramon Berenguer and the local Catalan nobility laid siege to it. The Lords of Besalu, Ampurdan, Rosellon and Carcassonne across the Pyrenees camped with their tents and their mangonels to await the surrender of the garrison. But Rodrigo was not there. In fact he was at the castle of Escarp (today's Granja de Escarpe) half a day's march away. He seems to have captured this castle quickly and taken all its inhabitants prisoner. He sent messengers to al-Mutamin (it is not clear where he was by this time) asking for reinforcements for Almenar. He knew the garrison could not hold out for much longer. Al-Mutamin and the Cid met at Tamarite and discussed the situation. The amir's order was for Rodrigo to attack al-Hayib's besieging army, but the Cid was unhappy with this. Twice in fifteen lines the author of the *Historia Roderici* uses the phrase 'gravely worried' and it seems likely that the Cid knew things that today we do not. He may have been outnumbered. From what followed, it does not appear that Sancho of Navarre was at Almenar; perhaps Rodrigo had no idea where he was and feared a counter-attack. The Cid's advice was to pay al-Hayib off.

This is the flesh and blood Rodrigo Diaz, a man of practical common sense who is prepared to compromise, double-back and use all the *realpolitik* of the *Reconquista*. The hero of the later *Poema de Mio Cid* would not do that; neither would Charlton Heston!

Al-Mutamin saw its wisdom, however, and Rodrigo sent messengers under a flag of truce to talk cash with al-Hayib. The younger brother, brave outside Almenar with the large army of Ramon Berenguer, refused. He had the Campeador on the run and probably took the request as a sign of weakness. The only alternative was confrontation. The *Carmen* says:

> The Count and his allies could not give up
> and did not allow [Rodrigo] to do what he wanted.
> He, then, prepares for battle.[25]

Then, somewhere near Tamarite, 'with a great noise of shouting and weaponry on both sides, the troops advanced and joined battle'.[26]

How long this one lasted, we do not know. The *Carmen* ends at this point, before battle is joined, with the Cid arming himself and praying. Again, Richard Fletcher attributes the Cid's victory to luck – 'to everyone's surprise',[27] he says. But simply being outnumbered does not explain victory or defeat. The author of the *Historia Roderici* talks of confusion and it may well be that a rout took place. All battles, especially those in pre-artillery days when men fought each other face to face, have a critical point at which the nerve of one side or the other is likely to crack. This seems to have happened outside Tamarite/Almenar. There were heavy casualties and Berenguer and several of his knights were taken in chains to Tamarite castle. They were passed to al-Mutamin, who, ever the gentleman, set them free after five days, apparently without ransom.

The *Historia Roderici* says that 'Rodrigo Diaz' returned with al-Mutamin to Zaragoza, where he was received by the citizens with the greatest honour and respect. In those days Rodrigo was raised up above his [al-Mutamin's] own son and over his kingdom and over all his land. He seemed to be, as it were, the lord of the whole realm.'[28] Some historians doubt that Rodrigo Diaz was given the title Cid in his own day because none of the contemporary texts use the term. If he was not already given it after Cabra, this would seem to be the fitting time for it, when a Christian general so impressed his Muslim allies that they called him al-Sayyid. The eulogies also made Rodrigo much richer: 'Al-Mutamin showered him with innumerable presents and many gifts of gold and silver.'[29] We do not know where he lived in Zaragoza, but his status now would have earned him a palace not much smaller than al-Mutamin's himself.

But trouble followed the Cid. At some time near Christmas 1082 there was a rising against al-Mutamin. The perpetrator, according to the *Historia Roderici* was 'a certain unworthy man' called Albofalac. Unusually, we have no other name for him, but he seems to have been the governor of the castle of Rueda, not far from Zaragoza. The historians Richard Fletcher and B.F. Reilly both believe that this seizure of a castle and its surrounding land was linked to the royal servant Ibn al-Royolo, who was executed on al-Mutamin's orders on suspicion that he was intriguing with Alfonso of Castile against him. In a passage of play that was depressingly familiar by now, Albofalac sent to Alfonso for support, and the king duly arrived with an army. At its head were two prominent members of the nobility, the *infante* (Prince) Ramiro, brother of Sancho of Navarre, and Count Gonzalo Salvadorez. Once again, we have men who were already the Cid's enemies marching to fight him, or at least his paymaster. Ramiro's brother-in-law was Garcia Ordoñez, who had been beaten and humiliated by Rodrigo three years before. As a man in Alfonso's service and the Lord of Calahora since 1076, he would have known the exiled knight from Vivar very well. So too did Salvadorez, who had also served the murdered Sancho before, like Rodrigo, offering his sword to Alfonso.

Before noblemen went on campaign – or even on a long journey, especially if it involved the always treacherous sea – it was the done thing to prepare spiritually in case of disaster. Salvadorez's documents have survived and offer a fascinating snapshot of the wealth, piety and Domesdaic fear of the times:

I, Count Gonzalo, in readiness for battle against the Moors with my lord [Alfonso], grant and concede to God and to the monastery of Ora[30] where my forebears rest, in order that I may be remembered there for evermore. . . . If I should meet with death among the Moors, may my soul be with Christ; and let my body be borne to Ora and buried there with my kinsfolk, together with 1600 gold pieces and three of my noble horses and two mules and from my wardrobe two silken robes and three of shot-silk taffeta and two vessels of silver. . . .[31]

'That I may be remembered there for evermore. . . .' How ironic that the only man remembered from those distant days of the *Reconquista* with anything approaching affection was the man against whom Salvadorez was now marching. But perhaps the count was not a popular man and he knew it: 'And if my vassals and retainers do not so bear me in the event of my death, they are nothing worth, like the traitor who kills his lord, because I made them rich and powerful.'[32]

We do not know whether the count made it home, but if he did, it was as a corpse. Rodrigo of Vivar was at Tudela, nearly two days' march away and not directly involved at all. Albofalac seems to have been working in conjunction with al-Mutamin's uncle Yusuf (called al-Muzaffar in the *Historia Roderici*), who had been a prisoner at Rueda under al-Muqtadir, his brother. For whatever reason, Salvadorez and Prince Ramiro decided to send for Alfonso in person and he duly arrived at Rueda, staying only a few days before going home.

In the midst of whatever strategy the trio were planning, Yusuf al-Muzaffar died, leaving Albofalac without a patron and culpably guilty of treason against al-Mutamin. The incident that followed, on 6 January 1083, makes little sense. As Salvadorez and Ramiro rode into Rueda, they were attacked by Albofalac's garrison. 'Albofalac's deceit and treachery', fumes the author of the *Historia Roderici*, 'were at once revealed.'[33] Both Salvadorez and Ramiro died under a hail of rocks hurled down on them from the battlements, perhaps through the machicolations (murder-holes) that were beginning to make their appearance in European castle construction. Had Albofalac planned this all along? Was he hoping that Alfonso would be riding under Rueda's gates too, to make the coup complete? He must have realized that al-Mutamin wanted his head for daring to rebel in the first place. Was this Albofalac's way of redeeming himself in the amir's eyes, that he could show him the corpses of two Christian noblemen?

At this stage the Cid seems to have contacted Alfonso, who was probably still on his way home to Castile-Léon. The *Historia Roderici* implies that Rodrigo re-enlisted in the king's service, but Alfonso still did not trust him, so he returned to Zaragoza. This is unlikely. So much of our understanding of what is happening in the Cid's exile is linked to where his family were and we have no clues about that. Were they still at Cardena, watched over by a careful and patient church, or were they with Jimena's high-born family in Oviedo? The attack at Rueda outraged Christian sensibilities, helping to forge the gulf between Christendom and Islam that lay at the heart of the crusading movement of the next generation. Perhaps Rodrigo merely wished to assure Alfonso that he had nothing to do with Rueda – and perhaps he felt he needed to do that because Alfonso had access at least to Jimena and the children.

In the spring of 1084, when the campaigning season began again, al-Mutamin and the Cid invaded Aragon. We have no idea of the size of their mixed army of Christians and Moors, but it was formidable. In five days, they 'ravaged the land of Aragon and stripped it of its riches and led off many of its inhabitants captive with them'.[34] Captives always posed problems in medieval history. Rich ones could be ransomed, bringing cash, valuables and even land to their conquerors. Poor ones were a nuisance; they could be used as serf labour, but in the short term they had to be housed and fed. Jails were the dungeons of castles, small and cramped. There are a number of instances in the eleventh-century texts of prisoners – even wealthy ones – being released after a few token days. It is likely that the symbolism of defeat and servitude was good enough. King Sancho seems to have stood by once again and dared not clash with Rodrigo.

Then al-Mutamin unleashed the Cid against al-Hayib. The author of the *Historia Roderici* is unusually virulent about this raid: 'There was not left in that region a house which he did not destroy, nor property which he did not seize.'[35] He took the castle of Morella, fighting what appears to be a battle outside its gates and all but destroying it. On al-Mutamin's orders, he rebuilt and refortified the neighbouring castle of Olocau, perhaps because it was stronger already than Morella or in a more strategically valuable position.

There is no doubt that by this time – probably the summer of 1084 – the Cid was a major thorn in the side of the Christian lords and a formidable asset to the Banu Hud, al-Mutamin's ruling family in Zaragoza. Al-Hayib intrigued once more with Sancho of Navarre and the pair led a joint army along the Ebro in search of him. Medieval battles usually followed a set pattern with messengers galloping backwards and forwards in parley to arrange exact times and places. We have seen that open battles were unusual in eleventh-century Spain – raids on villages and towns were more common, as were prolonged sieges of castles and cities. Sancho ordered the Cid to withdraw and never to return. Again, the author of the *Historia Roderici* puts words into Rodrigo's mouth: 'If my lord king wishes to pass by me in peace, I shall willingly permit him; and not only him, but all his men as well. Furthermore, should he wish it, I shall give him a hundred of my troops to attend upon him and be the companions of his journey.'[36]

The courtesies dispensed with, both sides stood their ground and the battle opened the next day, probably 14 August. The site remains unidentified, but was somewhere along the banks of the River Ebro, but in terms of what it accomplished it was the Cid's most spectacular victory. 'The fight was long,'[37] the *Historia Roderici* tells us, implying that it was hard fought and bloody. Once again, the Cid's enemies broke and this time his cavalry chased them over a long distance. Some commanders held their men in check, because the timing of a rout was crucial and exhausted horses would be useless in the event of a surprise counter-attack. At other times the victors had so narrowly won and their casualties were so heavy that any pursuit was impossible. Sancho's camp was looted, his guy-ropes ripped up and his tents burned. 'Unreckonable booty' was loaded on to mules and packhorses and taken back to Zaragoza, much to the delight of al-Mutamin and his sons and the vast crowd that flocked to meet them at the village of Fuentes, some 25 miles down the Ebro from the capital.

What was even more remarkable was the long list of nobility who surrendered to Rodrigo on the field. It reads like a 'who's who' of the eleventh-century elite. There was Ramon Dalmacio, the Bishop of Roda between 1076 and 1094. Today Roda is a tiny 'city' with the cathedral perched picturesquely on a hilltop and a population of thirty-six! The Romanesque crypt of San Ramon is still there, much as it was in the days of Bishop Ramon. There was Count Sancho Sanchez of Pamplona, probably the son of an illegitimate brother of the King of Navarre and perhaps the most powerful nobleman in Aragon. After him is listed Count Niño of Portugal, Gudesto Gonzalez, Nuño Suarez of Léon, Anaya Suarez of Galicia, Calvet, Inigo Sanchez of Monclus, Jimeno Garces of Pamplona (Count Sancho's nephew), Fortun Garces of Aragon and Sancho Garces of Alquezar. All these men, whose territory covered the whole of northern Spain, can be identified from other records of the day as *tenantes* (landholders) of various estates. Garcia Diaz of Castile is last on the list, preceded by Blasco Garces, the *mayordomo* or chamberlain of King Sancho of Navarre.

What strikes us as perhaps a little odd today is the fact that these men were *prisoners*, not counted among the dead. We have similar roll-calls in English history, from the battle of Ashingdon in Essex in 1016, between Edmund Ironside and his rival Cnut Sweynson, to Agincourt in France in 1415, between the forces of the dauphin and Henry V. These list the principal dead, in both cases a serious blow to the infrastructure of the state. Perhaps the nobility of Spain did not find the cause worth the candle. Cnut, Ironside, Henry V and the dauphin were fighting for kingdoms and even their very survival; perhaps the Cid's prisoners saw no profit in a glorious death.

The *Historia Roderici* tells us what happened next:

Rodrigo Diaz stayed at Zaragoza until the death of al-Mutamin. After his death, his son al-Mustain succeeded him as king.

Rodrigo remained with him at Zaragoza in the greatest honour and respect for nine [months].

After this he returned to his native land of Castile.[38]

8

Out of Afriquiya

Medieval Africa was a strange land inhabited by demons and monsters, as far as most Europeans were concerned. No one quite knew how far south it extended; the Cape of Good Hope was not found until 1488 by the Portuguese navigator Vasco da Gama. It would be five hundred years before the whole of the central area was seen by white men – Englishmen like Burton and Speke, Scotsmen like Livingstone – and until then it remained the Dark Continent.

The narrow northern strip from Mauritania in the west to Egypt in the east had been a Roman province since 164 BC when the burgeoning superpower had first moved against Carthage. The area later known as the Maghrib, from which the Moors had arrived in Spain in 711, was hugely profitable to Rome – an astonishing six hundred towns existed in Tunisia alone in the second century AD, based on a well-established farming economy begun by the Carthaginians. Wealthy Romans bought up estates and merged them so that by the reign of the Emperor Nero the elder Pliny claimed that half of Africa was the property of six men! Wine, oil and above all wheat were ferried across the Mediterranean to feed Rome's ever-hungry mouths. 'Smiling estates', wrote Tertillian a century later, 'have replaced the most famous deserts, cultivated fields have conquered the forests, flocks of sheep have put wild beasts to flight – certain proof of the increase of mankind.'[1]

The empire of Ghana was composed of various tribes who by the third century had collected near the modern city of Timbuktu, their societies developing under a single clan that controlled the western Sudan and the valley of the Senegal river. There had probably been trade links between the northern coastal strip and the Africa of the Gulf of Guinea for a thousand years before the Romans arrived, but the natural barriers of the vast Sahara desert and the formidable Atlas mountains to its north combined to slow this development. Not until the eighth century did the West African world open up, and by then the Romans had long gone and the Muslim conquest had changed the outlook of its native peoples. The forests and savannah of Ghana (the name actually being the title of its warrior-king) produced iron ore for smelting, ebony and ivory for objects of art. Gold came from here too, much of it carried up the Niger to Timbuktu on the southern edge of the Sahara. Food was also taken that way, in exchange for salt from the flats at Idjil and Taghaza in the centre of the desert. And the trade routes were two-way: glass, oil lamps and pottery made in the Mediterranean were taken by camel train to the city of Jenne-Jeno, one of the largest in Africa and already well established by AD 200.

It may have been this city that the Arab geographer al-Bakri, a contemporary of the Cid, was describing when he claimed that its king's hounds had collars made of solid gold. By the fourteenth century, when the still-extant copy of the *Poema de Mio Cid* was written, another geographer, Ibn Khaldun, believed that the King of Ghana owned a lump of gold that weighed a ton. Five hundred years later British novelists like Henry Rider Haggard and John Buchan could claim that the vast continent held the gold mines of Solomon[2] and the fabled, miraculous kingdom of the deathless Christian king, Prester John.[3]

The desert was endless and it produced its own strange, spiritual people. The trade route across the Sahara in the Cid's day ran from Sijilmasa in Morocco for 1,400 miles to Timbuktu. Trade north and south of the great desert produced a mingling of very different races. The forest and savannah dwellers of the far south were black Africans who formed a loose confederacy of tribes of the Soninke peoples. The Muslim tribes of the north were largely paler-skinned Berbers, of mixed Indo-European and Negro descent. They were the original inhabitants of North Africa and resisted waves of invasions by Romans, Vandals and Byzantines, retaining their tribal and linguistic culture partly because they were nomadic, following their herds and flocks from oasis to oasis and never really accepting the sedentary city life of the (for example) Roman interlopers.

113

It took the Arabs nearly half a century to subdue the Berbers, but their acceptance of Sunnite Islam was only ever skin-deep and the Arabs always regarded them as subject peoples from whom they exacted a tribute not unlike the *paria* of the Christian Kings of Spain. In the tenth century the Berbers were not only fighting the Ghanaians to the south, but also waged unremitting warfare against attempts by first the Umayyad and then the Abbasid dynasties to control them. They were the 'veiled ones', their faces covered against the vicious blasts of the wind-driven sand, and they experienced a mystical conversion some eight years before the birth of Rodrigo Diaz. In that year a warlord of the Sanhaja tribal confederacy of the Berbers, Yahya Ibn Ibrahim, travelled to Mecca in search of spiritual enlightenment and on his way back met an Imam, Abu Imran, who sent a Moroccan pupil of his, Abd Allah ibn Yasim, to lead the religiously ignorant Berbers into the ways of Allah.[4]

Ibn Yasim had a hard time of it. His mission fell on deaf ears and after the death of his protector, Ibn Ibrahim, he fled south with a handful of supporters to an area near the estuary of the Senegal river, where he established a ribat, a religious centre not unlike the strongholds of the later Christian Templars[5] in that Ibn Yasin's disciples were part ascetic zealots, part warriors. They came to be known as al-Murabitun in Arabic, a term that was corrupted to Almoravid by Christian Spain. And by the time Rodrigo Diaz was a small boy, they were on the march.

It is difficult to know what inspired new converts to the Almoravids. Perhaps the essential fundamentalism of Allah's message via Mohammed appealed to a people used to hardship and prepared actually to believe, rather than just pay lip-service to, the old mantras – 'There is no god but Allah and Mohammed is his prophet' and 'Prayer is better than sleep'. Unlike the earlier Muslim invasion of Spain and the later Ottoman invasion of eastern Europe, the Almoravids brought muscular Islam and conversion at sword-point. From 1042 the tribes of the southern Sahara fell under the influence. When Ibn Yasin was killed during a raid in 1059, his place was taken by a disciple, Abu Bakr ibn Umar, who gave the northern area of the ribat to his cousin, Yusuf ibn Teshufin.

Like many fanatics who came out of the African desert over the centuries,[6] Ibn Teshufin was probably unstable. He was certainly extraordinarily single-minded, an uncouth semi-literate who spoke poor Arabic and smelt of camels. He drank only milk and ate only barley bread, but he was a fine general and invaded Morocco, establishing his headquarters at Marrakesh at an uncertain date in the 1060s. While Rodrigo Diaz was earning a name for himself in the armies of King Sancho of Castile many miles to the north, Ibn Teshufin embarked on a relentless military campaign that saw him take Fez in 1075, Tlemcen the next year and Tangier in 1079. Fez had been established in 789 by Idris I as his capital and in the century before the Cid it was a constant battleground between the Fatimid and Umayyad dynasties of Spain. From 980 until 1012 it was effectively ruled by the Umayyad caliphate of Cordoba, and after that clan's collapse Berber tribes fought over it for years. Under the Almoravids Fez became a famous centre of textile manufacture and leather work. In all these cities those Berbers who rejected the Almoravid austerity or had not been slaughtered by Ibn Teshufin fled to the mountains, so that the area became far more orthodox than it had been for nearly three centuries and there was, at least on paper, a rapprochement with the caliphate of Baghdad. Tlemcen in particular became an important centre of pilgrimage for Muslims, its beautiful mosques attracting travellers from all over Islam before its sudden decline in the fourteenth century.

The Almoravid invasion of the Maghrib was very similar to that of the Middle East at the same time by the Seljuk Turks,[7] whose conquest of the Christian Holy Land sparked the First Crusade in the year of the Cid's death. It was partly explained by the fanaticism of the Almoravid warriors and partly by Ibn Teshufin's almost animal magnetism. And, far more than al-Andalus or Christian Spain, the Almoravids were a whole people geared to war. Marrakesh had a single stone-built fortress with double walls and an external perimeter of viciously thorned hedges made from the local plant zizyphus lotus. We have seen already, from the Cid's victories, that Christian nobles were all too ready to throw down their swords on the battlefield and submit to captivity. The Almoravids did not do

115

that. Like the Zulu of the nineteenth century and the Samurai of any century, their code and their mystic beliefs obliged them to die where they stood. As long as there were fanatical replacements for these losses, they were virtually unstoppable.

Despite the military ardour of the Almoravids, who were all too eager to embrace the Islamic concept of holy war – *jihad* – because it suited their mass temperament, there is no evidence that Yusuf Ibn Teshufin would ever have crossed the Straits of Gibraltar unless he was invited to. And just such an invitation arrived from the amir al-Mutamid of Seville, probably in the autumn of 1079. Another messenger sailed south at about the same time bearing letters from al-Mutawakkil of Badajoz. Even so, it would be an astonishing six years before Yusuf did anything concrete. Why the delay? He certainly owed al-Mutamid a favour, because the Andalusian had lent the Almoravid a fleet to blockade Cueta, which Ibn Teshufin was besieging. Perhaps the prospect of galvanizing the soft, alcohol-drinking amirs who dealt with Jews and allowed Christians to worship in their *taifa* states did not appeal. Ibn Teshufin had spent twenty years subduing Morocco and cannot by this time have been a young man. Some accounts say that he was 70 in 1086. He must also have realized that an invasion of Spain would bring him into headlong confrontation with the kings of the Christian north, not least the slippery Alfonso of Castile. And then there was a brilliant general who fought for the amir of Zaragoza, a man known to the Arabs as al-sayyid, the Lord.

But Alfonso was pushy. The weak al-Qadir was the king's puppet in Valencia and a Castilian army laid siege to Zaragoza. Alfonso wrote belligerent, threatening letters to al-Mutamid at Seville and perhaps to Ibn Teshufin across the Straits in Tangier. Then he marched on Toledo. This was now the largest city in al-Andalus with a population of perhaps 28,000. Its pleasure-loving amir, the poet al-Mutawakkil – precisely the soft traitor to a religious cause that Ibn Teshufin despised – had been sent packing by Alfonso in 1080, and al-Qadir installed in his place. There had been rumblings of discontent here for years and Alfonso had half-heartedly besieged the city on and off before. On 25 May 1085, however, and with minimal violence, he entered the city, which would for ever remain in the Christian ambit of Spain.

'After this,' wrote the author of the *Historia Roderici*, 'divine clemency granted a great victory to the Emperor Alfonso. . . . He incorporated [Toledo] into his empire with its dependent settlements and territories.'[8]

There can be little doubt that Alfonso was squaring up for some sort of final showdown with Islam. Difficult though it is to discern an overall game plan, it is clear that he saw himself as an integral part of the *Reconquista*, certainly as his father's successor and perhaps even with a divine mission. In another letter to Ibn Teshufin, which has survived, he contemptuously offered him a fleet to bring his forces across the Straits. And still he did not come.

In Toledo the tolerant government of Sisnando Davidez, a friend of the Cid and a man who, like him, had seen service in a Muslim state, was usurped within months by the rabid Christianity of Bernard, Archbishop of Toledo. This man was intent on restoring to his see the great prestige it had had under the Visigothic kings before the original Muslim conquest had swept it aside. He was also a monk from Cluny, in the Cid's day the most powerful and influential monastery in western Europe. It is no coincidence that his friend and fellow monk Odo of Châtillon would emerge in the next decade as Pope Urban II to demand that Christians descend on Jerusalem to free it from the Seljuks, thus sparking the First Crusade. Bernard and Odo between them were proof that it was not only the Sahara that produced fanatical bigots. The great mosque at Toledo became a Christian cathedral just before Christmas 1086. Its charter carried the words, 'the abode of demons [has become] a tabernacle of celestial virtue for all Christian people'.[9]

The *taifa* rulers were now between a rock and a hard place. Should they tolerate the increasing arrogance and territorial aggrandisement of Alfonso of Castile-Léon or invite Ibn Teshufin and his veiled ones from over the sea? Al-Mutamid summed it up brilliantly: 'I would rather be a camel-driver in Morocco than a swineherd in Castile.'[10]

The *Chronicon Regum Legionensum* lists Alfonso's territories by this time. Twenty-five towns fell to him after the taking of Toledo, and three in today's Portugal – Coria [actually conquered in 1079], Cintra and Santarem [these not until 1093]. A further nine cities – 'all of Extramadura' – were his by the turn of the century. 'This Alfonso', wrote Bishop Pelayo, 'was the father and defender of all the Spanish churches, and he did this because he was a Catholic in all respects. He was so terrifying to evil-doers that they never dared to show themselves in his sight.'[11] But there was one who did: Yusuf ibn Teshufin.

The long-awaited clash between them came on 23 October 1086, at Sagrajas near Badajoz. This was the most serious defeat inflicted on a Christian army for years and it seems in part to have been caused by Alfonso's complacency. Christian sources are remarkably reticent about it. Pelayo's *Chronicon* merely says 'In the Era 1124 [1086] was a battle on the field of Sagrajas with King Yusuf.'[12] Stanley Lane-Poole unfortunately did not quote his sources when he wrote: 'Alfonso, as he looked upon his own splendid army, exclaimed "With men like these I would fight devils, angels and ghosts!" Nevertheless, he resorted to a ruse to score a surprise over the joint forces of the Berbers and the Andalusians.'[13]

We do not have accurate numbers for either side. Some sources talk of 20,000 Almoravids stiffening the Andalusian army, which surely could have doubled that. Alfonso's troops, according to Muslim sources, numbered between 50,000 and 60,000 men, many of them mercenaries from France and Italy. It is likely that these figures are exaggerated, but Sagrajas was no skirmish in the valleys of the Cordillera Cantabrica and Ibn Teshufin, at least, had literally had years to prepare for it.

Alfonso's centre would have been composed of his knights, *caballeros*, *ricoshombres*, *hidalgos* and *infanzones* from Castile, Léon and Asturias. We know he had a strong Aragonese contingent too and all the great and good of Christian Spain would have been there, save one – Rodrigo, the Cid. The Campeador was still persona non grata in exile in Zaragoza and Alfonso was to regret his absence bitterly. The king's infantry, with their spears, billhooks, shields and swords, waited for the signal to attack just before dawn on the Muslim Sabbath – the ruse to which Lane-Poole refers. Most of

Alfonso's archers carried crossbows, weapons that the Church would try to ban sixty years later because of the appalling wounds they made. But the fact was that a crossbow was heavy and slow to reload. Even a skilled man could probably not get off more than two bolts (arrows) a minute, and this was woefully slower than the firing rate of the Almoravid short bows.

The Almoravid army, whose black tents were pitched a way to the rear of those of al-Mutamid, looked very different. We do not know where Ibn Teshufin was positioned, but it would probably have been, like Alfonso, in the centre, where he could direct operations. Ibn Yasim's original men of the rabat had fought on tribal lines, but Yusuf, like the original he was, had reorganized the Almoravids to create a well-oiled military machine. His own bodyguard – the Black Guard – surrounded him on the field, so that any Christian knight intent on galloping out, as Rodrigo Diaz was wont to do, roaring defiance and offering individual combat, would get short shrift and an early death. The Guard was composed of 500 cavalry, comprising Arabs, Turks and even Europeans, with an extra 2,000 black African cavalry. The horses they rode were Arabs, faster and lighter than Alfonso's destriers, and their speed and manoeuvrability were to prove decisive in the hours that followed.

In the psychological battle at Sagrajas the element of surprise was with the Almoravids. Alfonso's troops had faced Andalusian armies before. They were used to the light horses, the lightly armed troops, the short stirrups and low saddles of the cavalry and the short, curved composite bows of the archers. They had never seen before the black-skinned, black-veiled, black-coated Almoravids, whose banners danced everywhere, woven with verses from the Koran to boost their courage. They advanced in endless waves, three-ranks deep, dark men behind huge oryx-skin or hippopotamus-hide shields. And the Christians were terrified by two tactics unknown in all Spain – the use of camels and the terrible, relentless thunder of the drums. Camels had been seen in southern Spain for about a century by this point, but only as beasts of burden. True, the dromedaries were better suited, with their flat feet and prodigious lack of thirst, for desert warfare, but their speed, noise and smell threw

Alfonso's cavalry into total confusion. Drums to act as battle signals became commonplace in the centuries ahead, but Europe had never seen them before 1086. Mule-riding drummers, their drums across their animals' necks and black turbans swathed around their heads, sounded the death roll for thousands that day.

'Drums, only drums,' wrote novelist Robert Krepps as part of the Cid legend nine hundred years later, 'but drums that shook the adversary's courage as they shook the ground. . . . Only drums – drums that would now decide the fortunes of war. . . . The drums launched the Moors into attack, the drums called them to retreat. The drums paced their horses and their pumping legs. The drums directed, commanded, cajoled, heartened, led, fought.'[14]

Still at prayer and kneeling on their mats in the direction of Mecca, the Andalusian camp was quickly routed by a charge of Aragonese knights who drove them from the field. According to the modern version of the tale

> The camp erupted men, tugging on pieces of armour and clapping on light headpieces as they ran, slamming the short Arabian saddles on the bare backs of chargers that snorted and reared in surprise. Messengers galloped at full speed. . . . Boys still naked from the sleeping rugs dashed about carrying scimitars and spears and screeching for their unarmed masters. Concubines rolled out of bed and knelt in feverish prayer that the infidel would not reach the encampment.[15]

Alfonso himself probably led his main army against the second fortifications, the black-skinned tents of the Almoravid encampment. Here he met stouter resistance, but even so the day seemed to be going well, after the initial visual and aural shock was over. Then the Christians found themselves struck in the flank by the sledgehammer blow of Ibn Teshufin's cavalry, camels and all, which forced Alfonso to pull back to a line of defence in front of his own camp. Everywhere the bare-footed Berber archers darted in and out of the Castilian cavalry, while Ibn Teshufin's infantry hurled their bamboo spears and cut the Christians' throats with their murderous curved daggers:

Bronze statue of the Cid in Seville. *(Ken Welsh, Seville, Spain/Bridgeman Art Library)*

Silver coin of King Alfonso VI of Castile, Léon and Asturias. *(Author's collection)*

The coffer of the Cid in Burgos Cathedral. Was this the chest Rodrigo Diaz used to dupe the Jews of Burgos? *(Postcard in author's collection)*

The tomb of Ramon Berenguer, Count of Barcelona (1024–76), the man twice defeated by the Cid in the political turmoil of the eleventh century. *(Index, Barcelona Cathedral, Spain/Bridgeman Art Library)*

Duel between Rodrigo of Vivar and Martin Gomez, from *The Chronicles of Spain* written on vellum in 1344. *(Giraudon, Academia das Ciencias de Lisboa, Lisbon, Portugal/Bridgeman Art Library)*

The sixteenth-century Cid from *Chronica Particular del Cid* showing the warrior on Babieca. *(Hulton Archive/Getty Images)*

Dominic Vivant Denon reinters the bones of the Cid in his tomb at the monastery of San Pedro de Cardena, from the painting by Alexandre Fragonard. *(Musée Antoine Lecuyer, Saint-Quentin, France/Bridgeman Art Library)*

The Oath of St Gadea. The Cid extracts an oath from King Alfonso of his innocence in the death of his brother Sancho, from a nineteenth-century painting by Marcos Hiraldez de Acosta. *(Index, Palacio del Senado, Madrid, Spain/Bridgeman Art Library)*

LE CID.

The Cid as portrayed in Corneille's play *Le Cid*, from an engraving by Alexandre Marie Colin and Edmond Geffroy. *(Private collection/ Bridgeman Art Library)*

Statue of the Cid unveiled at Burgos by Franco at the height of his power. *(Manuel Belver/Corbis)*

The celluloid Cid – Charlton Heston on the battlements of Valencia watches the approach of the Almoravid fleet. From the film *El Cid* directed by Anthony Mann in 1961. *(Silver Screen Collection/Hulton Archive/Getty Images)*

Tizona del Cid. One of two weapons obtained, according to legend, by the Cid in his wars against the Moors. Experts today cannot decide its authenticity. *(Lindsay Mastro)*

Gateway to the Monastery of San Pedro de Cardena showing the Cid as Santiago Motamoros (St James the Moor Slayer). *(Luc Buerman/zefa/ Corbis)*

The plain of Sagrajas resounds with the pealing of weapons on shields, the raging of oaths and prayers, the loudness of hate and brutality hurled together in the beginning of the bloodiest combat that Spain has ever seen. . . . The squad of Turkish archers, front rank kneeling, second rank shooting over their heads and third rank standing quietly with nocked arrows to take the place of those who fell . . .[16]

The Aragonese cavalry trotted back – how far they had pursued al-Mutamid we do not know – and now their horses were blown. They held off, perhaps waiting for the horses to recover, or perhaps uncertain as to what to do, and then withdrew when fresh Almoravid forces – almost certainly a well-hidden reserve – appeared on the scene. Al-Mutamid may have been able to rally his men too, although checking running soldiers is a difficult task, and the attack on the Christians became merciless. Beaten back from their camp, which the Almoravids tore to pieces, Alfonso's knights took up position on a nearby hill, forming a ring of steel around their king until nightfall gave them a chance to escape.

'Christendom broke and fled the field,' wrote Krepps, 'while the storm of Islam followed on behind, whooping at the heels of the rout.'[17] Lane-Poole has a similarly chilling signing-off: 'Alfonso barely escaped with some five hundred horsemen. Many thousands of the best sword-arms in Castile lay stiff and nerveless on that fatal field.'[18]

We must always be wary of extraordinary numbers. One Muslim source claims 300,000 Christian dead and even conservative ones quote between 10,000 and 24,000, with only 3,000 Muslim casualties. Such figures invariably were compiled years later by men who were not there and, as always, history is written by the victors. The heads of the slaughtered were lopped off by the Almoravids and piled high enough that a muezzin could climb to the top of one such pile in the redeeming dawn of another day to call the faithful to prayer.

But while Alfonso licked his wounds and tried to grasp the enormity of what had happened, not only did Ibn Teshufin not pursue the shattered Castilians and Léonese, but he actually went home to the Maghrib. Robert Krepps has the neat excuse that Ibn Teshufin's son had died and he went home to bury him, but there is no mention of this in any contemporary source. The only death recorded is that of his cousin, Abu Bakr, but perhaps this would have caused instability at home and all in all Ibn Teshufin does seem a rather reluctant conqueror. The point to remember is that he was an old man, brought up in the early days of the Almoravid when strategy, like tactics, was immobile and solid. The whole of the Almoravid invasion of al-Andalus could be seen as a defensive measure, designed to save Moorish Spain from the Christian onslaught from the north. In that sense Ibn Teshufin had saved Badajoz, cut, at least temporarily, the *paria* (funds that were to be diverted to Baghdad from now on) and generally drawn a line in the sand. The chronicler Abd Allah's words, put into Ibn Teshufin's mouth, have a curiously modern, devolutionary ring to them: 'We have not come here for this kind of thing. The princes [amirs] know best what to do in their own territories.'[19]

Ibn Teshufin retained the vital port of the old Roman town of Algeciras which he had taken on his march north and probably left a token force behind at the disposal of the amirs. But in fact he was no friend of theirs either. If they despised him for his uncouth manners and lack of sophistication, he loathed them for their softness and lack of faith.

'After this,' wrote the author of the *Historia Roderici* chirpily, 'he [the Cid] returned to his native land of Castile'[20] – as though he was coming back from a holiday. In fact, a panicky Alfonso sent for him, as he sent for others too, and this reconciliation speaks volumes both for the nature of exile in the eleventh century and for the seriousness of the body-blow that was Sagrajas. 'King Alfonso received him honourably and gladly', but the reception cost him dear. It was a seller's market and both men knew it. We do not know enough about the personalities of either the Cid or his king to know how the encounter went. But out of it, Rodrigo got the castles of Gormaz (one of the most powerful in Spain),[21] Ibio, Campoo, Iguna, Briviesca, Langa and Duañez. The castle of Gormaz today receives few visitors, partially because of the steep rocky climb to its huge walls. It was built by the Moors in the middle of the tenth century and is one of the largest castles still standing in Europe. Its walls are nearly a mile in circumference. The Caliph's Gate still stands as a horseshoe reminder of its origins. This list is so astonishing (presumably Rodrigo's former estates, including Vivar, were returned to him too) that some historians have doubted the *Historia Roderici*. A glance at the map, however, shows Alfonso's craftiness. He gave the fortresses to Rodrigo rather as his contemporary William I of England gave counties to his barons. They were to 'hold' these lands in the name of the king, and in the infant feudal system of northern Spain that was precisely how Rodrigo held his castles. They were mostly built along the Duero, the river that fringed the *tierras desplobadas* and offered the most likely direction of attack either from Yusuf ibn Teshufin's veiled ones or perhaps even a renewed and invigorated al-Andalus. But, for Rodrigo, it just got better: 'Furthermore, Alfonso pardoned him and gave him this privilege in his kingdom, written and confirmed under seal, stipulating that all the land and castles which he might acquire from the Saracens in the land of the Saracens, should be absolutely his in full ownership, not only his but also his sons' and his daughters' and all his descendants.'[22]

This is a more important passage than Cid scholars have realised. First, it was 'written and confirmed under seal', implying that at one time some sort of contractual document existed. How much horse-trading Rodrigo had to do with Alfonso to get it we do not know. Second, it talks of 'full ownership', implying that this is different from the demesne-holding of the earlier listed castles in Castile-Léon. In theory, under the feudal system lands and castles could revert to the monarch who leased them should, for example, the tenant-in-chief displease his lord in some way. Third, it implies that the Cid will be unleashed at some time in the future to invade al-Andalus. His famous taking of Valencia makes perfect sense in this context and even gives royal authority for Rodrigo to take the title of Prince of Valencia in his own right, something that historian Menendez Pidal missed or dismissed, as the case may be. And fourth, the reference to plural sons is fascinating. We know that Rodrigo and Jimena had two daughters, but only one son – Diego –

is known by name. Were there others, perhaps, who died in infancy and whose names went unrecorded?

Because we do not know where Rodrigo's family were during his exile in Zaragoza, we can do no more than speculate on any reunion now. If Jimena and her children (who would have been between 8 and 12 by now) had been at the monastery of San Pedro de Cardena or with Jimena's family in Oviedo, then no doubt Rodrigo would have sent for them at once and established himself in comfort in whichever of Alfonso's castles suited him best.

However, the *Historia Roderici* is plainly wrong in sequence at this point. Chapter 27 makes the rather lame point that not all of the Cid's 'wars and rumours of wars' are contained in the book, as if the author suddenly had an attack of the jitters about his accuracy or even pointing to the fact that an earlier manuscript was lost. For some reason Alfonso rode out of Toledo on campaign and left Rodrigo behind, paying the king's troops. But this was the spring of 1089 and what had happened in the intervening two and a half years is largely a blank page.

Maria and Cristina would have been entering their teens by now, learning all the etiquette of Alfonso's court which would make them loyal and dutiful wives in the not-too-distant future. Diego would have been practising with sword and buckler the moves his father used for real on the battlefield. We know that Rodrigo witnessed Alfonso's charters as a prominent *ricohombre* in July 1087 and again in March 1088. The rest is silence.

In the spring of 1089 Rodrigo undertook what may have been his first chevauchee (raid) on Alfonso's behalf. With an army of 7,000 (William of Normandy had taken an entire country with about this number just over twenty years earlier), he crossed the Duero 'by the middle ford',[23] camping at Fresno not far from his own castle of Gormaz. On 20 May he celebrated the feast of Pentecost[24] at Calamocha and received ambassadors from Abu Marwan Abd al-Malik ben Hudhayl ibn Razin, amir of Albarracin. No doubt the amir's scouts had watched Rodrigo's dust for some time and the Cid's advance south was leisurely, pausing to observe the overtly Christian niceties before talking politics. He was entering the Spanish Levante now and the mere presence of his army seems to have had Albarracin's ruler falling over himself to pay tribute to Alfonso and curry favour with him. This done, the Cid marched due east to the River Turia and followed its course to Murviedro, north of Valencia. And here history was almost to repeat itself.

The *taifa* state of Valencia was still ruled by the obnoxious al-Qadir, who was causing as much of an outcry by his arbitrary rule here as he had before he was kicked out of Toledo. A local governor had risen against him, enlisting the aid of Murdhir al-Hayib, amir of Lerida and Denia, who in turn enlisted the aid of his old comrade-in-arms Count Berenguer of Barcelona. By the spring of 1089, therefore, we find an almost identical line-up to that of eight years earlier. Al-Hayib and Berenguer had been half-heartedly besieging the city for two years. Of course, we must remember that even in siege warfare there was a 'season'. Encampment in tents or peasants' hovels throughout the winter was nobody's idea of entertainment, but each time a siege was lifted it in effect had to be restarted, because breaches in the walls could be repaired and garrisons strengthened.

To avoid this problem, Berenguer was busy building and improving the castles of Cebolla and Liria, to enable him to keep his forces within striking distance of Valencia but without them being dangerously exposed on the plain below the city's walls. The last thing he wanted to see was the Cid's dragon banner on the horizon – he had gone down before that once previously. His men, however, perhaps already a new generation of hotheads who had never faced Rodrigo, had other ideas. They 'began to boast and to utter many curses against Rodrigo and to scorn him with much mockery'[25] but Berenguer called them to heel. He hauled down his tents, abandoned his castles and retreated north to Requera, then to Zaragoza and finally home. The *Historia Roderici* seems schizoid at this point. On the one hand, Rodrigo had no intention of attacking Berenguer, 'for he respected his lord King Alfonso, whose relative the Count was',[26] but on the other hand 'Rodrigo . . . remained at the place where [Berenguer] had fixed his tents, attacking his enemies on all sides.'[27]

It is unlikely that the Alfonso–Berenguer kinship would have caused the Cid a moment's doubt. Berenguer was trying to take

Valencia in effect from Alfonso's control. The attack at the camp was probably some sort of mopping-up operation, designed to clear the area. The arrival of Rodrigo at Valencia must have sent al-Qadir into a spin of panic. He sent envoys with 'innumerable and very valuable presents' to Rodrigo and swore homage to Alfonso, as did the governor of Murviedo to the north.

The Cid rode north and 'fought fiercely there and mastered and laid waste the country'[28] before establishing his army at Requera. Exactly who he was fighting and why is not recorded, but the scene was the Cordillera Alpuerte and perhaps these were stragglers of Berenguer's army or those of al-Hayib. He was still at Requera when news reached him of the return of Yusuf ibn Teshufin.

Al-Mutamid of Seville had sailed to Africa some time in the winter of 1088/9 with exactly the same request he had made before. Despite the defeat at Sagrajas, Alfonso had set up a garrison in the castle of Aledo far to the south of the Spanish Levante and about 40 miles from the sea. It was an isolated outpost, but it was at the heart of a Christian enclave in the Muslim wilderness and would act as a gentle reminder to al-Mutamid that he was, as far as Alfonso was concerned, still supposed to be paying him tribute. Reprisal raids were the order of the day here, with neither Christian nor Moor venturing too far from the castle walls and never without a coat of mail. This time there was no delay. Ibn Teshufin, a very old man by this time, crossed the Straits in his black-sailed dhows and joined forces with the amirs of Seville, Almeria and Granada. The *Historia Roderici* calls these veiled ones variously 'Ishmaelites'[29] and 'Moabites'[30] – both Hebrew terms from the Old Testament – as opposed to the 'Saracens' of al-Andalus.

When it was obvious that Aledo was the Almoravid target, Alfonso raised his army, probably in Toledo, and sent a letter to Rodrigo to support him. But then it all went wrong in a classic example of the communication difficulties that medieval armies habitually faced. Rodrigo had at most 7,000 troops and they were 400 miles away from Ibn Teshufin. The size of the Almoravid/ al-Andalus army by this time is anybody's guess, but since it was composed of the forces of the three largest *taifa* states in Spain, it very possibly outnumbered Rodrigo's by five or six to one. He was not about to get himself outmanoeuvred by such superior numbers and duly moved into position to link up with Alfonso. At Jativa, south of Valencia, the royal messengers caught up with the Cid with the news that Alfonso was marching from Toledo with 'an infinite multitude of horsemen and footsoldiers'.[31] It was three years since Sagrajas and the king had clearly replenished his army. Rodrigo marched to Ontoniente, in a direct line towards Aledo, and stocked up with supplies. Still he waited for Alfonso but still the king did not come. He sent his scouts, men armed to the teeth and riding fast genets, as far south as Villera, five days' march from Aledo and the Almoravids.

For reasons that are not clear, Alfonso had taken a more easterly route to arrive at Hellin, two days' hard riding away from the Cid's encampments. Rodrigo hurried east, riding ahead of his army with a handful of knights, no doubt with the loyal Alvar Fañez among them, but Alfonso had already left, marching directly against the Almoravids. Then, a bizarre thing happened; Ibn Teshufin upped sticks and left. The explanation given by the author of the *Historia Roderici* is not altogether satisfactory: '[The Almoravids] turned in flight at once, terrified by the fear of the king even before his arrival and fled before his face in confusion.'[32]

Why? Ibn Teshufin had shattered Alfonso at Sagrajas and even though his black drummers no longer had the element of surprise, there was at least a fifty-fifty chance of victory. Perhaps these odds did not appeal to the desert ascetic and they certainly did not to the amirs of al-Andalus, whose squabblings among themselves would cause an exasperated Ibn Teshufin to turn on them the following year.

But if both sides got off lightly in the non-battle that was Aledo, Rodrigo Diaz did not. Medieval kings ruled by hedging themselves around with the superstitious trappings of religion and by not suffering fools or betrayal at all. In Alfonso's eyes the Cid was anything but a fool, but the king felt betrayed. Where was the Campeador when he needed him most? And what would have happened if the battle at Aledo had materialized and turned into another Christian rout?

Rodrigo went back to his camp at Elche as bewildered and confused by Alfonso's inexplicable actions as the king was by the Cid's. Men began to desert Rodrigo, perhaps distancing themselves from the royal retribution that was to follow. In Toledo the gossips were busy again, perhaps the same ones who had poisoned the king against his erstwhile champion before. The Cid, they said, had deliberately disobeyed orders. At best, he had dragged his feet, ridden slowly, rested too often on the road. At worst he was 'an evil man and a traitor',[33] who was prepared to stand by and let the Ishmaelites and Moabites slaughter his own lord. It was nonsense, but Alfonso began to believe it. He was furious and stripped Rodrigo of all his honours. All the castles granted to his care by the king, as well as the Cid's own hereditary lands, for example in Vivar, were taken from him. His gold, silver, hawks, dogs, furniture – anything belonging to the traitor became the property of Castile-Léon and the charter granting all this to the Cid's children for ever was conveniently forgotten and perhaps, in that it has not survived, torn up. Worse still, Jimena and her children were arrested. We do not know what happened to them in Rodrigo's first exile, but now 'his wife and children, arrested by trickery, [were] cruelly retained in custody'.[34] Exactly where and what that cruelty entailed or what the trickery involved, is not known.

Rodrigo sent an ambassador, a trusted knight who may have been Alvar Fañez, to declare his innocence. 'My lord himself,' the *Historia Roderici* quotes, 'will fight in person in your court against another equal and similar to him; or his champion will fight on his behalf against another equal and similar to him.'[35] What Rodrigo was offering was trial by combat, portrayed in a different context in the Charlton Heston film as how God judged a man's guilt or innocence. The idea was a northern European one, passing from the Vikings via England to Normandy and so across the Pyrenees into Spain. It appealed to notions of chivalry and the fact that the Cid, now in his mid-40s, was willing to put his life on the line speaks volumes for his belief in his innocence of the charges laid against him. But Alfonso would not listen to Rodrigo's protestations and sent Fañez away empty-handed. He did, however, after what time-lag is uncertain, send the Cid's family back to him.

In an extraordinary document – which we cannot actually prove is either original or genuine – Rodrigo sent a detailed legalistic defence to his king, probably in the autumn of 1089. It is quoted in full in the *Historia Roderici* in a series of four oaths. The first was a repetition of the offer to stand trial by combat plus the assurance that Rodrigo had ignored no order from Alfonso, merely that the king had changed his route and that he, Rodrigo, could not find out where he was. The second oath was that had he reached either Aledo or Molina, he would have been honoured to fight with his king. Third, the Cid denied the charge of wishing harm to Alfonso or his army and contended that the 'great and unheard-of shame'[36] of the king stripping him of his honours was totally unjustified. And finally, Rodrigo swore that from the time he had kissed Alfonso's hand in Toledo (the reconciliation) until the moment he heard of Jimena's imprisonment, he had always supported his king: 'I spoke no evil of him, thought no evil. . . .'[37]

This extraordinary statement is not the eleventh-century equivalent of a court-martial testimony. Although it contains evidence, common sense and a rational – if limited – explanation of what went on, it places far more stress on the Cid's loyalty to Alfonso and his willingness to go to any lengths to clear his name. If Alfonso did not like the trial by combat idea, then Rodrigo was willing to undergo any other trial the king wished. It is difficult after a thousand years to understand the mindset of men in relation to trials by ordeal. The cynical stance was that Rodrigo of Vivar was the Campeador, a battle-hardened veteran whose skill as a swordsman was legendary. Who could Alfonso find to stand against him? On the other hand, the Cid was middle-aged; perhaps a younger man could best him? And where, in all this, was the wisdom and omniscience of 'the truest and most pious Judge of all?'[38]

In the event, Alfonso of Castile, Léon and Asturias and now nearly half of Spain declined Rodrigo's offer and ignored his protestations of innocence. He was in exile once more. And he would never see Vivar again.

9

Valencia the Shining

One of the themes common to the later epic sources on the Cid is that of wanderer. He is portrayed as constantly on the move, restless and misunderstood, rather like the grim, laconic gunfighter hero of the wild west tradition. The Christmas of 1089 saw him at his castle in Elche with his family. Alfonso was busy stripping the Cid of his lands and estates, but presumably Elche, in the Spanish Levante, was too far away to be affected. Christmas was a hallowed time, of course, in the Christian year, but it was a time for celebration too. No doubt Rodrigo felt dismayed and aggrieved by his king's attitude, but he may have put a brave face on it for the days of entertainment. That far south the weather was probably good enough for outdoor activities like jousting. Indoors, in the great hall at Elche, lute music would fill the evenings with songs and dancing.

How many men accompanied the Cid in exile this time is not known. Scholars of the later epics point out the obsession with wealth that runs through them. It might jar a little to find the 'noblest knight in the world' grubbing about to make a buck, but he had obligations in the feudal sense. If men had gone into exile with him, forfeiting their estates, he had to provide for them; if they did so voluntarily, then he was doubly obliged. The *Historia Roderici* says he spent only Christmas at Elche and 'after the feast' marched north to Polap where there was a 'great cave full of treasure'.[1]

This town, near the modern city of Benidorm, was a part of the amir Mundhir al-Hayib's *taifa* state of Denia. After a few days' siege the Cid took the place and helped himself to its valuables – gold, silver and 'innumerable precious stuffs'[2] – which probably means Moorish silks. This was in no sense a conquest: Rodrigo was merely paying his troops with the spoils of war, acting out the role of renegade and freebooter. Portum Tarvani was his next target, although we are unsure precisely where that was, and he spent Lent and Easter at Ondara, restoring and refortifying the castle for his own safety. We can be sure of the dates here. Lent began on 6 March and Easter Day was 21 April. The author of the *Historia Roderici* is keen to show the piety of his hero, who never fails to observe Christian festivals, even in the middle of wholesale slaughter or bandit raids.

Al-Hayib hurriedly sent ambassadors to buy Rodrigo off. So did al-Hayib's rival, al-Qadir of Valencia. So did those prominent Andalusians who opposed al-Qadir's detested rule. The Cid was, in effect, receiving the *parias* usually due to kings. He was carrying out precisely the kind of 'protection racket' begun by Fernando of Castile and continued by all three of his sons. By the summer he was north of Almenara, the site of the campaign that had earned him the first epic on his life, the Song of the Campeador, and sitting in the castle of Burriana 'as still as a stone'.[3] It is perhaps a little odd that the *Carmen* should be written in these years. Perhaps it was no longer sung during the Cid's second exile; perhaps, on the contrary, it was used by Rodrigo himself as a propaganda tool, to boost his own (no doubt flagging) ego and even gain support.

It was his very immovability at Burriana that prompted al-Hayib to ask for help. As so often in the previous fifty years, a beleaguered ruler of al-Andalus begged support from the Christian north. And the coalition was a formidable one: Alfonso of Castile, Sancho of Aragon, Berenguer of Barcelona, Ermengol the Count of Urgel and the amir of Zaragoza all promised aid. It was a mark of how formidable an enemy they believed the Cid to be. In the event, however, al-Hayib was to be disappointed. Alfonso had his hands full defending Toledo against the Almoravids and his troops probably never set out. Sancho of Aragon also had other priorities, as did Ermengol. Al-Musta'in of Zaragoza was the Cid's friend, and while feigning support for al-Hayib, promptly kept Rodrigo apprised of the situation as regularly as he could.

The coalition may have vanished in the fog of impending war, but Berenguer could still put a huge army into the field and his forces must have seriously outnumbered Rodrigo's. The Cid, perhaps unhappy with the defensibility of Burriana, retreated into the mountains of Morella where there was plenty of food in the form of sheep and goats. This was probably the pinewoods of Tevar to the north and nearer the sea.

According to the *Historia Roderici*, Berenguer took his army through Albarracin and accepted tribute from al-Musta'in at Daroca, taking the amir to meet Alfonso camped near Oron. Clearly, either Berenguer believed Rodrigo was still active or he was unwilling to take no for an answer. That was, however, precisely the answer the Castilian king gave him. Either Alfonso did not want to risk his army because of the Almoravid presence or he felt he had punished Rodrigo enough. So Berenguer came on alone.

We know his commanders. 'Bernardo' was Deudat Bernat de Claramunt from Tarragona. 'Giraldo Aleman' was Guerau Alemany de Cervello and 'Dorca' was Dorca de Castellvell. The Catalan names always sound odd, but they may well have represented even more cosmopolitan interests. Bernat's name was French and Guerau was 'the German'. It is another reminder of the multiculturalism that was the Spain of the early *Reconquista*. We also know that the faithful al-Musta'in's gallopers brought Rodrigo news of Berenguer's troop movements.

Two letters, one from Berenguer to the Cid and the other the Cid's reply, are quoted in full in the *Historia Roderici*. Historians are divided on their authenticity, but if genuine they give us a fascinating insight into battlefield protocol of the period. The Berenguer letter expressed fury that Rodrigo was in correspondence with al-Musta'in and that he had appropriated cash which was 'rightfully' the *paria* payable to Barcelona: 'You are still in possession of our money, which you stole from us.'[4] Berenguer then took the moral high ground by refusing to lower himself to the Cid's apparent contemptuous remark that the Catalans were much like their wives. What Berenguer was trying to do was to annoy Rodrigo so much that he abandoned his impregnable mountain stronghold: 'We see and understand', he wrote, 'that your gods are mountains, ravens, crows, hawks and eagles and nearly every sort of bird; you trust more in their auguries than in God.'[5]

This is an extraordinary statement and it was taken up by later chroniclers. We have already seen that there may have been pockets of paganism in eleventh-century Spain, but they are likely to have been in the Catalan/Basque territory rather than on the more prosaic *meseta* of Castile that was Rodrigo's home. In the curiously Celtic heritage of Catalonia the spiritual, supernatural power of birds of prey was a tradition that may have died hard. Ravens, crows, hawks and eagles all held the same place in Celtic mythology. The raven carried the souls of the dead from the battlefield to the afterlife, while both the hawk and the eagle were associated with death and evil.

Berenguer's next taunt is more predictable: 'If you will abandon your mountain and come out to meet us on the plain, you will indeed be the Rodrigo whom men call the warrior and the Campeador. If you do not do this, you will be what they call in Castilian *alevoso* [traitor] and in French *bauzador* and *fraudator* [deceiver].'[6] Finally, the count, no doubt waiting with his exposed army and watching the mountains for signs of life, threatened the Cid: 'God will avenge his churches which you have broken into violently and violated.'[7]

This charge has been raised by all modern commentators on the Cid, totally at odds as it is with the later legends of the perfect Christian knight. It is a classic example of the complex paradox at the heart of chivalry. On the one hand men like Rodrigo and King Alfonso could endow churches and monasteries and on the other they could physically pull them down. Churches were houses of God, but they also contained gold and silver, the lifeblood of the mercenary. We have no actual proof of course that the Cid was genuinely guilty of iconoclasm, but we cannot disprove it either.

Rodrigo's reply was not long in coming. He agreed he had reviled Berenguer and his knights and he still did. And he explained why. It annoyed him that Berenguer had told all and sundry that he (Rodrigo) was afraid to face the count – he had of course defeated him once before – and that Berenguer's claim that he only held off against the Cid so as not to offend Alfonso was so much rubbish. Rodrigo then turned to the present. He was waiting, he said, to see Berenguer fulfil his boast. He was on high but flat ground, ideal for battle, and he promised to 'pay you the wages I usually pay you'[8] (death). If the count failed to meet him, however, Rodrigo would let all Spain know that he was a coward. In a brilliant sentence, the Cid answered the jibe about the birds and the caustic attempt to outdo him in semantics: 'You have hurled boastful words at me, saying that you would defeat me and possess me as a captive dead or alive; but this lies in the hand of God, not yours. You have most falsely made sport of me in saying that I have acted *aleve* [treacherously] in the speech of Castile or *bauzia* in that of Gaul, an obvious lie uttered by your own mouth.'[9]

He then accused Berenguer of being a liar, in a phrase which some historians have assumed refers to the belief that the count killed his own brother in 1082. Certainly Berenguer was found guilty of that murder after failing a trial by battle in the presence of Alfonso of Castile in 1096/7, but since the Cid is so outspoken against Berenguer in his letter, why does he not come straight out with it? He merely had his clerk write: 'Never have I acted thus [treacherously]. Rather has he [Berenguer] who is already renowned for it in such stories as you will know; and what I refer to is widely known to many, both Christian and pagan.'[10] This is merely underlining that Berenguer Ramon was a dishonest, duplicitous character – and there were few in Spain who could doubt it.

In the clash that came with first light, Rodrigo, unusually, was caught napping. Berenguer's scouts had clearly found his camp in the sierras and under cover of darkness a detachment climbed to higher ground still, overlooking the Cid's tents. At dawn Berenguer's main force attacked uphill and the Campeador found himself surrounded. Rallying his men as quickly as he could, Rodrigo led an attack that smashed the Catalan formations, but the Cid himself was wounded and unhorsed. This is the only time in his career that any wound is recorded and the implication from the *Historia Roderici* at least is that it was the difficulty of the ground which caused the horse (Babieca?) to slip and that the Cid was wounded on the ground. Contrary to the rather feeble and fatalistic behaviour of Rodrigo's warriors when he is fatally wounded in the Charlton Heston film, falling back in disorder along the curve of the bay outside Valencia, Rodrigo's troops held their ground against Berenguer and drove them back to total defeat.

Again, as with so many eleventh-century battles, we have no clear idea of the numbers involved. The *Historia Roderici* cites 'an innumerable multitude' slain, and again, curiously, all the leading commanders surrendered rather than died fighting. The chronicler records that Deudat Bernard, Giraldo Aleman and two others with 'very many other noble men', Ramon Mir and Ricart Guillem, were held in chains separate from the rest. 'Thus was accomplished', wrote the author of the *Historia Roderici*, 'the victory ever to be extolled and remembered of Rodrigo over Count Berenguer and his army.'[11]

The camp on the plain below the battlefield was sacked and the list of spoils was impressive: 'many vessels of gold and silver, precious textiles, mules, horses, palfreys,[12] spears, coats of mail, shields and all objects of worth . . .'.[13] Berenguer was certainly not travelling light. And, 'chastised and confounded by God and made captive at the hands of Rodrigo',[14] we can imagine his sense of humiliation.

Then the horse-trading began. Ransom was first on the agenda. Berenguer and Aleman between them agreed 80,000 gold mancuses,[15] a vast sum, with rather less, one supposes, for their subordinates. Such cash was not available quickly and the ransom terms were met in the weeks and months ahead – in gold, silver, children and even relatives as pledges that all would be paid. In the event Rodrigo the knight overcame Rodrigo the bandit and he sent everyone home in an act of largesse worthy of his legend.

Afterwards the Cid went north to Zaragoza, the scene of his first exile, and spent a few days at Daroca. He may have been recuperating from his wound there, or he may simply have been ill. The *Historia Roderici* merely records in passing that he was recovering his health when ambassadors returned from Zaragoza to report that Berenguer was there anxious to make peace. This is an intriguing episode in the annals of the Cid, because he was clearly still contemptuous of the Catalan and had no wish to deal further with him. It was his knights who persuaded him, although the words put into their mouths by the author of the *Historia Roderici* are hardly compelling: 'What ill has Count Berenguer ever done to you, that you do not wish to be at peace with him?' No doubt the flies on the wall enjoyed Rodrigo's answer!

It must have occurred to the Cid to wonder what the Count of Barcelona was up to; in eleventh-century Spain nobody's virtue was over-nice. We must conclude that the victory at Tevar had been so complete that Berenguer was willing to pull out of the Levante – 'the count placed in Rodrigo's hand and protection that part of Hispania which was subject to his [Berenguer's] overlordship'.[16] The alternative was to fight Rodrigo again and it is likely that Berenguer had no wish to face the man a third time. Al-Hayib's death at this crucial time (whether by accident or design is not recorded) left a boy, Sulayman, on the throne and those viziers appointed regents split al-Hayib's state into three, making them all the easier for the Cid to rampage through if he so wished.

The next Christmas Rodrigo spent at Cebolla, today's El Puig de Santa Maria, and he settled down to besiege, in the new year of 1091, the castle at Livia ,where he 'handed out enormous wages to his troops'.[17] The *Historia Roderici* contains two chapters at this point which some historians have doubted. Letters reached the Cid from Constance of Burgundy, Alfonso's second wife and thus Queen of Castile-Léon. The much-married Alfonso wed Constance in 1079 when Rodrigo Diaz was still in royal favour, so we can suppose that the queen and her husband's subject knew each other well. She told Rodrigo that Alfonso intended another campaign against the Almoravids, partially to stop their new advance and partially, no doubt, to avenge Sagrajas.

Yusuf ibn Teshufin, defying the conventions of mortality (he must by now have been nearly 80), crossed the Straits again in June 1090, no doubt delighted to learn that two Christian armies were tearing each other apart at Tevar, and besieged Toledo. But the city proved too strong and the Almoravids pulled back to Granada, nursing a grievance over the womanly behaviour of the *taifa* amirs.

Queen Constance's request, echoed by various Castilian friends of the Cid, was that he should bring his army to the king's aid; the last time Alfonso had gone in to battle without him, he had suffered a very bloody nose. By this time Livia was on the point of surrender but Rodrigo lifted the siege, no doubt to the great bewilderment and relief of the populace, whose belief in miracles was probably reaffirmed, and then he marched to join Alfonso at Martes, near Cordoba. 'When the king heard that Rodrigo was on his way he immediately went out to meet him and received him in peace with great honour.'[18]

For Alfonso to make the first move and ride or even walk forward to greet the Cid was indeed a mark of respect. We are left wondering why. Did Queen Constance write her letter at Alfonso's instigation, because he was too proud to ask help from the man he had twice sent into exile? Or did this incident never happen at all? The two armies, the Cid's and Alfonso's, then apparently marched on Granada and the veiled ones. The *Historia Roderici* claims that Ibn Teshufin declined battle because he was 'terrified' of Alfonso. This is unlikely. The man was a wily old fox and a highly talented general and as such he knew when discretion was the better part of valour. He had smashed the Castilian king before, but the Castilian Campeador was another matter. No doubt Ibn Teshufin's scouts would have reported that the Cid was with Alfonso and the Cid had never lost a fight. Ibn Teshufin dithered for six days, then slithered away without giving battle.

In an unidentified mountainous area called Libriella, Rodrigo pitched his tents in front of the king's and Alfonso was furious – 'Look at the insult and shame which Rodrigo inflicts upon us!'[19] – and launched a vicious verbal attack on the Cid accusing him of all sorts of things, true and untrue. Rodrigo took it all on the chin, but when Alfonso threatened to arrest him, the Cid turned on his heel and marched back to his own camp. If some historians have doubted all this, they have failed to grasp the essential pettiness and touchiness of Alfonso VI. The chroniclers paint a flat, two-dimensional portrait: the king is good and just and pious – typical eleventh-century superficiality. We know enough about Rodrigo and his king to know that the pair had a love-hate relationship. Alfonso needed the Cid – sometimes desperately – to keep his state together. On the other hand Rodrigo could be insufferable, as with the tent incident and his failure to link up with the king's forces two years earlier. On his part, the Cid was torn between the oath of homage he had probably made to his king and the fact that the man had kicked him out – twice – and imprisoned his family for a time. On top of all that, Rodrigo was now receiving the *paria* from *taifa* states and was de facto ruler of a sizeable portion of eastern Spain. Perhaps, by 1091–2, the Cid knelt to no man.

Men began to leave Rodrigo at this point, as they had before, drifting to Alfonso's tents under cover of night, and the Cid packed up his tents and marched towards Valencia. He was now riding through the Sierra de Benicadell, where he had failed to find the king's army in 1089. Probably believing Alfonso was on his tail (although the king had in fact gone back to Toledo), he refortified the derelict castle of Peña Cadiella and stocked it for a siege 'with an ample supply of bread and wine and meat'.[20] He spent Christmas at Morella.

He was on his way to lay siege to the castle of Borja near Tudela when he was interrupted by a galloper from al-Musta'in of Zaragoza with the news that Sancho Ramirez of Aragon was pressing him again. Rodrigo seems to have left his army behind and gone ahead to Zaragoza, probably to see the lie of the land himself. According to the *Historia Roderici*, a large turnout of the 'great and small' approached the Cid and prompted a renewal of the understanding that the man had had with his former ally. It is this relationship, as much to do with honour and mutual respect as it was with booty, power and land, that later generations signally failed to understand.

Sancho and his son Pedro had taken Monzon from al-Musta'in in 1089 and seemed ready to resume hostilities. The arrival of the Cid's army, camped along the river at Fraga, some miles from Zaragoza, made him reconsider. Armies massed, their tents flapping in the Zaragozan wind, and messengers rode backwards and forwards. This time, there would be no battle. Not only did Rodrigo bury the hatchet with Sancho, but he acted as go-between for al-Musta'in and the Aragonese king, who promptly rode home with honour satisfied. For those who persist in seeing the Cid as a war-mongering thug, this piece of diplomacy proves otherwise. Like any good negotiator, of course, he found it helped to be working from a position of strength – in his case with an army at his back.

Chapter 50 of the *Historia Roderici* is odd. In the midst of what historian Richard Fletcher calls its 'literary bleakness', it suddenly means what it says. Rodrigo marched through the Rioja, past the castles of Calahorra and Najera, taking Alberite and Logono: 'all those regions did he lay waste with relentless, destructive, irreligious fire. He took huge booty, yet it was saddening even to tears. With harsh and impious devastation did he lay waste and destroy all the land aforesaid. He altogether stripped it of all its goods and wealth and riches and took these for himself.'[21] The repetition of those lines, the implication for a second time that the Cid destroyed churches, very possibly tells us that the Rioja was the home of the author of the *Historia Roderici* and that he was taking the Cid's predations personally.

What all this meant was that Rodrigo had invaded Castilian territory for the first time, in effect making a direct challenge to Alfonso himself. The king was by this time (1092) besieging Valencia with his own army by land and with Genoese and Pisan warships by sea.[22] He had no wish to relinquish such a rich prize, so he sent Count Garcia Ordoñez, whose territory the Cid had destroyed, to bring the upstart to book. There is no doubt that the relationship between these men went beyond the mere rivalry of one *alferez* or *armiger* replacing another. Ordoñez may have orchestrated the on-going systematic verbal attack on Rodrigo at Alfonso's court, poisoning the king against him at every turn, and this may have prompted such a ruthless outburst.

Ordoñez reached Alberite with an immense army and sent out the usual challenges. The Cid held his position in Alfonso's castle for a week, by which time Ordoñez had thought better of the encounter and dispersed his troops. Rodrigo set fire to the woodland and vineyard before making his way back to Zaragoza. If it was the Cid's intention to take the great city state of Valencia for himself as early as this, then the preliminary invasion of the Rioja was a master-stroke. It made Alfonso fear for his own frontier and abandon the siege. The Italian navies sailed home. But there were more pressing matters. The Almoravid forces may have refused battle in 1090, but they had certainly not gone away. In the campaigning season of 1092 Ibn Teshufin had at last handed the reins of command to his son, Mohammed Ibn Aisa. First Murcia, then Aledo fell to him, followed by Denia, Jativa and Alcira. He was now within a day's ride of Valencia, where a palace coup took place at the end of October. The detested al-Qadir was overthrown by Ibn Jahhaf, the *qadi* or mayor of the city, and despite a pantomime attempt to escape disguised as a woman, al-Qadir was caught and beheaded in his own city square. It was well known that Jahhaf was Ibn Teshufin's man and it could not be long before Valencia fell to the Almoravids. First the Cid's army took Cebolla 9 miles to the north, then it marched on Valencia itself.

'In the month of July, at harvest time, Rodrigo encamped beside Valencia.'[23] His cavalry rode through the cornfields, burning the crops as they stood in the fields and tearing down the flimsy wooden huts built in the lee of the great walls. All this is rather odd. It is not surprising that the Cid should attack quickly to catch the Valencians napping, but they had been under siege for some weeks or even months by land and sea and very recently. Why was corn still growing in the fields and why were the extramural houses occupied at all? The clear implication in the *Historia Roderici* is that the Almoravids were already in the city, stiffening the Valencians' resolve rather as the presence of German troops did among the Turks at Gallipoli in 1915. Modern historians have doubted this, but there were certainly those in Valencia, like the new ruler Ibn Jahhaf himself, who would much rather have welcomed the veiled ones than the Cid and his Christian knights. Rodrigo systematically destroyed the suburbs beyond the walls – Villaneuva and Alcudia must have fallen in hours rather than days – and in a magnanimous gesture returned the food, chattels and plots of land of all those who went over to him. This systematic destruction of the suburbs was characteristic of siege warfare throughout the *Reconquista* period and both sides carried it out. What remains unexplained is what the Cid hoped to gain by returning property to those who surrendered – this only makes sense if it happened after the fall of the city.

What little we know of the mechanics of warfare in this early period comes from the thirteenth-century *Primera Cronica General*, which recounts the early tenth-century siege of Zamora by the Moors. It was a failure and the leader of the attacking forces, Ibn al-Qitt, had his head hacked off and impaled on the town's gate. Three years before the Cid took Valencia, Yusuf ibn Teshufin had camped outside Toledo, the symbolic and strategic stronghold of the Christian north. But the place was virtually impregnable, built as it was on steep cliffs over a bend in the River Tajo, with walls thickened by the Moors themselves. Alfonso VI had taken the city in 1085 because he had spent nine months in exile there and knew every inch of its defences.

We do not know exactly what sort of equipment Rodrigo had with him in the summer of 1093. The *Chronica Adefonsi Imperatoris*, the chronicle of the Emperor Alfonso, mentions siege gear – 'He [the King of Léon] built catapults, machines and many siege engines'[24] – but that refers to a siege thirty-seven years after the Cid's investiture of Valencia and was probably written nearly sixty years later. The *Historia Roderici* mentions no siege engines in this context at all. What were the Cid's options? He could surround Valencia by land and wait for the city's food and water supplies to run out. This was cheap in terms of lives, but could prove very costly in other ways. There is no mention of ships at Rodrigo's disposal, so the Valencians could have supplied themselves – potentially indefinitely – by sea. Added to that, the Almoravids were somewhere to the south, in unknown numbers, and the Cid could not afford to sit this one out for long. He could attempt to get inside the city's walls with scaling ladders, but the walls would have been between 20 and 30 feet high and the casualties would have been appalling, with no guarantee of success. That left undermining and the range of siege weapons available to him. Undermining was notoriously difficult. It involved experts (sappers) getting close enough to the walls to chip away at the foundations with picks and shovels. Such a party would be continually under missile fire from the battlements above. Once a tunnel was established, it was held up by wooden beams and joists and when it was deep enough a fire was lit inside. The flames would burn the timbers which in turn would bring the masonry crashing down and a breach would be made in the wall. A determined frontal assault could then hack its way in.

Siege weapons like the mangonel had been known since Roman times when the legions had taken with them on campaign any number of *onagers* ('wild asses', named after their tension spring which resembled the animals' kick). Variants of these continued to be used into the Middle Ages, but experts are divided as to what form they took. Later versions were huge, but manoeuvrable, wooden engines, with spoon-ended arms winched into a firing position by twisting animal gut 'straps'. The 'spoon' hurled rocks, burning tar, pots of Greek fire (a sort of napalm), corpses, body parts, dung or rotting vegetables, depending on the purpose of the attack. Rocks cracked city walls, Greek fire burned the skin off city occupants and dung and corpses filled them with terror. Modern experimental archaeology has proved that these weapons had an effective range of 1,300 feet, well out of crossbow range of Valencia's defenders on the walls. Our problem arises in that we do not know if these weapons were known in eleventh-century Spain or whether the Cid had any at Valencia. Less likely still is the trebuchet, a larger and less manoeuvrable contraption that relied on a tall, crane-like counterpoise mechanism for its operation. This was probably originally a Chinese invention from the third to fifth centuries BC, but it was unknown in Europe until AD 500. Its use crept very slowly westward from Byzantium, but it was unknown in Italy or England before the siege of Dover in 1216. The Anglo-French rebel Simon de Montfort owned one called Malvoisin ('bad neighbour') and Edward I, fighting Robert the Bruce's Scots at Stirling, ordered one built with the name Warwolf. Poetically, in the context of the Cid, the last recorded use of a trebuchet was by the Spanish *conquistador* Hernando Cortez in the siege of the Aztec capital Tenochtitlan in 1521. Rodrigo may well have had siege towers or belfries, 20-foot-high towers on wheels that could be rolled up to town walls rather like slow, lumbering, engineless tanks. Once against the masonry, soldiers could climb up inside the wood and leather tower via ladders and leap from the top on to the battlements to cross swords with the defenders. The battering ram was simply a tree-trunk slung under a wheeled roof that could be driven by manpower against solid doors, be they Christian or Moorish in design.

Back in July 1093 the Cid was engaged in a propaganda war. He wrote to all the rulers of Spain, Christian and Muslim, explaining that Yusuf Ibn Teshufin was afraid to face him and to the Valencians he sent the following message (perhaps hurled by mangonel, perhaps delivered by messenger): 'I freely offer you a period of truce until the month of August. If Yusuf should come in the meantime to your assistance and should defeat and expel me from these lands and liberate you from my dominion, serve him and remain beneath his rule. But if he should not do this, serve me and be mine.'[25] Rodrigo then withdrew to the north, ransacking villages as far as Villera and carting off prisoners and plunder to his castle at Cebolla. While there he took the opportunity to collect the back *paria* due to him from the *taifa* state of Albarracin. In his absence the Valencians, clearly more Muslim than Christian, having been so for three centuries, sent an urgent message to Ibn Teshufin, who duly crossed the Straits again as he had so often before. It was probably September by now and the conventional campaigning season was drawing to a close. According to the *Historia Roderici*, the Almoravids did not give battle – 'greatly fearful of him, they dispersed by night and retired to their bases in confusion'.[26]

We have only the vaguest notion of a time-scale now. Rather as the Heston film encompasses the siege of Valencia in what appears to be days and is of course, in running time, only minutes, the Cid did not enter Valencia until Thursday 15 June 1094. It was taken by assault, so one or more of the siege weapon options must have been used and Rodrigo let his army run amok in the streets, helping themselves to whatever they found. It was all part and parcel of medieval warfare – to the victors the spoils – and if it was not very pretty, it was the essential cement of loyalty. 'He found', wrote the author of the *Historia Roderici*, 'and took possession of vast and innumerable riches: immense, uncountable quantities of gold and silver, precious jewellery, gems set in fine gold, treasures of various sorts, silken textiles decorated with precious gold.'[27]

We know what the Cid's Valencia looked like because of the writings of the Arab geographer al-Udri, who died there nine years before Rodrigo took the city. The sea was much nearer to the city walls then, lapping at their foundations, with black Arab fishing boats bobbing on the blue water. The ground was level, with nothing like the impressive scarp slopes of Toledo, and the city was built between two tributaries of the River Turia. Al-Mansur's grandson, Abd al-Aziz, had built the enormous walls that Rodrigo had spent nine months admiring with various degrees of impatience. There were seven gates for the Cid's battering rams: one was unnamed but the others were the Bab al-Qantra, the Bab al-Warraq, the Bab ibn

Sajar, the Bab al-Hansas, the Bab al-Qaysariya and the Bab al-Sarin. The market, specializing in silk, stood on its present site, and the great mosque, over which Rodrigo built a church, is the site of today's cathedral, with al-Qadir's royal palace, where the Cid now made his home, beside it.

The poet al-Muranabbi lamented the fall of Muslim Valencia as others had lamented the *Reconquista* elsewhere:

> Valencia! Valencia! Trouble is come upon you, and you are in the hour of death . . . your strong wall which is founded upon these four [corner] stones trembles . . . your lofty and fair towers . . . little by little they are falling . . . your white battlements which glittered afar off have lost their truth with which they shone like sunbeams . . . your pleasant gardens which were round about you, the ravenous wolf has gnawn at the roots and the trees can yield no fruit. . . . The fire has laid waste the lands of which you were called mistress and the great smoke thereof reaches you. There is no medicine for your sore infirmity and the physicians despair of healing you. Valencia! Valencia! From a broken heart have I uttered all these things. . . .[28]

All this of course was part of the romance of the lost world of al-Andalus, and it was to have far more poignancy after 1492 when the last Moorish ruler in Spain, Mohammed Abu Abd-Allah, called Boabdil, surrendered to the Christian 'kings' Fernando and Isabella of Aragon and Castile. 'Weep like a woman,' Boabdil's mother scorned her son, 'for what you could not defend like a man.'[29] In fact, the actual fabric of Valencia probably changed little. A church replaced the mosque, but Rodrigo's main and immediate task was to rebuild the walls, barbicans and gates against a possible Almoravid attack.

Yusuf ibn Teshufin had now passed command of his army to his nephew Mohammed (what happened to his son is unknown), who with his 'infinite multitude of barbarians and Moabites and Ishmaelites drawn from all over Hispania'[30] promised to bring the Cid in chains to the old man. The *Historia Roderici*'s figures are nonsense, claiming 150,000 cavalry, no doubt with mules and camels, and 3,000 infantry. Camped just 4 miles away at Cuarte, the Almoravids spent ten days – and more importantly nights – wearing down the Cid's garrison with shrieking and screaming, no doubt punctuated by the terrible thunder of the drums. It was probably October by this time, the sacred Muslim month of Ramadan, and the Cid was on his own. The nearest Christian stronghold was nearly four days' hard riding away and a potential ally, King Sancho Ramirez of Aragon, died days before Rodrigo took Valencia. Bearing in mind his relationship with Count Berenguer, swearing undying love or not, he could forget any help from there. Alfonso of Castile-Léon may have offered help, but that relationship too was edgy and bent with the wind. In any case the Almoravid threat was not confined to Valencia; Badajoz had fallen to Ibn Teshufin and Toledo had to be the king's priority. Rodrigo was paying the price of Christian *realpolitik*, snatching a *taifa* state geographically too far to the Muslim south.

Abu Abd Allah Mohammed ibn al-Khalaf ibn Alqama was in the city. Not all of his report has survived, but enough of it to give us a striking glimpse of the situation. The Cid was heavily outnumbered, with no ships for escape and the veiled ones harassing his walls and sending random volleys of flaming arrows to burn the temporary tents of his garrison inside the walls. Troublemakers were kicked out of one of the six gates, all iron was confiscated to melt down for weapons and the Cid told the besiegers that at the first sign of assault every Muslim in the city would be put to the sword.

Typical of the man, Rodrigo did not wait for the drums of the Almoravids to destroy his people's nerves and he led a sudden surprise attack some time in mid-October. Ibn Alqama probably watched from the walls as the Cid moved out at dawn, his army divided into two. The first wing was a feint, apparently riding at speed to smash through the black circle of tents. Then, when the 'veiled ones' moved to defend the tents, Rodrigo himself led the second wave and shattered Mohammed's forces: 'By God's clemency,' wrote the author of the *Historia Roderici*, 'Rodrigo, the invincible warrior . . . defeated all the Moabites . . . a multitude of them fell to the sword.'[31]

The Almoravids panicked, rushing headlong to their ships, and the booty the Cid brought back from their encampment was astonishing – the usual gold and silver, most of it probably looted from the cities of Badajoz, textiles, horses, mules and above all weapons. In fact, this victory was a vital one. Cuarte went down in the annals of all Spain as it marked the first defeat of an Almoravid army. In Aragon, far to the north, a clerk wrote, 'in the year when the Almoravids came to Valencia and Rodrigo Diaz defeated them and took captive all their troops'.[32]

Using his time profitably, the Cid now rode north to the castle of Olocau where al-Qadir had stashed much of his loot. He knew perfectly well that the Almoravids would be back, however many of their deadly drums he hung on church altars to reassure his Christian followers, and he may have carried out something of a scorched-earth policy, helping himself to anything from the surrounding area that would help him hold out in another siege.

By 1096 help had arrived. Sancho Ramirez lay with the saints in the crypt of the monastery of San Juan de la Peña and his son Pedro now ruled Aragon. While he was patrolling his southern territory with a sizeable army, ambassadors reached him from the Cid. The *Historia Roderici* implies that this happened in reverse, i.e. that Pedro made overtures to the Cid, but this seems unlikely, however much prestige there was in an alliance with the 'invincible' Campeador. It was while these negotiations were under way, near Peña Cadiella, that the Christian army ran into a larger force of Almoravids under Mohammed. Unusually Rodrigo was caught in bad battle country, at Bairen on a narrow ridge about 4 miles long. He had the sea on one side, with volleys of arrows from the Almoravid ships thudding down on his men's raised shields, and a large force on his landward side. The *Historia Roderici* gives us Rodrigo's words as he cantered along his army's line: 'Listen to me, my dearest and closest companions. Take a firm grip on yourselves. You must be fearless. Do not quail before the enemy numbers. Today our Lord Jesus Christ will deliver them into our hands and into our power.'[33]

The Cid led an assault at midday, driving the Almoravids back into the sea – 'and enormous numbers . . . were drowned'.[34] Another victory, another humiliation for the veiled ones, and more loot. Rodrigo and Pedro paused briefly during their triumphal return to Valencia to sack the castle of Montornés, whose people were rebelling against the king.

The last two years of his life saw the Cid in the thick of battle where, it seemed, he was born to be. Abu al-Fateh, the governor of Jativa to the south, led an army north to Murviedro in a direct challenge to Rodrigo's authority. The Cid hunted al-Fateh to the town of Almenara, which he besieged and captured in three months. He set his prisoners free and ordered the building of a church dedicated to the Blessed Virgin. Slowly Allah was bowing out of Spain, although it would take him another four hundred years to leave altogether.

Murviedro was crucial to Valencia's safety and Rodrigo had to take it. The colossal size of the task is underscored by the author of the *Historia Roderici*, who puts a prayer in the Cid's mouth: 'You know, O Lord, that I do not wish to enter Valencia before I have with the aid of your power secured Murviedro by siege and conquest and sack . . . and if the town, by your gift, will fall under our possession and authority, there I will cause Mass to be celebrated to you and your praise, O God.'[35]

Like Toledo, Murviedro was built on solid rock. It was the Roman stronghold of Saguntum that had been destroyed by Hannibal in 219 BC. It was a vast site of 9 acres, with deep wells and complex fortifications. Rodrigo sealed off all escape routes and bombarded the city with his engines (the only mention of these weapons in the *Historia Roderici*). The inhabitants were thoroughly rattled, and asked the Cid for that quaint courtesy he had granted to the people of Valencia four years earlier. They were dying of hunger and asked permission to send gallopers to 'the king and our lords' for help, the usual desperate missives to anybody who would listen. Rodrigo gave them thirty days. Alfonso was not likely to be very helpful – 'I prefer that Rodrigo should have the town of Murviedro rather than any Saracen king'[36] was his predictable answer. Even less likely to thunder to their aid was the Cid's friend al-Musta'in, amir of Zaragoza, who said 'Rodrigo is a hard man, a very brave and invincible friend, such that I do not care to engage with him in battle.'[37] Similarly, Abu Marwan, the amir of Albarracin, told the Murviedran ambassadors: 'If our king Yusuf shall choose to come, we shall all together accompany him and willingly come to your aid. But without him we should never dare to fight against Rodrigo.'[38] Ramon Berenguer III, the Count of Barcelona, also declined, although he did agree, in exchange for 'vast tribute', to attack the Cid's castle at Oropesa as a feint to draw Rodrigo away while the Murviedrans restocked their city. In the event, Berenguer did not even do this, but kept the tribute anyway. Yusuf ibn Teshufin was also approached by the desperate Murviedrans, but his reply was not recorded.

Alone and terrified, the besieged townspeople begged for a twelve-day extension, although both they and the Cid knew it was a ploy. He warned them: 'When the twelve days have expired . . . if you do not at once surrender the castle to me, as many of you as I can lay hands on I shall burn alive or execute after torture.'[39]

This was no idle threat. Three years earlier the Muslim leader of Valencia, Ibn Jahhaf, was put on trial by Rodrigo for lying to him over the whereabouts of al-Qadir's treasure. Even Muslims like Ibn Bassam, whose account of the Cid's occupation of the city is understandably hostile, believed that Ibn Jahhaf could expect little else. They dug a pit in the city square in Valencia and buried the treacherous rebel leader, who almost certainly had a hand in the murder of al-Qadir, up to his armpits. A fire was lit around him and he died in agony, desperately dragging the flaming brands nearer to quicken his end. Burning like this was unusual, but the Cid, according to Muslims in Valencia, wanted to kill Ibn Jahhaf's wife and children this way too. There is a nauseating echo to all this – five hundred years later the furze branches crackled around heretics in Spain in the appalling *auto da fé* of the Inquisition.

Finally, on the feast of the Nativity of St John the Baptist,[40] Rodrigo sent assault troops into the city. It was largely deserted because he had allowed the inhabitants to leave with the barest essentials. The Cid's men knelt and celebrated the first Christian Mass in the city for nearly three centuries. Murviedro was sacked and large numbers of prisoners taken back to Valencia in chains.

The last five chapters of the *Historia Roderici* gloss over the Cid's government of Valencia and the marriages of his daughters and the death of his son. Some of this would appear later in the fictionalized versions that followed his own death. Rodrigo's son, Diego, is an enigma. He is mentioned in only one source, the late twelfth-century Aragonese text *Liber Regum* (the king's book), and that tells us that the boy was killed at the battle of Consuegra near Toledo in August 1097. The battlefield today forms part of the Cid tours that take bemused tourists over the campaign trails of Rodrigo Diaz. Diego was, of course, no longer a boy, and must have been in his 20s by this time. But Consuegra was an Almoravid victory over Alfonso of Castile-Léon, which must mean that Diego was with the royal army. What was he doing there? There are two possibilities, one more likely than the other. The less likely is that Diego was a hostage at Alfonso's court, perhaps never released when the king set Jimena and the girls free and kept under Alfonso's watchful eye to make sure his father behaved himself. After all, Rodrigo had been twice exiled, was notoriously insubordinate when it suited him and by 1094 was Prince of Valencia, de facto king of a *taifa* state. Furthermore, his military reputation was awesome and men flocked to his banner. Unlikely as it was that the Cid would turn against his native Castile for real, rather than merely terrorizing its frontiers, it was not impossible; he had already invaded parts of it. Such hostage-taking became the stock-in-trade of rulers later in the Middle Ages. The future Vlad the Impaler, called Dracula, spent several years at the Ottoman court to ensure his father's good relations with the advancing Turks. The more likely possibility is that the relationship between Rodrigo and Alfonso was much more complicated – and subtle – than the chroniclers make out. They quarrelled, certainly, but they also kissed and made up; the fact that Alfonso seemed perfectly happy to have the Cid as ruler of Valencia is perhaps evidence of this. If there had been no quarrels and no exile, there was nothing more natural than that young Diego should be brought up at Alfonso's court, as Rodrigo had been brought up at his brother Sancho's. Arguably, of course, if there had been no quarrels and no exile, the Cid himself would have been at Consuegra and would probably not have been Lord of Valencia.

We are on surer ground with Rodrigo's daughters. Throughout the Middle Ages men like the Cid extended their power and wealth through military adventuring and diplomatic marriages. It was the lot of Diego to make his way in the world by the sword, as his father had, and he was unlucky. It was the lot of Maria and Cristina to marry and carry the Cid's blood on to generations yet unborn. Maria married, bizarrely enough, Ramon Berenguer III, Count of Barcelona, whose family had long been at odds with the Cid. Again, it is a measure of the *realpolitik* of the time that men trying to kill each other on a Spanish battlefield one day should attend their children's wedding in a Spanish church the next. Cristina married Ramiro, whose father was Lord of Calahorra and whose grandfather was King Garcia III of Navarre. Their son (Rodrigo's grandson) became King of Navarre in 1134.

The church of St Mary the Virgin, Mother of Our Redeemer, replaced the 'Saracen building which they call a mosque'[41] and the Cid presented it with a golden chalice worth 150 marks as well as two hangings woven of silk and gold whose beauty had never been seen before in Valencia. One of the grants of land to this church has survived intact and is in the cathedral archive at Salamanca.

Among other documents which we can still read is the charter of 1098 which probably contains Rodrigo's signature – 'Ego Roderici, simul cum coninge mea affirmo oc quod superius scriptum est' (I, Rodrigo, together with my wife, confirm what is written above).[42] It also contains the Christian names at least of the men who were his faithful retainers in the last days – Ramiro, Nino, Rodrigo, Martin, Diego, Fernando. Some of these men can be positively identified as the great and good of Castile and Léon who may well have followed the Cid into one or both of his exiles and fought at his elbow in battles without number.

'Rodrigo died at Valencia in the month of July in the Era 1137.'[43] It was probably 10 July, in the Christian year 1099. The Campeador died in his bed, but of what cause is unknown. He was probably 56 and his passing was the signal for a renewed Almoravid attack on Valencia. A chronicler in Poitou, far to the north across the Pyrenees, wrote 'in Spain, at Valencia, Count Rodrigo died. This was a great grief to the Christians and a joy to their pagan enemies.'[44]

10

The Poem of the Cid

The Cid is dead. Long live the Cid. It may seem odd that only part of the way through this book our hero's story should come to an end. But that is precisely the point: the death of Rodrigo Diaz, a hard man in a hard land, heralded the birth of El Cid the Campeador, the national hero of Spain.

The *Historia Roderici* sweeps on, concerned with the shock news of the man's death and the military effects it had. The news would have reached Marrakesh by the end of July, perhaps sooner, and another army was sent against Valencia. Astonishingly Yusuf ibn Teshufin was still alive and it seems Valencia may have become an obsession with him. It was not the strategic lynch-pin that the Heston film makes it out to be, but it was a symbol of a once-great Muslim *taifa* state that had now been ruined by the cold and alien hand of Christendom.

Jimena, her son and husband dead, her daughters respectively in Navarre and Barcelona far to the north, would have to hold out alone. The *Historia Roderici* claims the siege by Ibn Teshufin lasted seven months. During that time Jimena almost certainly sent messages to her sons-in-law, Ramiro of Navarre and Ramon Berenguer III, but both were waging war elsewhere. The only other hope was Alfonso of Castile-Léon, with all the bitterness of the love-hate relationship of nearly forty years between him and the Cid. But Alfonso may have been related to Jimena and we know that he did ride to her aid. His charter dated 14 May 1100 is headed 'on the road to Valencia when I was going to put myself at the head of the Christians'.[1] Historians have overlooked the fact that the King of Castile and Léon must have been 60 by now. Unlike Ibn Teshufin, he does not seem to have passed command of his armies to a subordinate general and perhaps he was not as keen for glory as he had once been. It may be that his arrival north of Valencia was enough to deter the Almoravids, who had failed to face him before, for all they had beaten him twice. A year later Jimena was still talking big in a charter that confirmed her husband's grants to the church of Santa Maria, promising fresh conquests 'which, with God's help, we shall make by land or sea'.[2]

In fact, of course, the reverse situation was the reality. Three months after Jimena's boast, the Almoravid general Magdali laid siege to Valencia again and this time Jimena sent the Bishop of Valencia, Jeronimo, to beg Alfonso again for help. It was March 1102, the beginning of the campaigning season, before the king could muster his army. The Almoravids pulled back, as they probably had two years earlier, but Alfonso knew this game of cat and mouse could not go on for ever. As the *Historia Roderici* tells it: 'So he [Alfonso] returned to Castile, taking with him Rodrigo's wife with the body of her husband and all the Christians who were with them there with their household goods and riches. When they had all left Valencia, the king ordered the whole city to be burnt; then he led all these people to Toledo.'[3] It was something of a pyrrhic victory for Ibn Teshufin and Magdali. All they found was a blackened husk of a city, with the frightened inhabitants flinging themselves to kiss the feet of the new conquerors as they had nine years earlier kissed the feet of the Cid. It was the lot of town-dwellers in eleventh-century Spain.

'[The Almoravids] have not lost it [Valencia]', wrote the author of the *Historia Roderici* ruefully, 'since that day.' But that day would not last for ever. The Spartan Almoravids became as soft and decadent as the Andalusians and fifty years after the Cid's death a new sect, the Almohades, came out of Africa, bent on *jihad*. This sect was founded by the Berber leader Mohammed ibn Tumart, seeking to reaffirm the fundamental values of the faith. The Almoravids refused to accept his vision and he declared war on them in 1122. By 1145 his successor Abd al-Mamun had conquered Morocco and the Maghrib. In 1150 he crossed the Straits, as Ibn Teshufin had done, to 'rescue' al-Andalus from itself. In a series of successes the Almohades held up the *Reconquista* for forty years.

They were fanatical and intolerant, enforcing conversions, especially of Jews, and it was not until 1238 that Valencia passed into the hands of a Christian king, James of Aragon, the Conqueror, a Cid of the thirteenth century. Even so, the city kept a kind of semi-autonomy over its local affairs until the eighteenth century, reflecting that the Cid's Valencia was always, somehow, different.

But, long before that, the Cid was to be reinterred in the monastery of San Pedro at Cardena. The cult of death is one of the most fascinating aspects of medieval history. The stiff upper lip and lack of emotion of the modern Englishman was totally lacking everywhere in the past. Men and women, Christian and Muslim, screamed and cried hysterically on the death of a loved one. They tore their clothes, drew blood from their flesh with their nails and daubed their heads and faces with ashes. Such scenes were almost certainly widespread in Valencia at the Pentecost of 1099 and very possibly again at Cardena three years later.

Men, even heroes like Rodrigo Diaz, believed in the realities of purgatory and 'stinking' hell and they were terrified of them. Wealth, power and pride were not tickets to heaven – humility, remorse and a pure life were. No doubt as he lay dying in his bed with the shadows lengthening about him, the Cid Campeador had time to reflect on the purity of his life. He had slaughtered men; broken faith with his anointed king not once, but twice and possibly three times; had, according to some, despoiled churches; and according to all sources had a man burned alive. Yet medieval men were realistic too. War was war – people died, buildings were burned down. And as far as the burning of Ibn Jahhaf went, he was not only a Muslim but a regicide, responsible for that most appalling of medieval crimes, the murder of a king; even other Muslims believed his end was justified. The Cid would doubtless have made a will, ensuring that Jimena and his daughters were well cared for. 'And when he arranged these things,' records the fourteenth-century *Chronicle of Morcea* on the death of the knight Guillaume Champlitte in 1278, 'he surrendered his soul and the angels took it and bore it to where all the righteous are found. Commemorate him, all of you; he was a good prince.'[4]

Around his bed the bevy of churchmen would have been led by Jeronimo, his archbishop, who administered the last rites and kissed him, placing the sword Tizona vertically on his chest, with the cruciform hilt at his lips and his hands clasped over it. We are unsure of the exact procedures that followed, because there were slight variations from region to region, country to country and time to time. In St Albans in England, a century and a half after the Cid's death, we have a detailed description of the burial of Abbot William of Trumpington:

> The body was stripped and washed and . . . his . . . beard would certainly have to be shaved. Then some . . . of the more senior monks . . . were admitted and the body was opened with an incision from the trachea to the lower part. Everything in it was placed, sprinkled with salt, in a cask, which was reverently interred in the cemetery with blessings and psalms. The body was washed and soaked inside with vinegar, a great deal of salt was sprinkled into it and it was sewn up. This was done with care and prudence lest the body, which had to be kept for three or more days, should give off an offensive smell. . . . By this time . . . the body was so clean and spruce and the face so rubicund and unblemished, that to many it seemed pleasant and desirable to touch it with their hands and carry it on their shoulders like some saint.[5]

To understand how the Cid passed, literally, from history to legend, we have to look at the later Cid chronicles, always critically aware that as we distance ourselves from 1099 so the mythology creeps in. With considerable hindsight, according to the 'Chronicle of the Cid', compiled by the English poet Robert Southey in 1813, Rodrigo expressed a wish before he died to be buried in the monastery of San Pedro. Southey's work was a compilation of a number of Cid legends, dating from the fifteenth to the seventeenth century. Whether he sacrificed historical accuracy on the altar of poetic metre, we do not know.

Rodrigo's will gave grants of land to those knights who had followed him into exile, while to those not so long in his service he gave grants of between 1,000 and 3,000 silver marks. Squires got between 500 and 1,500. He commanded that at San Pedro the company give clothing away to 4,000 paupers, in the shape of a 'skirt of escanforte [a sturdy fabric] and a mantle'.[6] This of course conveniently ignores the fact that the Cid in Valencia – a city he had spent nine months besieging, six years holding and of which he was lord in his own right – was, in effect, a king. Would he really have wanted to give that up, even in death, for a burial place in a monastery that was only linked – and that indirectly – to his wife? This is just one of the ways in which the legend corrupts reality.

With these last instructions given, the Cid asked Jeronimo to 'give him the body of our Lord and Saviour Jesus Christ'[7] (the holy sacrament he had taken all his adult life), and he still, at this stage, had the strength to kneel and to manage a prayer when back in bed: 'Lord Jesus Christ, thine is the power and the kingdom, and thou above all kings and all nations, and all kings are at thy command. I beseech thee, pardon me my sins and let my soul enter into the light which hath no end.'[8]

Then the Cid died and his body was washed twice with warm water and a third time with rose water and then it was anointed and embalmed. We shall see later that the Cid legends are particularly bizarre relating to his corpse, but it is worth noting that Southey was translating here from a Spanish source written four centuries after Rodrigo's death. The source claims that he was surrounded by men we know were not there at the time (for example Alvar Fañez), that he died at Quinquagesima (29 May) – it was actually 10 July – and that he was 73 (he was probably 56). The same source contends that the Cid looked so lifelike after death that he was strapped by an ingenious frame into the saddle of Babieca and thus brought to the monastery of San Pedro, where 'the king [Alfonso] beheld his countenance and seeing it so fresh and comely and his eyes so bright and fair and so even and open that he seemed alive, he marvelled greatly'.[9]

Rodrigo's companions explained that for a week before he died, the Cid had eaten nothing and had only drunk a concoction of myrrh and balsam. This and the embalming made more sense to Alfonso now, 'for he had heard that in the land of Egypt they were wont to do this with their kings'.[10] Three days of solemnities followed, with the Cid's body lying in state in front of the high altar, and then, at Jimena's request, Alfonso brought an ivory chair from the council of Toledo and had the body placed on it, sitting upright:

> And he laid a cloth of gold upon it and upon that placed a cushion covered with a right noble tartari [costly silk fabric] and he ordered a graven tabernacle to be made over the chair, richly wrought with azure [blue] and gold, having thereon the blazonry of the Kings of Castile and Léon and the King of Navarre and the Infante [Prince] of Aragon and of the Cid Ruydiez the Campeador.[11]

Still according to this source, Alfonso, the King of Navarre and Prince of Aragon, along with Bishop Jeronimo (now the prelate at Salamanca), arranged Rodrigo in the chair in a rich purple robe sent to the Cid by the Sultan of Persia, as a mark of the man's international renown: 'And in his left hand they placed the sword Tizona in its scabbard and the strings of his mantle in his right. And in this fashion the body of the Cid remained there ten years and more, til it was taken thence, as the history will relate anon.'[12]

Robert Southey's 'Chronicle of the Cid', which is a further extrapolation from those general works, takes us further: 'After the body of the Cid had been there [on his ivory throne] ten years in all, the Abbot Don Garcia and Gil Diaz weened that it was no longer fitting for the body to remain in that manner.'[13] This was presumably because the Campeador's embalmed body was literally falling to pieces. Embalming was an imprecise science; even the corpses of the Egyptian pharaohs, the most famous examples of the skill, are, while fascinating, hardly attractive. If the chair story is true – and it seems a little too bizarre for it not to be – then Rodrigo's organs would have been removed at his death and the body cavity filled with salt and any combination of herbs and spices. He had of course been buried initially in the tomb of his cathedral of Valencia, so what state the body was in when it was taken to

Cardena is anybody's guess. Similar examples of embalming have all
gone the same way. In England the philosopher Jeremy Bentham had
his last wish fulfilled that he should watch over the students of his
'working man's college' in Gower Street, London, by being
embalmed in a chair at the end of the main corridor. The bones of
his thighs protrude through his breeches and his head is a wax copy,
the original being in the hat-box between his feet. Likewise,
Vladimir Ilyich Ulyanov – Lenin – still lies in state in Red Square in
Moscow, despite the loss of his ears and nose-tip over time.

Three local bishops held Masses and vigils and buried the Cid
again: 'They dug a vault before the altar, beside the grave of Doña
Ximena, and vaulted it over with a high arch and there placed the
body of the Cid seated as it was in the ivory chair, and in his
garments, and with the sword in his hand and they hung up his
shield and his banner upon the walls.'[14]

The 'Chronicle of the Cid' tells us that Jimena died four years
after Rodrigo, in other words in 1103, and that her daughters Elvira
and Sol attended her funeral. Already the mythmakers were at work.
The names Elvira and Sol come from the *Poema de Mio Cid* and an
elaborate description of Jimena's funeral is provided. Sol was the
younger (no notion here of the twins of the Heston film) and she
arrived first at the monastery of San Pedro because she was coming
from Navarre and thus had less far to travel than her sister.
According to this version, her husband Prince Sancho had died,
childless, in the previous year. Elvira, however, arrived in state with
her husband King Ramiro, their infant son Prince Garcia, the Bishop
of Pamplona and half the court. Jimena was buried at the feet of the
Cid, who was still sitting out eternity on his ivory throne. After a
week of Masses King Alfonso of Castile arrived, with Jeronimo,
Bishop of Salamanca and a large retinue. In Jimena's will the servant
Gil Diaz received a lifetime's annuity and the rest of the cash went to
San Pedro, with instructions to the monks to pray on certain
anniversaries for 'the souls of the Cid and Doña Ximena'.[15] The
daughters then split the remaining legacy between them – all the
gold, silver and expensive clothes. The childless and husbandless Sol
pledged her share ultimately to her little nephew and adopted him

on the spot, taking him to Aragon until he should receive his full inheritance as King of Navarre.

The historical evidence shows us a different picture and a less satisfactory one, which is a clue to the existence of the fiction: later chroniclers felt compelled, in the absence of evidence, to create it! Experts today believe that Jimena died in 1116, seventeen years, not four, after her husband. Assuming as we have that she was younger than the Cid anyway, this would make perfect sense. We know that in 1113 she sold the church of Valdecanas, probably to the cathedral of Burgos. Of her daughters we know nothing. Since Ramon Berenguer III remarried in 1107 we must assume that Maria had died by then, but there is no hard evidence about either of them.

It is in what happened next in the affairs of northern Spain that the myth of the Cid was born. He may have been petty, touchy and fickle, but Alfonso VI was one of the great Kings of Spain, providing the same kind of stability, ultimately, that his father had. But whereas Fernando had left three warring sons, Alfonso left (despite five marriages) no sons at all, only Urraca, the daughter named after his favourite sister. In her husband, Alfonso of Aragon, there should have been a second Cid. Known as el Batallador, the Battler, he proclaimed himself Emperor of Spain as his father-in-law had done, but the Alfonso-Urraca match was not made in heaven and the couple were soon at war with each other for real. Alfonso invaded Castile, taking territory that had once been the Cid's near Burgos. When Urraca's sister Teresa and her husband Count Henry of Portugal also began to kick over the traces, it seemed as though all the consolidation work done by Fernando and Alfonso of Castile was about to be destroyed.

In the south the Almoravids flexed their muscles again, taking, after Valencia, one *taifa* kingdom after another so that the *paria* tribute to the Christian north dried up and everybody despaired that a new dark age was about to descend. It is in moments like this, when the currency is devalued and military defeat stares people in the face, that men become legends, and the past assumes a golden glow. In England, as the Saxons sought to extinguish Romano-British culture in the sixth century, Arthur was born. After the Saxon defeat at Hastings, the obscure Hereward the Wake became a Fenland champion. As ambitious Austrians extended their power into the Swiss cantons in 1307, the crossbow ace William Tell was there to stop them. The fact that Arthur, Hereward and Tell may actually be purely fictional characters does not detract from their importance or from the power of their respective myths. Rodrigo Diaz was real, but now, in these grim times, he must become the Cid Campeador, the perfect knight. So, before the year 1118, the anonymous author of the *Historia Silense* took up his quill in Léon and began the epic story of a greatness that was past. It was only a handful of years after that that Bishop Pelayo of Oviedo wrote the *Chronicon Regum Legionensum*. It was at some time in this decade, although there are historians who place it later, that the *Historia Roderici* was written, giving the fullest 'historical' source of the Cid's life.

As we have seen, what makes the *Historia Roderici* so important and unusual is that it is written about a subject, not a king. And it is doubly important because it was written with possible access to men who had known him and fought with him. One of these was Alvar Fañez, the Cid's right hand, who went on after Rodrigo's death to defend Toledo against another abortive Almoravid siege. His exploits were recorded in the *Chronica Adefonsi Imperatoris* on the invasion of the *taifa* state of Alameria by Alfonso VII of Castile and Léon. And in it is this verse:

> Rodrigo, often called 'My Cid', of whom it is sung that he was never defeated by the enemies, who subdued the Moors, subdued our counts, himself used to praise this man [Fañez] and used to say that he himself was of lesser reputation; but I proclaim the truth, which the passage of time will not alter – my Cid was the first and Alvar the second. Valencia mourned at the death of friend Rodrigo, neither could the servant of Christ hold on to her any longer.[16]

But it was not just in the written record that the Cid's reputation was beginning to loom larger than life. The monastery of San Pedro at Cardena had a vested interest in him. In the ever-shifting fortunes of the medieval Church, which was always ready to cash in on the gullible and superstitious, the Benedictine order was in decline soon after the Cid's death. We do not know how much money Rodrigo and Jimena left them but it cannot have lasted for ever. Running a monastery was an expensive business, with important guests to house, alms to distribute and vast acres to maintain.[17] As the Christian frontier of the *tierras desplobadas* moved south again under Alfonso VII, so San Pedro was no longer the great bastion of Christianity it once was. It had become a backwater by 1142 when Alfonso ceded it to the mighty abbey of Cluny, itself struggling with serious financial difficulties. The Benedictines fought to prevent this by appealing directly to Rome, but it took four years and in the meantime the avaricious Cluniacs had helped themselves to most of the monastery's movables.

Luckily for San Pedro, the remains of the Cid and his wife were not among them. It was an age of relics. Saints' bodies were often 'translated' from one tomb to another, as we have seen with the body of Isidore of Seville, so sweet with the odour of sanctity that the experience was positively delightful and the corpse's hair could be combed. One saint was so annoyed at being disturbed by the Viking king Cnut of England that she rose out of her coffin and caught the king a powerful right hook for the indignity she was suffering.[18] In the pass at Roncesvalles in the Pyrenees pilgrims on the way to Compostela could see the hero Roland's footprints in the stones. For a small fee they could also see his famous hunting horn, his sword and even, for a time, the bloody cloth that bound his wounds.

And there was a militarism growing in Spain that reached a new plane in terms of the *realpolitik* of the Middle Ages. Five days after Rodrigo Diaz died, the armies of Godfrey de Bouillon smashed their way into Jerusalem, the first and last time that crusaders would get that far into the heartlands of Islam. It was becoming a more rigid, bigoted, black-and-white world than anything the Cid had known. Pope Urban II, the former monk of Cluny, wrote to the Counts of Besalú, Empurias, Roussillon and Cerdaña over a three-year period from 1096. One such letter read:

You know what a great defence it would be for Christ's people and what a terrible blow it would be to the Saracens, if, by the goodness of God, the position of that famous city [Tarragona] were restored. . . . No one must doubt that if he dies on this expedition for the love of God and his brothers, his sins will surely be forgiven and he will gain a share of eternal life through the most compassionate mercy of our God.[19]

This seems a little rich. Urban was making the point that he wanted Spanish warriors to fight Islam at home rather than undertake the reconquest of Jerusalem, but in doing so he was preaching to the converted. The counts to whom he wrote, and their ancestors, had been fighting Muslims for three and a half centuries. In comparison with that, Godfrey de Bouillon was a mere beginner.

Out of this impasse of *jihad* and crusade, the military orders were born. In the century after the death of Rodrigo, no fewer than eight were created in Spain, each modelled on the earliest and best known, the Templars and Hospitallers.[20] Only twenty years after the Cid's death the Order of the Knights of St James of the Sword was set up at Santiago and the ex-disciple became Santiago Motamoros, the Moor-killer. As Cardena was being eclipsed by Cluny the Knights of St Benedict of Evora were born, confirmed by the papacy twenty years later. In 1156 the Knights of San Julian de Pereyo first pulled their white habits on over their mail, followed the next year by the Order of Calatrava, founded by Navarrese Cistercians, similarly dressed. In 1173 the Knights of Monte Gaudio shook off convention by wearing scarlet surcoats. Seven years later the order of Our Lady of Montjoie (or Trafac) was created, followed by the Knights of Trujilla and the Knights of St George of Alfama, founded in Aragon ninety-nine years after Jimena had taken the body of her husband out of Valencia.

This obsession with the martial and the religious, blended into single orders of varying wealth, power and importance, played absolutely into the hands of the abbot of San Pedro, who was keen to cash in on the Cid as a Christian legend par excellence. Historian Richard Fletcher points up the problem in tracing this transfer from reality to fiction, from man to myth: 'The cult of dead heroes at their tombs is too perennial (from Hector to Elvis Presley), too enduring a human instinct for any individual manifestation of it to be neatly docketed and explained by the historian.'[21] Even so, there are pointers along the way and the most obvious was the *Poema de Mio Cid*, the Poem of the Cid. As we have seen, the very first poetry on the man was the Song of the Campeador, written during his lifetime at some point in the 1080s. But the *Poema* was different, more complicated, and whole books have been written about it. There is huge debate about when the *Poema* was written, driven by the fact that the only existing copy, written in Spanish, not Latin, dates from about 1350. It lies in the Bibliotecha Nacional in Madrid and was made at a period very different from that of Rodrigo of Vivar. The last sentence in this manuscript takes us nearer to him: '*Per Abbat le escrivió en el mes de mayo en era de mill e CC xlv anos*' (Per Abbat wrote it in the month of May in the Era 1245).

This takes us to the Christian year 1207, but it does not explain who Abbat was, or whether he created the poem or merely copied it from an earlier manuscript. This is where the greatest controversy arises, Colin Smith arguing that Abbat was the author, Menendez Pidal and Richard Fletcher contending that he was merely a copyist. Pidal went further, as we shall see, claiming that the *Poema* dates from the 1140s, in other words not long after the *Historia Roderici*. Few scholars accept this today and there are several clues in the text which prove their case.

The *Poema* is divided into three sections or *cantars*, a reminder that the work was written to be sung, like the Song of Roland or the Song of the Campeador. It was an age of mass illiteracy and the production of the written word was slow, laborious and expensive. If a troubadour sang the *Poema* from a vantage point in the market square of Burgos or Toledo, he would reach potentially hundreds of passers-by. Although little can be gained by a minute analysis of the *Poema* (much of the research has been concentrated, rightly, on the work as a wonderful example of Spanish literature), various facts actually add to our understanding of the Cid and his time.

The first *cantar* is 'del destierro', the exile, and it takes us to the first exile imposed on Rodrigo by Alfonso in the autumn of 1081.

A scattering of names strikes a chord – Garcia Ordoñez, Fortun Sanchez, Lope Sanchez – these men were real and we can trace them elsewhere. Al-Andalusian amirs were given Latinized versions of their names but Almutamiz and Almutafar are not quite right. Throughout, Rodrigo is referred to as Ruy Diaz Cid, the 'Ruy' presumably being a shortened version of the Latin Ruderici with which he signed charters in Valencia. The first pages of the poem are missing and Per Abbat substituted prose instead, making it more likely that he was copying the rest from an earlier incomplete version. Once we move into the realms of pure poetry, problems arise. Historians are trained to be sceptical, dubious, honestly critical of evidence, and there is a deep-rooted assumption that the more poetic something becomes, the less realistic and 'true' it is. So Julian Grenfell may have been killed in the First World War (1916) but his 'Into Battle' is a hopelessly romanticized version of the appalling, muddy slaughter on the Western Front:

> The thundering line of battle stands,
> And in the air death moans and sings,
> But day shall hold him in safe hands,
> And night shall clasp him in soft wings.

The *Poema* suffers similarly. The poetic convention of the time has a great deal of repetition, with parallel verses that were perhaps originally there to underscore a point or even to remind a listening audience where the singer had got to after a 'comfort break'. Rodrigo is referred to continually as 'he who in good hour was born' or 'in good hour girded on a sword', and there are innumerable references to his splendid beard. Lurking beneath the surface of Rodrigo the Christian knight is a darker element of the supernatural, the pagan. We have seen already the omens of the birds wheeling in the sierras and the jibe delivered by the Count of Barcelona. The propitious time of the Cid's birth may have a similar relevance here. The beard is fascinating. Was Rodrigo secretly rather vain, seeing his huge beard as a mark of manhood? Was this a peculiarly Spanish notion, bearing in mind that four centuries after the Cid, the English pirate Francis

Drake would famously send his fireships into Cadiz harbour to singe the beard of the King of Spain?

In the first *cantar* the Cid is a doomed hero, larger than the sum of things:

> And one sentence only was on every tongue;
> 'Were his lord [Alfonso] but worthy. God, how fine a vassal!'[22]

A similar sentiment was repeated in Philip Yordan's screenplay for the Heston film. The first verse of the *Poema* may contain a prayer from the lips of Rodrigo, but the second is already discussing omens:

> At the gate of Vivar on their right hand the crow flew;
> as they rode into Burgos it flew on their left.[23]

Outlawed by Alfonso and given nine days to leave his kingdom, the Cid finds himself abandoned by a terrified people:

> We dare not let you in nor lodge you for any reason,
> or we shall lose our goods and our houses,
> and besides these, the eyes out of our faces.[24]

A little girl of 9 warns him away and the Cid stops to pray at the church of Santa Maria in Burgos before camping beyond the city limits near the banks of the River Arlanzon. At this point a new name emerges, that of Martin Antolinez, 'the good man of Burgos', who brings the Cid food and wine and ultimately follows him into exile. Antolinez is described as 'a hardy lance' and it is likely that he was a captain of the Burgos militia of the *caballeros villanos*. He represents a type rather than any specific individual, and his loyalty to the Cid is unwavering.

What follows in the first *cantar* is one of the most baffling of the Cid stories, which has been ignored by both the *Historia Roderici* and the Heston film, at both ends of the Cid spectrum in terms of time. With Antolinez's help, the penniless exile swindles two Burgos Jews, Raquel and Vidas, by borrowing money from them against the collateral of two coffers of gold. He cannot take his land nor even these 'movables' with him, because of their great weight, but he will accept 600 marks to fund his exile. The chests are in fact filled with sand and the gullible Jews part with the cash, kissing Rodrigo's hands to seal the bargain. The story is hardly worthy of a Christian hero and is unlikely to have any basis in fact, so why is it here at all? Attitudes towards Jews varied from a grudging acceptance to murderous loathing. In Spain, especially al-Andalus, Jewish communities were large and flourishing, the Jews themselves often taking up key roles in local *taifa* administration. From the eleventh to the thirteenth century Jewish mysticism was growing in importance in the south of France and the Kabbalah doctrines, centred on Catalonia, were the result. As the *Reconquista* gathered strength from the mid- to late twelfth century, so it became a crusade against Judaism as well as Islam. Christian kings no longer borrowed money from Castilian Jews and by 1381 the Sephardic sect had crossed the Straits to the relative safety of Morocco. In 1492, when Fernando and Isabella drove the Moors from Granada, they drove the Jews out too. And this is precisely why the Jewish tale of Raquel and Vidas is included in the *Poema*. Whether purists liked it or not, Rodrigo Diaz was beginning his metamorphosis. A Christian knight of the *Reconquista* must be an enemy of Jews, because, put simply, the Jews had killed Christ. By the time the *Poema* was written, out-and-out hostilities had not yet begun, but to con greedy and avaricious Jews out of their stereotypical gains was seen as a fair game and the triumph of good over evil.

Leaving a slice of the Jews' money at the cathedral for a thousand Masses to be sung, Rodrigo rides from Burgos to San Pedro of Cardena. It is grey morning when he gets there, and Abbot Sancho is busy with the Matins service. There, too, is Jimena, with five ladies in attendance, praying to St Peter, the patron saint of the monastery:

> Thou who guidest all creatures,
> bless my Cid the Campeador.[25]

Rodrigo Diaz leaves 50 marks with the abbot for the care of his family – there is no mention of a son – and bids them a tearful farewell:

165

He stretched out his hands, he of the splendid beard; his two daughters, in his arms he took, drew them to his heart for he loved them dearly. He weeps from his eyes and sighs deeply; 'Ah, Doña Jimena, my perfect wife, I love you as I do my own soul.'[26]

But before he can leave Cardena, he is joined by a retinue of over a hundred knights prepared to follow him into exile. He can offer them nothing now, he tells them, but that will all change in the future. Jimena's very long prayer is a cleverly placed reminder that the Cid is, above all, a Christian lord. There is no mention in the entire *Poema* of his ever having been in the service of a Muslim amir or of fighting alongside one. Her prayer ends:

> Thou art the King of Kings, and of the whole world Father. I adore thee and believe with all my will and I pray to St Peter that he may aid my prayer that God may keep from harm my Cid the Campeador.[27]

Rodrigo's journey is described in minute detail, camping at Espinoza de Can, riding past the 'goodly city' of San Estaban, crossing the River Duero at the Figuerala. Clearly, whoever the author of the *Poema* was, this was home territory for him. And all the time men flock to his banner. In the Sierra Miedes the angel Gabriel appears to Rodrigo, promising him 'as long as you live that which is yours will prosper'.[28]

Military action soon follows and in this first *cantar* of the *Poema* Alvar Fañez Minaya emerges not only as the Cid's right hand, often dripping with enemy blood up to his elbow, but as a kind of staff officer given to dazzling tactical ideas which he suggests to the Cid:

> With one hundred of our company,
> after we have surprised and taken Castejon,
> do you remain there and be our fixed base.
> Give me two hundred to go on a raid.
> With God and good fortune, we shall take rich spoils.[29]

Interestingly, although Rodrigo and Fañez are planning an ambush, the author sees nothing sneaky or unheroic about that. The realities of mountain warfare were clearly known to him. At the gates of Castejon, the Cid thunders into action:

> My Cid Ruy Diaz rode in at the gate;
> in his hand he carried a naked sword.
> Fifteen Moors he killed who came in his way,
> took Castejon and its gold and silver.[30]

Fañez, raiding along the River Guadalajara with his two hundred, is equally successful. Rodrigo names some of his men – Muno Gustioz 'who was his vassal' and Felix Munoz, the Cid's nephew, Alvar Alvarez, Alvar Salvadorez, Galindo Garcia, 'excellent knight of Aragon' – but it is not possible to be certain whether these characters really existed or are simply fictional creations.

Fañez emerges as a true hero and a steadfast friend. The mercenary theme of money that runs through the *Poema* makes it clear that the leaders of raids took one-fifth of the prize money as their own, for personal use. It was this loot that made the Cid and his lady seriously rich during their lifetime. But Fañez turns down his cut, saying:

> I thank you from my heart, famous Campeador,
> for this fifth part which you offer me;
> it would please Alfonso the Castilian.
> I give it up and return it to you.
> I make a vow to God who is in heaven;
> Until I have satisfied myself on my good horse
> with joining battle in the field with the Moors,
> with handling the lance and taking up the sword,
> with the blood running to above my elbow,
> before Ruy Diaz, the famous warrior,
> I shall not take from you one wretched farthing.[31]

Rodrigo may not be portrayed as fighting with the Moors in the *Poema*, but, rather like his relationship with the Jewish money-

lenders, he is quite prepared to do business with them. He sells his
share of the spoils to the Moors for 3,000 silver marks, and then
he's on the move. Again, we are in country familiar to the author –
from Castejon the Cid rides on past the caves of Anguita, crossing
the river into the Plain of Taranz. He defends a camp on a round
hill surrounded by water near Alcocer, helping himself to spoils as
he goes. It is entirely feasible that the clashes the Cid had here
represent some of those battles that the author of the *Historia
Roderici* says it would be tedious to recount or about which he had
no knowledge. And at Alcocer, we have a glimpse of Rodrigo as
general. Reinforcing his hillfort by digging a ditch to create a moat,
the Cid settles down to a fifteen-week siege. The villages go over to
him – Terrer, Calatayud – but Alcocer remains firm behind its stone
ramparts. So the Cid feigns a withdrawal, leaving only one tent
standing, and the citizens, thinking the evacuation is genuine, open
their gates and give chase:

> The Campeador turned his face around;
> he judged the distance between the Moors and their castle,
> bade them turn with their banner . . .
> Halfway across the meadow they came together.
> God, their hearts were glad upon that morning.[32]

With the Moors caught out in the open, it was no contest:

> Know, in this manner, my Cid took Alcocer.[33]

A new name now appears as Rodrigo's man Pedro Bermudez plants
the Cid's banner at a high point in the city, as a symbol of
Christianity and power. Whether this was the golden dragon of the
Carmen or some other device we do not know, but by the time the
Poema was written, and certainly by the time Per Abbat copied it,
true heraldry was an exact science and all the colour of the Heston
film would have been a reality in Spain.

Retribution is soon on its way when the local citizenry beg King
Tamin of Valencia to eject the Cid. He sends the minor kings Fariz

and Galve to besiege Alcocer and they try to cut off the water supply to the city. Again it is Fañez who suggests a sortie at dawn and the Cid appoints Pedro Bermudez as his standard-bearer:

> What haste among the Moors. They set to arm.
> It seemed the earth would split with the noise of their drums
> . . . and as for the coloured pennons, who could count them?
> . . . They clasp their shields over their hearts,
> they lower the lances swathed in pennons,
> they bared their faces over their saddletrees . . .
> 'I am Ruy Diaz, the Cid, the Campeador of Bivar!'[34]

What we have here is an important affirmation of the battle tactics of the Cid's time or shortly after it. His knights are charging the enemy with their lances at rest, under their arms, and to bend low over the saddle they would have to ride with straight legs and long stirrup-leathers. The self-announcement by the Cid can be taken as a sort of battle cry, rather as the Saxons at Hastings when Rodrigo was a young man shouted 'Out! Out!' and the crusaders in Jerusalem as he lay dying bellowed '*Deus Lo Volt*'.[35]

Chapter 36 gives an encapsulation of the traditional Cid-against-the-Moors scenario:

> You would have seen so many lances rise and go under,
> So many bucklers [shields] pierced and split asunder,
> So many coats of mail break and darken,
> So many white pennons drawn out red with blood,
> So many good horses run without their riders.
> The Moors call on Mohammed and the Christians on
>   St James.[36]

True to the poetic tradition that continued into the Shakespearean era and beyond, leader fights with leader, as was the natural order of things. So Rodrigo duels personally with King Fariz, hitting him so hard with his third sword stroke that the enemy breaks and the field is won. Martin Antolinez goes one better fighting with Galve:

169

> He broke in pieces the rubies of his helmet;
> he split the helmet, cut into the flesh.[37]

With the spoils of this battle, Rodrigo sends 'a bootful' of gold and silver to Santa Maria in Burgos to pay for a thousand Masses, the remainder to go to his wife and daughters, then he sells Alcocer back to the Moors. He does this several times in the *Poema*, contrary to historical evidence elsewhere, but it does show the Cid's fascinating nature. War was a way of life to him, as was loot. As he tells his men:

> Lances and swords must be our shelter,
> or else on this meagre earth we cannot live.[38]

The birds wheel overhead again as the Cid leaves Alcocer and he is on the road again. Alvar Fañez is sent with a share of the loot to Alfonso of Castile, who promptly pardons him on the spot, but 'of the Cid Campeador I [Alfonso] will say nothing'.[39] This is an important passage because it creates the myth, still current today and blessed by the eminent historian Menendez Pidal, that Rodrigo was unswervingly loyal to his king and did all that he did, including the taking of Valencia, in his name and out of devotion to Castile. It is simply not true.

Large numbers follow Fañez with Alfonso's backing to join the exile. For fifteen weeks (the usual time attributed to sieges in the *Poema*) the Cid lays waste to the Martin valley near Zaragoza and camps on the stone ledge of El Poyo:

> As long as there are Moors and Christian people,
> it will be called the Chair of the Cid.[40]

Rodrigo's raiding now takes him into the lands of the Count of Barcelona – the Pass of Olocau, Huesca and Montalban. The count is miffed:

> It weighed on him heavily.
> He took it as an affront.[41]

It is clear from the *Poema* that there is already bad blood between the count and Rodrigo –

> He offended me once in my own court;
> he struck my nephew and gave no reparation.[42]

– and this incursion with his outlawed bandits is the last straw. He gathers his mixed army of Christians and Moors and finds Rodrigo in the pine grove at Tevar. Again we have a tantalizing glimpse of the Cid's battle tactics:

> Cinch tight the saddles and arm yourselves.
> They are coming downhill, all of them in breeches.
> Their saddles are flat and the girths loose.
> We shall ride with Galician saddles, with boots over our hose.[43]

The exact meaning of the different riding techniques is now lost to time. Rodrigo is confident and is successful, of course, and in the heat of battle he wins an important prize – 'the sword Colada, worth more than a thousand marks'[44] – (a third of the price of the city of Alcocer).

Ramon of Barcelona now goes on hunger strike, playing a psychological game of cat and mouse with the Cid which does not end until Rodrigo lets him go. It is perhaps based on fact and perhaps represents an attempt by Ramon Berenguer to go home with some of his dignity intact. In fact, of course, he had lost men, territory and a sizeable chunk of tribute to the Cid, who probably never intended to kill his man anyway. Here, with the Cid's men 'so rich they cannot count all they have', the first *cantar* ends.

The opening of the second *cantar* – The Wedding – follows on and takes the story on to Valencia, with Rodrigo growing in reputation as his army prospers. Almenar, Jerica, Burriana, Murviedro – the place names are accurate and they echo what we know about the real Rodrigo:

> They are frightened in Valencia, they do not know what to do.
> Know, the fame of my Cid has gone everywhere.[45]

And the poet gets it more or less right when he explains the lack of support from Yusuf ibn Teshufin: 'he was so deep in war with the King of the Atlas [mountains] that he neither sent to advise them nor came to their rescue'.[46]

The taking of Valencia is reasonably accurate too – a nine-month siege followed by the acquisition of vast riches: Rodrigo's fifth is worth 30,000 marks in cash, let alone goods, and

> His flag flew from the top of the Moorish palace.[47]

Once again, the faithful Cid sends presents back to Alfonso of Castile.

In dealing with Rodrigo's government of Valencia, the poet is again well informed and pulls no punches. The Cid is ready to hang men who attempt to desert him and he welcomes the fighting cleric Jeronimo – 'Bishop Don Jerome'. He is:

> learned in letters and with much wisdom
> and a ready warrior on foot or on a horse.[48]

Valencia has a bishop again and all Christendom is delighted.

In the *Poema* Alfonso has in effect been holding the Cid's family prisoner at Cardena and the long-suffering Alvar Fañez is once again at his court, giving the king the Cid's present of a hundred richly harnessed horses. He asks for Jimena and her girls to be released and Alfonso complies:

> It pleases my heart;
> I shall provide them with escort while they go through my
>   lands
> and keep them from harm and grievance and from
>   dishonour.[49]

Only once in the entire *Poema* does the Cid admit to having Moorish allies:

172

Ride forward through Santa Maria to Molina, which is
     further on;
Abengalbon [Ibn Ghalbun] is lord there, my friend, at peace
     with me.[50]

In Chapter 86 we learn that Babieca is not only a stallion, but that
the animal was acquired from the amir of Seville:

He who was born in good hour did not delay;
he put on his silk tunic, his long beard hung down;
they saddled for him Babieca and fastened the
     caparisons [harness].
My Cid rode out upon him bearing wooden arms.
On the horse they called Babieca he rode, rode at a gallop;
it was a wonder to watch . . . from that day Babieca was
     famous through all Spain.[51]

Reunited with his adoring family, Rodrigo goes to the highest
vantage point in Valencia and

their eyes behold the sea.
They look on the farmlands, wide and thick with green.[52]

The King of Morocco, called Yusuf in the *Poema*, is greatly
annoyed, remarking:

'For in the lands that are mine he has trespassed gravely
and gives thanks for it to no one save Jesus Christ.'[53]

So Yusuf ibn Teshufin sails across the Straits with an army of 50,000
and Rodrigo makes a curious comment:

'My wife and daughters will see me in battle,
in these foreign lands they will see how houses are made,
they will see clearly how we earn our bread.'[54]

173

It is almost as though the taking of cities and destroying of country-side is just a day-job like any other, and the battle-hardened veteran takes a teenage delight in 'showing off' in front of his family.

In his description of the battle of Cuarte, in which yet again the Cid achieved a surprise victory by striking out from a beleaguered and apparently hopeless situation, the poet has Rodrigo encountering Ibn Teshufin personally, wounding him three times with his sword. Again, vast riches fall to the Cid's men –

> a thousand horses of the best and best broken
> . . . precious tents and jewelled tent poles[55]

– one of which, Ibn Teshufin's, Rodrigo sends back to Alfonso.

At this point the *Poema*'s version of the Cid's exploits, with various minor exceptions that are not all that far from the truth, now descends into fairytale. Two Castilian noblemen, Diego and Fernando, called usually the Heirs of Carrion, an area to the west of Burgos, press Alfonso to give them the Cid's daughters in marriage. It is clear throughout that these men are Machiavellian schemers in league with Garcia Ordoñez, the Cid's implacable enemy at court, and they are blatantly after the Cid's money. Carrion is real, but nothing else about this interlude rings true. The girls are called Elvira and Sol, as though the poet had no idea of their real names. The Cid smells a rat, but as the loyal subject of Alfonso, who also wants the weddings to take place, he reluctantly agrees.

The third *cantar* continues the theme. Once the poet is locked into the fiction of the daughters' weddings, the Outrage at Corpes is a particularly unlikely way to get back to reality. This section opens with the Cid's pet lion escaping and so terrifying the Heirs that they end up hiding under the furniture. Rodrigo, of course, calmly sorts the problem out:

> My Cid rose to his elbow, got to his feet,
> with his cloak on his shoulders walked towards the lion;
> the lion, when he saw him, was so filled with shame,
> before my Cid he bowed his head and put his face down.

My Cid Rodrigo took him by the neck, led him as with a halter,
and put him in his cage.[56]

It is entirely plausible that Rodrigo Diaz did own a lion. Presents of
exotic beasts stretch back to the ancient world and the fact that this
animal was caged in Valencia may mean that it was originally a pet of
al-Qadir, the last amir before the Cid took the city. The incident is
bizarre, but of course its purpose in the *Poema* is to point up the
cowardice of the Heirs of Carrion, which becomes even more apparent
when a new Almoravid army arrives under King Bucar, 'of whom you
have heard tell'.[57]

This may refer to Ibn Teshufin's nephew Mohammed, but
rather than seeing it as Rodrigo did, with the grim determination
of the fortress mentality, in the *Poema* it is a cause for rejoicing
because here is another opportunity for plunder. In the battle that
follows the Cid crosses swords with Bucar and the result is
devastating:

> The Cid overtook Bucar three fathoms from the sea,
> raised Colada and struck him a great blow,
> and there he cut away the jewels of his helmet,
> split the helmet and driving through all below,
> as far as the waist his sword sank.[58]

In the right hands a broadsword could split a skull, but anything
beyond that is a work of imagination. Stories of Saxon two-handed
axes doing similar damage at Hastings in 1066 are probably equally
'tall'. From this encounter the Cid obtained his second sword, Tizon,
'worth a thousand marks of gold'.[59]

In an unusual aside Rodrigo allows himself a little vanity:

> I win battles, as pleases the Creator;
> Moors and Christians go in fear of me.
> There in Morocco, where the mosques are,
> they tremble lest perhaps some night I should take them
>   by surprise . . .[60]

We can almost hear him pausing and winking to his audience

> . . . but I plan no such thing.
> I shall not go seeking them, but stay in Valencia. . . .[61]

Rodrigo gives his splendid swords to his sons-in-law as they ride back to their homes with their new brides – 'The Heirs have ridden out from Valencia the Shining.'[62] And on the way the dastardly pair plot to kill Abengalbon, who quickly rumbles them and only lets them pass on because of his respect for the Cid.

In the wood at Corpes where the Heirs and their wives are camped, the pair suddenly turn on the women, stealing their clothes and leaving them with 'nothing on their bodies but their shirts and silk undergarments'; then they beat them with horse-harness and spurs:

> and over the silken cloth the clean blood ran . . .
> Doña Elvira and Doña Sol could no longer speak;
> they left them for dead in the oak grove. . . .[63]

The rest of the *Poema* deals with the Cid's revenge. Naturally outraged, he brings the Heirs to trial in Toledo under Alfonso as judge and demands that honour be satisfied in trial by combat. Interestingly he does not fight them himself, but gives the honour to Pedro Bermudez and Martin Antolinez.

The *Poema*'s description of the dress of the Cid's company at court seems to come from an altogether later period than the 1090s:

> Put on your armour over padded tunics,
> put on your breastplates, white as the sun,
> furs and ermines over your breastplates
> and draw the strings tight that your weapons be not seen.[64]

Rodrigo is clearly expecting trouble. As for the Cid himself,

> he covered his legs in stockings of fine cloth and over them he put
> shoes of elaborate work. He put on a woven shirt as white as the

sun, and all the fastenings were of silver and gold. The cuffs fitted neatly for he had ordered it thus. Over this he put a tunic of fine brocade worked with gold shining in every place. Over these a crimson skin with buckles of gold, which my Cid the Campeador wears on all occasions . . . his beard was long and tied with a cord, for he wished to guard his person against insult.[65]

This is the fullest description we have of Rodrigo's appearance and if we are right about when the original *Poema* was written, it is possible that the poet learned it from someone who knew the man in his last years at Valencia.

Alfonso gives the go-ahead and first Pedro Bermudez, who seems to have a speech impediment –

> you call me Pedro the Mute!
> But you know well that I can do no better

– then Martin Antolinez challenge the Heirs. Since the Heirs have powerful backing in the form of Garcia Ordoñez, the combats that follow become a three-way event with Muno Gustioz for the Cid fighting Asur Gonzalez, Martin Antolinez fighting Diego Gonzalez and the ubiquitous Alvar Fañez fighting Gomez Pelaez. It is now that we have the scathing insults thrown at Rodrigo that we have cited earlier:

> Still when might we receive honour from my Cid of Vivar!
> Let him go now to the River Ubierna and look after his mills
> and be paid in corn as he used to do![66]

It is the old slur that Rodrigo's family is second rate in the fiercely hierarchical pecking order of the Castilian nobility. Gustioz gives as good as the Cid gets in his reply:

> First you have your breakfast and then you say your
>   prayers . . .
> you are false to all and still more false to the Creator.[67]

The clashes in the lists are excitingly told, no doubt by someone who had seen duels like this:

> When this blow was struck, Muno Gustioz returned another; he split his shield in the middle of the buckler. Nothing withstood his stroke, he broke the armour; he sheared it apart and though not close to the heart, drove the lance and pennon into the flesh so that it came out an arm's length on the other side. Then he pulled on the lance and twisted Gonzalez from the saddle.[68]

Then Rodrigo speaks again:

> Praised be the King of Heaven,
> my daughters are avenged.[69]

In a lightning postscript suitors arrive from Navarre and Aragon and the wronged Elvira and Sol marry the men their real counterparts actually married:

> See how he grows in honour who in good hour was born.
> His daughters are wives of the Kings of Navarre and Aragon.
> Now the Kings of Spain are his kinsmen
> and all advance in honour through my Cid the Campeador.[70]

As a piece of history the *Poema* presents problems. Much of it is nonsense, a medieval example of what today we would call a historical novel and not a very convincing one at that. Yet some of it is verifiable by other evidence, especially the places and people that colour it. What is marked is the personal touches – the Cid's appearance, the acquiring of the swords Colada and Tizona, the brilliance of Babieca, the reliance on Alvar Fañez as the Cid's sword arm. What is impossible to measure is how much of this was invention and how much may have been based on fact not recorded by earlier chroniclers. Modern research, into the structure of the trial scene for example, indicates that the *Poema* was probably written about a century after Rodrigo's death, but some of the details in it could still have been handed down through the generations as folklore.

We know the poem was written by a Castilian – the original language is pure Castilian and the sentimentality shown by the Cid as he leaves for exile seems to be from the heart. The place-names are intensely local.

Ultimately, what we have in the *Poema* is the first phase of the legend of the Cid. He is proudly Castilian because the poet was and because his work was almost certainly sung at the court of Alfonso VIII, whose crushing defeat of the Almohades at Las Navas de Tortosa in 1212 is considered the finest victory of the entire *Reconquista*. Cordoba and Seville fell to his son Fernando III and never again would any fanatical sect cross the Straits to al-Andalus. The period of Alfonso VIII's infancy was an action replay of the early years of the Cid's life, with Christian princes squabbling and killing one another while the Muslim menace spreads swiftly from the south. Already the Cid was a hero, a rallying cry from the tomb to point the way towards Christian – and Castilian – victory.

11

. . . and into Legend

Alfonso X, el Sabio, the learned, was one of those all-rounders who drive a country forward. King of Castile and Léon for over thirty years, he was also elected Holy Roman Emperor in 1267. He played his part in the ongoing *Reconquista* by conquering the west of Spain and entering into a Cid-like alliance with the amir of Granada, which gave him a rare period of peace in which to pursue his other interests. His importance in the legend of Rodrigo of Vivar is that he was, perhaps unusually among the warrior-kings of Christian Spain, a scholar, fascinated by science and astrology, and very ready to milk the Arab world of its culture by having key works translated into Spanish. It is not an exaggeration to say that he was the founder of Castilian as the national language of Spain and he personally wrote poetry as well as treatises on philosophy and what today we would call chemistry. The sixteenth-century historian Juan de Mariana wrote of him that 'He gazed so much at the sky that his crown fell off'[1] – not an altogether fair summation of the man's achievements. His law code of the 1260s, the *Siete Partidas*, was the first written in the vernacular in Spain and he even got a team of Toledan Jews working on a translation of the Old Testament from its original Hebrew.

He came across the Cid while he was compiling, with yet another team, this time Christians, a general history of the peninsula. Probably completed in the 1270s, this has come down to us as *Primera Cronica General*. It is incredibly convoluted and was originally part of a much larger work which no longer exists and to which sections were added for thirty or forty years after Alfonso's death. What its writers did was to cobble together everything to do with the Cid that they could find, which included the *Carmen*

180

Campi Doctoris, the *Historia Roderici* and the *Poema de Mio Cid*, as well as other songs, poems and ballads now lost to time. As such, we have no way of knowing how much historical truth ended up in the *Primera Cronica*, but it was probably very little.

However learned Alfonso may have been – and we can assume that his scholars were even more so – he was not a historian in the modern sense. Nor were any of his team. They did not weigh evidence, look for corroboration or refutation, interpret documents or apply critical standards. Rather they were antiquarians, who simply collected everything and wrote it all down as though it was the truth. One classic example of this is their inclusion after 1272 of the details from the *Estoria de Cardena*. The cult of the Cid in the monastery where he was buried was clearly still going strong nearly two hundred years after his death, and during Alfonso's visit there he composed some beautiful verses to be chiselled into the stone sarcophagi of Rodrigo and Jimena. Still there when the literature expert James Fitzmaurice-Kelly visited it in 1908, it read:

> Belliger, invictius, famosus marte in triumphis,
> Clauditor hoc tumulo magnus Didaci Rodericus.
> (Shut up in this tomb is the undefeated warrior,
> famously victorious in war, the great Rodrigo).

It is likely that the monks gave the king a gorgeous calfskin-bound book on the Cid – the world's first 'biography' of the man – on this occasion. The work itself has not survived, but it is from this, as incorporated into the *Primera Cronica*, that the embalming story we have already heard was taken.

It would be another forty years before the next phase of the Cid legend appeared, the *Cronica del Famoso Cavallero Cid Ruydiez Campeador*. First written before 1312, it was printed at Burgos in 1552 by order of Prince Fernando. The actual text was prepared then by Juan de Velorado, the abbot, who seems to have made a whole plethora of mistakes, adding to the mythology of the subject and to our confusion. This *Cronica* was reputedly written by the Cid's loyal servant Gil Diaz, whose original name was Abenalfarax (Abu ibn al-Faraq), a Muslim who was the *qadi* in the Cid's palace at Valencia in the 1090s. As related in the *Cronica*, Abenalfarax (various spellings exist) came to Rodrigo one day asking that he be converted to Christianity because as a child he had been captured by Christians and 'I find that I have led a life of great error and that all which Mohammed the great deceiver gave to the Moors for their law, is deceit; and therefore, sir, I turn me to the faith of Jesus Christ and will be a Christian and believe in the Catholic faith.'[2] This glaring piece of propaganda must be set against the time in which it was first written and the time in which it was printed. Assuming, as experts do, that the *Cronica* was written by 1312 (although there is a school of thought which fixes it thirty years earlier), Spain had once again fallen into the internecine back-biting and sheer chaos that characterized the Cid's time.

As astonishing proof that history repeats itself and few of us learn by the mistakes of the past, Alfonso VII of Castile and Léon, dying fifty-eight years after the Cid, split his realm between his warring sons Sancho and Fernando. So while Castile and Léon were once again at each other's throats, as the century progressed there was a hardening of the Christendom–Islam relationship. The rulers of Barcelona, at loggerheads with Castile-Léon in the Cid's time, joined forces against the Almohades to stop the renewed expansion of fundamentalist Islam to the north.

Under Fernando III of Castile the kind of unity achieved by Fernando I and Alfonso VI was re-established, with the Almohades being smashed at Las Navas de Tortosa in 1212 and Léon being added to Fernando's territory in 1230. Eventually achieving the status of sainthood, Fernando set up a university at Salamanca, curbed the power of the warlords in his own domains (which in the eleventh century would have seen him go head-to-head with the Cid) and swept al-Andalus of its Muslim tendencies. With the creation of a Castilian navy, there was even talk – mentioned half-jokingly by Rodrigo in the *Cronica del Famoso Cavallero* – of an invasion of the Maghrib to stop the African threat once and for all.

The Cid's Valencia was retaken in 1238, and its territory re-populated by Catalans from Aragon. For the next two centuries

Spanish Christians employed much the same economic system they would use in sixteenth-century America. Arabs and Moors became, in effect, serfs and land ownership passed to Christians from the north. Increasingly Muslims were expected to convert, as Abenalfarax had done, to Christianity. Such people were labelled *moriscos*.

Now that the whole peninsula was virtually Christian (Gibraltar – the rock of Tariq – was taken from the Moors in 1312), the 'enemy at the door' no longer existed. Africa was quiet and soon to be dismembered by Europeans greedy for slaves, gold and ivory, and in the south of al-Andalus a nervous Granada kept its head down. So the nobles of Spain turned on one another, led by the *infante* Sancho who refused to accept the principle of primogeniture set up so recently by his own father in the *Siete Partidas*.

Sancho had won the support of the *cortes* (parliament) of Castile by 1282 and Alfonso X was deposed. Despite the fact that parliamentary power in Spain pre-dated that of England ('the mother of parliaments') by some years, the real power in the peninsula, as everywhere else in Europe at this time, lay in the personality, integrity and sheer brass-neck of the king. Sancho may have been a hard case, but he died young, leaving that nightmare for medieval society, a boy-king. Portugal, Aragon, even France saw this as an opportunity to meddle and to unbalance the knife-edge control created by St Fernando.

Luckily for Castilian royalty, the infant Fernando's mother was Maria de Molina, one of the handful of extraordinarily strong-willed women that the Middle Ages threw up. With skill and nerve she held the throne together until Fernando came of age and then proceeded to do the same thing again when he died seventeen years later, before she finally settled down to an honoured retirement. Like the Cid, her exploits were still being embroidered centuries later when the playwright Tirso de Molina wrote *La prudencia en la mujer* (The Wisdom in Women).

This was the period in which the *Cronica del Famoso Cavallero* was written, when boy-king and over-mighty subjects threatened havoc in Castilian society. Rodrigo Diaz may have been just such an over-mighty subject, but by this time his legend had grown. He was regarded as a saint by the monks of Cardena, and had acquired a chivalric status far above the squabbling *hidalgos* of Maria de Molina's time. To sum him up in these terms, we cannot do better than to take the genuine attitudes discussed by historian Maurice Keen. The knight was marked by 'his courtliness (especially in regard to women) and his skills in horsemanship, the hunting field and sword play and the social virtues expected of him, his courage and generosity, his loyalty to the plighted word, his independent spirit . . .'.[3] Rodrigo, the Cid Campeador, had all of these in good measure.

What of the Spain of the printed version of the *Cronica*? By 1552 many European countries had taken advantage of the printing press, originally a Chinese invention, to produce variants of their national histories. In England several versions of the Ballad of Robin Hood were available, printed by London 'stationers' who advertised their premises by the nearest inn, or at the publishing centre at Amen Corner, near St Paul's Cathedral. In Transylvania the evil Vlad Țepeș, the Impaler, was becoming known to a new generation anxious to believe every exaggerated word about their country's bloody past. The thread of violence that runs through these early printings is a world away from our views of Hood and Țepeș today, and it is also a world away from the sixteenth-century version of Rodrigo of Vivar. Perhaps a better comparison can be found in Thomas Malory's *Mort Artu*, printed in England in 1471. Like the *Cronica del Famoso Cavallero*, it was based on earlier versions of the legend but this is still the enduring image of Arthur that most of us hold today. The sixth-century Romano-British warlord, whose name is uncertain,[4] became, in Malory's hands, a full-blown medieval king, with a castle (Camelot), a queen (Guinevere) and a host of bold, plate-armoured knights, like Galahad, Gawaine and Lancelot, whose lives become a quest for the impossible – the acquisition of the Holy Grail. Rodrigo Diaz, by the sixteenth century, could easily have been a knight of the Round Table.

By the 1550s Spain was unrecognizable as the war-torn country inhabited by the Cid. Most obviously, the Moorish threat had long gone and the *Reconquista*, of which Rodrigo of Vivar was a part, was well and truly over. The historian Nebrija wrote:

Who cannot see that although the title of Empire is in Germany, its reality lies in the power of the Spanish monarchs who, masters of a large part of Italy and the isles of the Mediterranean Sea, carry the war to Africa and send out their fleet, following the course of the stars, to the isles of the Indies and the New World, linking the Orient to the western boundary of Spain and Africa.[5]

This was Spain's *sieclo d'oro*, the golden century, when the country of the Cid was the world's superpower. Cristoforo Colon, the Italian adventurer whom many thought mad because he believed the world was round, had discovered the New World (repeatedly called the Indies by Spain after Colon's famous error of navigation) in Spanish ships with Spanish crews backed by Spanish money. His expedition of 1492 had been funded by Isabella of Castile, so that technically Castilian became the official language and culture of the Americas and it was the Spanish flag that Colon had rammed triumphantly into the beach of Hispaniola.

In 1519 Hernando Cortes had brought the castles and lions flag again to overawe the Aztecs of Mexico, and seven years later the illiterate Francisco Pizarro did the same thing, with a great deal of slaughter, to the Incas of Peru. In our politically correct times, both these acts are seen as appalling examples of barbarity, aggrandizement and genocide on a terrifying scale, but they helped make Spain the most formidable power in the world at the time. Contemporary carvings and paintings of Cortes show him trampling naked Aztecs under his horse's hoofs exactly as Santiago the Moorslayer had done for the four centuries of the *Reconquista* and as the Cid himself is depicted doing on the Arca de Santa Maria, the sixteenth-century archway in Burgos.

Spain was now at the heart of the Holy Roman Empire, its Habsburg rulers revered and feared throughout Europe. While the *conquistadores* (conquerors) tramped the jungles of the Amazon in search of Eldorado, the legendary city made of pure gold, the Inquisition was making its presence felt to stem the growing tide of Protestantism. In 1539 the Basque soldier Ignatius Loyola set up the Society of Jesus, a plain, simple, fanatical and (for Protestants

185

anyway) deadly code of Catholicism. This was the second-generation Inquisition, because in the 1480s Tomas de Torquemada had become its first Inquisitor-General with papal and royal dispensation to use torture to discover secret Protestants, first in Spain and then throughout Europe. The resulting *auto da fé* was an orgy of garrotting and public burning which Protestant propaganda had no need to embellish. Consequently Spain remained one of the most dependably Catholic countries in Europe throughout the Reformation.

The problem was that the King of Spain, Carlos I, was also Charles V, Holy Roman Emperor. Initially – and apocryphally – he may have spoken Spanish only to his horse, but as time went on he became the champion of Spain's Catholicism and Spanish became his favourite language. The flipside was that Spanish money and Spanish troops were being diverted to pay for the emperor's political ambitions and grandiose schemes elsewhere.

The 'golden century' also saw an impressive outpouring of literature as part of the whole complex process of the Renaissance. While Bartolomé Murillo was founding the Academy of Seville, painting extraordinary scenes of everyday Spanish life alongside more conventional religious studies, and Domenico Theotocopoulos, El Greco, was creating his astonishing flame-like figures and neo-Impressionist scenes, Spanish writers were making names for themselves too. Garcilaso de la Vega was a soldier-turned-poet who introduced sonnet writing to Spain and produced odes along the lines of those of the Roman poet Virgil. Lopé de Vega produced an estimated 1,500 plays and countless ballads with a graceful musical verse, many of them 'cloak and sword' works full of excitement and adventure. Gabriel Tellez we have already heard from under his pseudonym of Tirso de Molina. Originally prior of the monastery of Soria, he wrote plays, mostly *Comedias*, and was particularly impressive in writing female characters for the stage.

These men, together with more serious scholars like the humanist Luis de Leon, who were persecuted by the Inquisition for using Hebrew sources in their Bible studies, were breaking new ground at the time when the *Cronica del Famoso Cavallero* was retreading old ground and the old tolerance had gone. Alfonso the learned had

186

employed a panel of scholarly Jews to translate the Bible; the Spain of Charles V officially had no Jews at all. The motive for printing the stories of the Cid now changed. In 1312 the handwritten version was created to remind a tottering, strife-torn Spain that men like the Cid had once existed; that they were an ideal to be admired. It was as though Rodrigo of Vivar had become the Moorslayer, Babieca's giant hooves trampling the severed heads of the Moorish enemy. Now, at the height of Spain's greatness, it was a reminder that Spain had always been great, producing heroes like the Campeador. When they opened Rodrigo's tomb in 1541 to remove it to another part of the church, the odour of sanctity rose from the sarcophagus. As it did so, the first rain in months fell – clearly the handiwork of a saint.

Southey's 'Chronicle of the Cid' throws light on this:

> . . . men of all nations and at all times have come from all parts to see and reverence his holy body and tomb, being led by the odour of his fame, especially knights and soldiers, who, when they have fallen upon their knees to kiss his tomb and scraped a little of the stone thereof to bear away with them as a relic and commended themselves to him, have felt their hearts strengthened, and gone away in full trust that they should speed the better in all battles into which they should enter from that time with a good cause. By reason of this great devotion and the great virtues of my Cid, and the miracles which were wrought by him, King Philip the Second gave order to his ambassador Don Diego Hurtado de Mendoza, to deal with the Court of Rome concerning the canonization of this venerable knight Rodrigo Diaz.[6]

There were – and are – of course, strict rules regarding canonization and we no longer have a record of the miracles attributed to the Cid. Mendoza took his task seriously, particularly since he personally claimed descent from Rodrigo and worked with the monks of San Pedro de Cardena to produce the necessary paperwork to impress the Curia.

As so often in the history of the papacy, however, politics intervened. While Mendoza was composing his dossier, a combined

Spanish and Florentine army was capturing the independent city-state of Siena in Italy. Even though Philip gave it to Cosimo de Medici, Duke of Florence, two years later, Spanish troops playing fast and loose with Italian cities and Italian lives did not encourage cordial relations. It did not help that the pope at the time was Paul IV (Giovanni Caraffa), a fierce hardliner who not only, as would be expected, opposed Protestantism, but even declared Ignatius Loyola a heretic! It was said that sparks flew from his feet as he strode through the Vatican. He hated all things Spanish, accused the Cardinal Primate of Spain of heresy and cheerfully went to war with the very country that was most loyal of all to Catholicism. Against this, the pleas of a Spanish scholar relating to a Spanish war hero dead for five centuries did not carry much weight. By the time Pope Paul died, to such rejoicings that the mob went on the rampage in Rome destroying his effigies and smashing open the cells of the Inquisition, it was too late to start again.

The reprint of the *Cronica* forty years later may well have appeared for different reasons still. In 1593 Spain was ruled by the infuriatingly enigmatic Philip II. The Spanish Netherlands had erupted into a Protestant-inspired, Dutch-led, English-backed revolt and Spain had lost not one but two armadas to England. The discovery of the 'mountain of silver' at Potosi in 1545 had flooded the Spanish market and created an inflation that quickly spiralled out of control. The stultifying effects of the monopolistic *Mesta* (sheep-herders) prevented expansion and experimentation in other forms of agriculture. Prices doubled in a generation and taxes shot sky-high. In human terms there was a huge drain of talent and energy out of old Spain as young men sailed for the golden opportunities of the New World. Increasingly foreigners were drifting into Spain, encouraged by its prestige, and business and trade were becoming controlled by Jews and outsiders, the natural greed of the free market proving more powerful than the anti-Semitic edicts of the long-dead Fernando and Isabella.

Philip was not the extrovert his father was and he established the obscure little town of Madrid as his capital, building the vast and gloomy palace – or was it a monastery? – of El Escorial just outside it. It was now that the Spanish legend of laziness – *mañana* (tomorrow) – came into existence. Everything became more hidebound, conservative and slow. 'If Death came from Spain,' wrote the viceroy of Naples, 'we should live a long time.'[7] Three years after the second edition of the *Cronica del Famoso Cavallero* was printed, Castile was bankrupt and Francis Drake sailed into the harbour at Cadiz and with his fire-ships sank every Spanish vessel at anchor. It was time for the Cid to come riding back into the Spanish psyche, to save the day as the real man and his legend had done so many times before.

But the heroism did not last. A new mood had alighted in Spain and on the world which has never quite gone away. In the fifteenth century the *Mocedades de Rodrigo* (The Youthful Pranks of Rodrigo) had appeared, running to over a thousand verses which had no bearing on history at all.[8] And in 1605 the *Romancero de Cid* continued this trend for fiction. In that same year Miguel de Cervantes published his imperishable *Don Quixote*. It appeared in two parts, the second following ten years later, and the whole thing was written in fits and starts between other works. Great as the literature is, it marked the end of the chivalric ideal that had obsessed intellectual Europe for six hundred years; gunpowder and shot now replaced the armoured knight on the battlefield. Henceforward, it was a world of technology and professionals, of trajectories, manoeuvres and counter-manoeuvres. Quixote, clattering over La Mancha in home-made armour and riding the under-nourished nag Rosinante, is a world away from Rodrigo Diaz on Babieca. The Cid rode against Christian kings and nobles, against amirs of al-Andalus and Berber fanatics out of Africa; Don Quixote rode, in his daffy, delusional world, at windmills. And Quixote himself says, in the book, 'That there was a Cid . . . is beyond doubt; but that [he] did the deeds which [he is] said to have done, I take to be very doubtful.'[9] It had all gone horribly wrong.

The ballad-reading public now wanted outrageous storylines, corny comedy and what today we would call human interest. And the writers of the day gave them exactly that. The *Romancero* was reprinted twenty-six times in ten years and by 1618 the first play had appeared.

Guillen de Castro may not be known today outside his native Spain, partly because he had the misfortune to be a contemporary of Marlowe, Shakespeare and Corneille, but his reputation in the early seventeenth century was matched by the frequent fact of such greats dying in poverty to be rediscovered – and their work 'lifted' – by later generations. De Castro was a native of Valencia, where it is likely that stories of the Cid still circulated, and in 1591 he became a member of a distinguished literary society, the Nocturnos. He was a key figure in the Spanish government of Naples, patronized by serious politicians like the king's right-hand minister Enrique de Guzman, the Count-Duke of Olivares. A knight of the Order of Santiago by 1623, de Castro's *Comedias* were hugely popular and he was a regular winner of national prizes for poetry at the religious festivals held in Madrid.

His *Los Mocedadas del Cid* may have been written as early as 1600 and the play, in two parts, was an immediate success, reflecting the old romances with their fierce patriotism and easy-on-the-ear poetry. For the story of Rodrigo of Vivar, however, a greater playwright was waiting in the wings: Pierre Corneille. An unsuccessful lawyer with a Jesuit education, Corneille began to write for the Parisian stage in 1629 with a comedy called *Mélite*, in which he parodied the obsessions of polite society – just as Oscar Wilde would do two and a half centuries later. Like most successful playwrights, Corneille attracted a powerful patron, in his case Armand Jean Duplessis, Cardinal Richelieu, who virtually ran France in those years. Something of a playwright himself, Richelieu founded a group of intellectuals – Les Cinq Auteurs – to write dramas based on the cardinal's own view of the world. A temperament like Corneille's found this difficult and after a spectacular row with Richelieu, the playwright retired to Rouen where he wrote *Le Cid*.

The importance of this play lies in the fact that the legend of Rodrigo of Vivar now appeared for the first time outside Spain.[10] Corneille had borrowed heavily from de Castro, especially in the version of Rodrigo killing Jimena's father and the tortuous love-hate relationship that existed between them. Two ballads of the several hundred that were churned out by Corneille's time caught his imagination. In the first, Jimena goes to Alfonso to demand justice for the Cid's killing of her father. Again, we have no specific details, and, in a reversal of the approach in the *Poema*, it is Rodrigo who asks Alfonso for the girl's hand in marriage. 'I am the one who made her lose her father when she was a very little girl'[11] reads the second stanza and it probably hits the right note in respect of their differing ages. In the fourth stanza it is clear that Rodrigo is a haunted man: 'Every night when the sun goes down, I see the knight [Jimena's dead father] on his horse and it reminds me of what I did.' We have strong echoes here of Hamlet's ghost, rising from the grave to demand vengeance. In this case Alfonso agrees to the wedding. As Rodrigo has deprived Jimena of the protection of her father, it is his duty to become her protector as her husband. Interestingly, in the ninth stanza the literary Alfonso assumes the likely attitude of the real king: 'I am not going to offend the Cid, as he is valuable and a defender of my realm.' Rather meekly, Jimena accepts Rodrigo with happiness; Corneille had a neat dramatic take on this.

In the second ballad the playwright used, the Cid's wedding takes place in the presence of Alfonso and Layn Calvo, the Archbishop of Léon. Rodrigo admits in the presence of God: 'I killed your father, Ximena; I killed him man to man to take revenge for an offence. I killed a man and I give you a man in place of your dead father, an honourable husband.'

There is no historical evidence at all for the feud between Rodrigo and Jimena's father as the background to their relationship. But what is important is that virtually all perpetuators of the Cid legend have kept this element in, with its fascinating human interest angle. 'So', says the second ballad rather cheesily, 'where love is present all evil that has happened in the past is forgotten.'

Dubbed at the time a tragicomedy in that it fitted both dramatic genres, *Le Cid* landed Corneille in a great deal of controversy. Richelieu's Academie Française, which he had founded the year before the play appeared, laid down strict rules about domestic construction. Plays had to be presented using unities of time, place and action – one setting (a gift, of course, for set designers!); one time-frame (usually a day); and one conflict. *Le Cid* did not follow this convention and Richelieu himself, no doubt out of personal pique with Corneille, demanded a rewrite.

Pamphlets followed accusing the playwright of immorality. The Academie insisted that all plays were to be instructive and morally uplifting. *Le Cid* failed there as well. The play tells us virtually nothing about eleventh-century Spain and the theme of love (lust?) overcoming duty was not acceptable. The 'querelle du Cid' raged for months, but subsequent editions of the play from 1648 were firmly labelled tragedies and were more conventional in style.

Although essentially a love story, *Le Cid* did have some heroic lines and concepts, including 'When we conquer without danger our triumph is without glory'[12] and the more famous 'And the combat ceased, for want of combatants.'[13]

The literary critic Sainte-Beaune summed up the play: '*Le Cid* marks the birth of a man, the rebirth of poetry, the drama of a great century.'[14]

We have to wait another 150 years before Rodrigo of Vivar appears again north of the Pyrenees. This time it was at the hands of an Englishman and the motivation was very different. If Corneille had been inspired by the relationship between Rodrigo and Jimena, Robert Southey was inspired by Spain itself.

One of the Lake poets whose own poetry was eclipsed by that of William Wordsworth, Southey was a Bristolian who followed the conventional upper-middle-class Englishman's education of the day. He attended Westminster School in London before going up to Balliol, Oxford, where he learned 'a little swimming . . . and a little boating'.[15] But if Southey's schools were conventional, his attitude was not. Expelled from Westminster for an outspoken attack in a magazine article on the evils of flogging in public schools,[16] he and the opium-smoking poet Samuel Taylor Coleridge dreamed of setting up a 'Pantisocracy' in America. Where his contemporary Robert Owen actually established a similar neo-Communist society in his

'villages of co-operation', Southey's ideas barely got off the ground.
He imagined a society in which 'the best books would have a place;
literature and science, bathed anew in the invigorating stream of life
and nature, could not but rise reanimated and purified'.[17] He was
not a defender of women's rights, however: 'Each young man should
take to himself a mild and lovely woman for his wife; it would be her
part to prepare their innocent food and tend their hardy and
beautiful race.'[18] No books for girls, then! It was in 1808, the year
before he began regular contributions to the influential *Quarterly
Review* and five years before he became Poet Laureate, that Southey
translated the 'Chronicle of the Cid'. As one of that dwindling band
of Englishmen who openly supported the French Revolution,
Southey set out for Spain in 1795. Two years earlier his government
had declared war on Revolutionary France and anyone still
espousing the republican cause was deemed a traitor. No doubt
Southey felt a lot safer wandering in Galicia. His original intention
was to write a history of Portugal, but he became attracted to the
Cid instead.

Southey was a poet by inclination, so the translations he made
came naturally to him. He was also a scholar, but of the generation
before modern criticism became the norm. Even so, his preface to
the 'Chronicle of the Cid' throws useful light on the legend:

If the *Chronica del Cid* be extracted from the General Chronicle,[19]
which is giving it the latest date, even in that case it was written
before the end of the thirteenth century; that is, little more than
150 years after the Cid's death, and whatever fiction has been
introduced into the story, must have been invented long before, or
it would not have been received as truth and incorporated into the
general history of Spain.[20]

Southey's translations for the 'Chronicle' came from three distinct
sources: the 1593 *Cronica de Famoso Cavallero*; the *Cronica de
España* and the *Poema de Mio Cid*. Of the particular edition (1604)
of the *Cronica de España* that he used, Southey explains that the
scholar Florian de Ocampo was approached by the printers of

Zamora 'to give him something which they might publish to the use and glory of those kingdoms whereof they and he were natives'.[21]

Southey points out the useful fact that printers notoriously altered words and phrases at will to make texts more intelligible to modern readers[22] and blames Ocampo for not doing more to control this: 'Ocampo was not a common Corrector of the Press; he was Chronicler to the King of Castile.'[23]

Finally the future Poet Laureate used various Romances of the Cid, those printed in vast numbers early in the seventeenth century as Spain's *sieclo d'oro* was turning back to iron. He is rightly dismissive of them, realizing that they were the popular entertainment – the soap operas – of their day, sung by *copleros*, *trouveurs* and *joculars*: 'I know none of any value among the many hundreds which I have perused. I have very seldom availed myself of the Romances del Cid.'[24]

So Southey's interest in the Cid lay in an almost accidental discovery of the man and his legend in the various libraries of Spain. But why did his translation do so well and capture the imagination of cultured Englishmen for the first time? The answer lies in politics. From 1791 the aggressive revolutionary government of France famously offered help to any country in Europe that wished to throw off the tyrannical yoke of their particular brand of the *ancien régime*. The ideals of liberty, equality and brotherhood which were the shallow slogans of the new rulers had a huge appeal in the increasingly liberal chattering classes across Europe, and Robert Southey was one who fell under the spell in England. But after an initial feeble attempt to keep France out of Spain, King Charles IV's chief minister, Manuel Godoy, felt forced to sign an alliance with the French in 1796. Southey was still in Spain while all this was going on but was at home before the going really got rough. Spain had already lost many New World possessions to Britain (Trinidad in the West Indies, for example) and to France (the notorious Louisiana Purchase of 1803), and in declaring war on Britain in 1804 she opened herself to an armada-style drubbing by Horatio Nelson off Cape Trafalgar the following year.

When France invaded Portugal in 1807 and the flamboyant cavalry commander Joachim Murat thundered into Madrid months later, Spain was transformed from a weak ally into yet another victim of 'la bête noire', Napoleon Bonaparte, now Emperor of the French. The king was deposed and Bonaparte's brother Joseph (much to Murat's fury) took his place on the Spanish throne. 'My position here is unique,' he wrote to his brother, 'I have not a single supporter here.'[25]

On 2 May 1808, led by local peasantry in Asturias, Spanish guerrillas began the War of Independence. It was bloody from the beginning, characterized by Francisco Goya's etchings of deaths by firing squads and limbs impaled on thorn bushes. French troops knew that if they straggled too far behind their marching columns, their likely fate was a slit throat from a Basque mountaineer and the final ignominious end; their penises cut off and stuffed into their mouths.

The reality of Spanish politics in this year was highly complicated, with local rivalries, traditionalists taking on reformers, and myriad shades of opinion on revolution and France and the state of the nation. In Southey's England, however, the guerrillas were portrayed as heroes, united in the same cause as Englishmen against a tyrant (Bonaparte) who had no right to be there. The result, from the British viewpoint, was to send to Spain a contingent of troops led by the relatively unknown general Arthur Wellesley, who had won his only laurels in India. If Wellesley, the future Duke of Wellington, had nothing but contempt for Spanish regular troops and even less respect for the guerrillas, this was not how it was perceived in *The Times*. Spain was filling everyone's conversation – Spanish customs, Spanish politics, Spanish dress – and of course Spanish heroes like El Cid.

It was while the French army was besieging Burgos that a regiment of dragoons broke into the monastery of San Pedro de Cardeña in search of gold and jewels. When they found the tomb of Rodrigo Diaz, they realized the symbolic significance of the place and all but destroyed it. The French governor of Castile, a little more civilized than the hard-riding *grognards* who were used to despoiling churches, was appalled at the sacrilege and had the scattered relics of the Cid collected and reburied in a new monument.

This dispersal of memorabilia meant that invaluable information was lost. We would love to know if Rodrigo was indeed seated on his ivory chair with his sword in his hand as Gil Diaz reputedly placed him. Some relics certainly left Spain and were found in Sigmaringen in Germany in 1921. Their tortuous journey from a regiment of French dragoons in 1808 is unknown, but the clue might lie with the Egyptologist Dominique-Vivant Denon. A remarkable Renaissance man who was a painter, illustrator, author and diplomat, he travelled with the more famous Champollion to Egypt as part of Napoleon Bonaparte's expedition there in 1798. He was subsequently made organizer of salon exhibitions in Paris and was given *carte blanche* regarding what artworks he included. He had a personal collection of relics of the famous, including the bones of Peter Abelard, the French philosopher who was a contemporary of the Cid; hairs from the moustache of the warrior-king Henri IV, who was stabbed to death by an assassin in 1610; and a tooth of the philosopher-cynic Voltaire. Denon was given the task of reassembling the Cid's bones, and although he may have replaced some at the monastery, it is certain that he kept the rest for the remainder of his life. His protégé Alexandre-Evariste Fragonard produced a painting of Denon reburying the Cid about 1811.

The half-century that followed Southey saw the birth of the modern historian. The French Enlightenment and the English Age of Reason, despite various false starts and sudden darts in the wrong direction, created an atmosphere in which a critical, honest, warts-and-all scholarship based on hard evidence could prevail. In the context of Rodrigo Diaz, it came in the form of a Dutch scholar of Arabic, Reinhart Dozy. Dozy came from a French Huguenot family, settling in the Netherlands in 1647. Born in February 1820, by which time English interest in Spain had waned, he attended the university of Leiden and became Professor of History by 1857.

His first published work was *A History of the Almohades*, written ten years earlier, but his main claim to fame rests on his *Histoire de Musselmans d'Espagne* (History of the Muslims in Spain), which spanned four centuries of al-Andalus, culminating in 1110, eleven years after the death of Rodrigo Diaz. Still regarded very highly, Dozy established a level of critical scholarship that went far beyond anything achieved on the history of Spain to this point. He slated the bigotry and bias of the medieval monkish chroniclers and portrayed the Cid as something of a thug. When the British historian and archaeologist Stanley Lane-Poole went to press with his *The Story of the Moors in Spain* in 1886, he was glowingly supportive of Dozy's scholarship. He was 'an historian as well as an Orientalist and his volumes are at once judicious and profound'.[26] Even so, Lane-Poole was not prepared to throw out the baby with the bathwater, as Dozy had done:

> Professor Dozy maintains that the romantic history of the Cid is a tissue of inventions and . . . he founds his criticisms mainly on the Arabic historians, in whom, despite their national and religious bias, he places as blind a reliance as less learned people have placed in the *Chronicle of the Cid*.[27]

Dozy's 1849 essay *Recherches sur l'Histoire et la Litérature de l'Espagne pendant le moyen age* appalled all Spain. In particular the chapter entitled 'Le Cid d'apres de nouveaux documents' caused huge controversy. By this time everyone had forgotten all they ever knew about the real Rodrigo Diaz, the hard and complicated man living in hard and complicated times. He was the crusader, the shining knight without peer, galloping under the banner of Christ on his Babieca. Charlton Heston's film was still over a century away, but it was the image every Spaniard – and many others besides – had in his head already. To Dozy, the Cid was a pragmatist. He was not chivalrous or generous. He fought for cash and loot – his army was dependent on such things. And Dozy repeated these accusations, despite a slamming from Spanish nationalists and intellectuals, twice more, in 1860 and 1881. Although today few of us would find much fault with Dozy's reassessment, the means by which he reached his conclusions are decidedly shaky. Lane-Poole was right: the 'nouveaux documents' to which the professor referred were the newly translated work of Ibn Basam – it is the medieval equivalent of a biography of Nicholas II written by Lenin and just as trustworthy. And Dozy is 100 per cent wrong when he says that the *Poema de Mio Cid* has no historical value. Legends and their place in time are hugely useful to the historian, and sometimes myth can be as important as truth. It was just that Professor Dozy was too busy pulling that metaphorical plug. He also seriously miscalculated the Cid's era. We now know that Rodrigo Diaz was playing the same two-edged game of *realpolitik* as everyone else, except that he was doing it better. Dozy clearly expected his medieval warriors to be chivalrous knights after all.

American interest in the Cid pre-dates the Hollywood connection by well over a century. Washington Irving spent three years in Spain in the late 1820s and produced a variety of works – *The History of the Life and Voyages of Christopher Columbus* and *A Chronicle of the Conquest of Granada* in particular – that caught the reading public's imagination. Similar work was being carried out at Harvard in the same decade when George Ticknor became Smith Professor of French and Spanish Literature. No systematic study of Spanish history was available at the time and his *History of Spanish Literature*, published in the same year as Dozy's bombshell, became a landmark in Spanish-American studies.

Dwarfing all these scholars of earlier generations, however, was Ramon Menendez Pidal, who first published his *La España del Cid* in 1929. Again, we have to leap forward in Spanish history to understand how the Cid legend fitted the mood of the moment. As historian Henry Kamen puts it: 'Spain was thrust reluctantly into the nineteenth century and has never quite emerged from it'[28] – and this remark is probably also true of Menendez Pidal's scholarship and his approach to Rodrigo Diaz. It is important to remember that Pidal was a child of the nineteenth century. Born in Corunna in 1869, he was still a baby when his family met a reversal of fortunes as a result of the Revolution of the previous year. Queen Isabella was forced to flee to France and a provisional government, essentially set up by the army, rather incongruously brought in democracy, freedom of worship and a Press that was outspokenly free. Pidal's father lost his position as magistrate for refusing to accept this new liberalism and the family, essentially broke, had moved six times by 1884 when they finally settled in Madrid. Pidal's father died in 1880, by which time the short-lived Republic had been replaced by the Restoration, during a painful twenty-year period in which a kind of stability was attained in Spanish politics based on the rule of king and *cortes*.

Ramon Pidal was hugely successful at university in Madrid, winning prizes from the Royal Spanish Academy for his work on the *Poema de Mio Cid*, the only known copy of which Pidal's uncle had bought in 1863. By the 1890s he held the post of Professor of Romance Philology at Madrid University and he and his wife spent their honeymoon on horseback, riding as far as possible the countryside crossed by the Cid as described in the first *cantar* of the *Poema*. It was at university that Pidal first came across the work of Dozy and he was furious that the great national hero should be dismissed with such contempt by a foreigner. When he came to write his own biography, he accused Dozy of 'Cidophobia' and refuted his attack point by point.

In this he was echoing the attitudes of Marcelino Menendez y Pelayo, a historian so brilliant that he made professor at the age of 21, before most students have attained their first degree. Pelayo's line, however, was stark and uncompromising: 'Spain', he wrote, 'the evangeliser of half the globe; Spain, the hammer of heretics; Spain, the sword of the Pope. This is our greatness and our glory: we have no other.'[29] Once again we are looking at motivation and once again Rodrigo of Vivar filled a niche. The last vestige of Spanish Imperialism vanished with the loss of Cuba, Puerto Rica and the Philippines to America in 1898. That year a group of intellectuals calling themselves 'the generation of '98' began a systematic search for what had gone wrong. The poets Antonio Machado and Ortega y Gasset, the philosopher Miguel de Unamuno and the novelist Pio Baroja all set out to find examples of the greatness in Spain's past to make a point about the present and the future. The fierce regionalism which was the legacy of the *taifa* states and the endlessly warring kingdoms of Castile, Léon, Navarre and Aragon re-emerged in the years that Pidal was writing his book on the Cid. And this was coupled with a working-class agitation to be found elsewhere in Europe: Winston Churchill sent troops into the mining community of Tonypandy in South Wales, and Nicholas II's panicky guard opened fire on unarmed peasants outside the Winter Palace in St Petersburg. In Spain itself the 'Tragic Week' in July 1909 saw over fifty churches burned in Barcelona alone. Laurie Lee found himself in a village near Segovia as later violence spread. The streets 'were black with priests and its taverns full of seething atheists. Some stood in a doorway heaving stones at the church, others sang obscenities about the bishop.'[30]

There were horror stories of nuns being raped, graves being smashed open and corpses strewn about. All this was ended by the military dictatorship of General Miguel Primo de Rivera. He delighted the generation of '98 and their adherents by settling the earlier Spanish attempt to colonize Morocco. Improvements were made in transport and farming. Even so, that great leveller, the Wall Street crash, destroyed him and his king, Alfonso XIII, who crept out of his palace in Madrid on 14 April 1931 and never came back.

La España del Cid (The Spain of the Cid) was published in 1929, just before the Republican balloon went up, and Pidal's scholarship was impressive. While dismissing the later Cid legends, rightly, as rubbish, he bent the earlier efforts, the *Poema de Mio Cid*, the *Primera Cronica General* and the *Estoria del Cardena*, as far as possible to underscore the greatness of Rodrigo Diaz and to restore him to pride of place as a sort of national saint of Spain. The historical Santiago of Compostela may have been a bit 'iffy' in terms of his actual links with Spain, but Rodrigo of Vivar was real, Castilian and a dyed-in-the-wool hero. And within five years of Pidal's second edition (1934), Spain was plunged into a civil war in which the propaganda of the Cid was at the forefront.

The Spanish Civil War was never simply a confrontation between Left and Right, although these groups had been squaring up to each other all over Europe after the armistice that ended the First World War in November 1918. Laurie Lee, who was there, wrote:

The 'Communist' label . . . was too rough and ready, a clumsy reach-me-down which properly fitted no one. The farm labourer, fisherman and handful of industrial workers all had local but separate interests. Each considered his struggle to be far older than Communism, to be something exclusively Spanish, part of a social perversion which he alone could put right by reason of his roots in this particular landscape.[31]

The Republic of 1931 became increasingly right wing, using police and the army to put down local insurgencies. In Andalusia a village called Casas Viejas saw the slaughter of twenty-five locals. Peasants, whose financial position had been grim for generations, threw in their lot with industrial workers hit by the world slump. In October 1933, as Hitler's Nazi party took up the reins of government in Berlin, workers attempted coups all over Spain. In an act with eerie echoes of the days of the Cid, Moorish troops were rushed over from Africa to quell the trouble. Two thousand civilians died. A local said to Laurie Lee at this point: 'It's true . . . the rebels [are] steadily building up their forces from Africa. . . . The Catholic kings were the first to drive the Moors from Spain. Now the Catholic generals are bringing them back.'[32]

By the early months of 1936 what was happening in the *cortes* and in general elections was irrelevant. The country was slipping into chaos as the right-wing Falangists clashed with the Popular Front on the Left, burning churches and murdering civil guards. On 18 July the Generals' Rising took the form of a plot spearheaded by Mola, Groded and Franco, and for three years Spaniard killed Spaniard to iron out their country's differences. The results were horrendous. Well over half a million people died, with a further two million languishing in government prisons in the years that followed. The arrival of the International Brigades gave the war a dimension beyond the confines and problems of Spain. As Laurie Lee put it: 'To Spain, so backward and so long ignored, the nations of Europe were quietly gathering.'[33]

Ernest Hemingway wrote *For Whom the Bell Tolls*, and the Condor Legion bombed the Republican port of Guernica – practice, cynics said, for the Blitzkreig that would terrify all Europe three years later. But it was Francisco Franco who called up the shade of Rodrigo Diaz. With his thinning hair, high voice and plump figure,

Franco was hardly the stuff of which heroes were made. He was not a great general, so he identified with a man who was. Deliberately moving his government during the war to Burgos, he daily crossed the square of St Gadea where the Cid of legend had forced a showdown with Alfonso VI. He directed operations from within 6 miles of the *sotopalacios* where legend said the Cid had been born at Vivar and less than a mile from the banks of the Arlanzon where he had begun his first exile in 1081. Others linked Franco with different heroes – Philip II, Charles V, Charlemagne, Alexander the Great, even the Archangel Gabriel, while the artist Salvador Dali thought him a saint – but time and again it was with Rodrigo of Vivar, the legendary Cid, that his contemporaries compared him in Spain. Even the title he took for himself – El Caudillo, the leader – was a reference to the *grans capitans* or warlords of medieval Spain, the Cid among them.

On 18 May 1939 Franco entered Toledo at the head of a 16-mile-long victory parade comprising 200,000 troops – more soldiers than Rodrigo Diaz would ever have seen in his life. The press release from his office in Burgos promised that 'General Franco's entry into Madrid will follow the ritual observed when Alfonso VI, accompanied by the Cid, captured Toledo in the Middle Ages'.[34] Marvellous. Except, of course, that the Cid did not accompany Alfonso into Toledo. He was in exile in Zaragoza at the time and the king took the city by himself.

On Sunday 1 October 1939 Franco established a national holiday, the *Dia del Caudillo*, and two weeks later the *alcalde* of Burgos made a flowery speech as Franco left for Madrid: 'The city says with all its heart, as it did to the Caballero de Vivar, "Caudillo, here is Burgos: glory to God on high and all praise to you, saviour of Spain".'[35] Nor did these links end with the close of the civil war. After Charlton Heston's film had given Rodrigo Diaz worldwide coverage, Franco was still riding the white gelding Zegri, a Babieca for our own times.

Perhaps the zenith of the propaganda of the Cid, however, occurred in July 1955, when the huge equestrian statue of the Campeador was unveiled in the square at Burgos. Joaquin Costa had once suggested that modern Spain was only a liberal shadow of its aggressive, imperialist past and that we should 'lock the tomb of El Cid with seven keys'.[36] As the stamping bronze Babieca, swirling cloak and uplifted Tizona of the Cid came into view, Franco said of Rodrigo, 'in him is enshrined all the mystery of the great Spanish epics: service in noble undertakings; duty as reason; struggle in the service of the true God'.[37]

And this was the Cid who sprang, fully formed, into celluloid six years later.

I make no apology for discussing the Heston film here, because it is as much a part of the legend of the Cid as the *Poema*, the *Cronica del Famoso Cavallero* or any of the Romances. I find it fascinating that Ramon Menendez Pidal approved of the production; many authors claim (wrongly) that he acted as historical adviser on the set. The reason that the aged historian liked it is that it re-created the man who had become his hero and perhaps his obsession.

'Meantime', wrote Charlton Heston, 'the new scripts on my stack included one based on a man I'd barely heard of; Rodrigo Diaz de Bivar, the Cid, the medieval Spanish hero who had fought against the Moors.'[38]

This was the thinking man's view of the Cid. Heston is a university graduate with an enormous respect for history, yet he had 'barely heard' of Rodrigo de Vivar and saw him in simplistic terms as a crusader. Heston was not impressed by the initial script but he was fascinated by a man whose reputation had lasted for a thousand years. Like all professionals, Heston researched his subject, focusing on the *Poema de Mio Cid*, although he acknowledged that it was incomplete and written long after the man and his times. 'Some modern historians,' he wrote, 'trying to clear the cloud of Arthurian legend that obscures him, have cast the Cid simply as a ruthless mercenary. . . . However politically correct that may be, I don't think it is a realistic view.'[39] Heston's meeting with Pidal in Madrid before the cameras rolled tells us a lot about this new direction of the legend. 'Dr Pidal was then in his 90s,' Heston remembered, 'but he clearly realized that our film would provide the permanent impression of the man to whom he had devoted much of his life.'[40] And that was precisely the point. In our glib, sound-bite world of visuals and instant experience, it is not the Cid of Pidal or Fletcher that people know, but the Cid of Charlton Heston. Rather depressingly, the average cinema-goer has very little grasp of history and Hollywood in recent years has notoriously rewritten it anyway from an American perspective.[41]

So Heston's storyline is a mish-mash of Cid legends. The film opens on Rodrigo's wedding day, in which the wedding party, complete with the ever-faithful Alvar Fañez, runs into a Moorish raiding party and defeats them in battle. We see a ruined church, a heartbroken priest and a huge Visigothic crucifix riddled with arrows. What is unlikely is that not one but two amirs (in fact, the total is five) should be captured – al-Mutamin and al-Qadir – in a single skirmish. When Rodrigo spares these men's lives, he incurs the enmity of his fellow Christians who do not understand his actions – 'We have always fought the Moors' is the incredulous line from Jimena (Sophia Loren), when she and Rodrigo finally meet. It is Mutamin who gives Rodrigo his title: 'Among my people we have a word for a warrior who has the wisdom to be merciful. We call such a man Al Sayyid.'

In the squabble that arises from the release of the Moors, Rodrigo's father, Diego Lainez (Michael Hordern), clashes with Jimena's father Gomez de Gormaz (Andrew Cruikshank). The accusation of lying between two proud men leads Rodrigo to fight Gomez and kill him, lending substance to the ballads that Corneille used, but this duel takes place without witnesses and with his dying breath Gomez demands that Jimena avenge him. For over half the film, therefore, Jimena wears funereal black and engages a rival for her love, Count Ordoñez, the villain of the *Poema* and of actual history, played by Raf Vallone, to kill Rodrigo.

In the meantime the celebrated tournament takes place between Rodrigo and Don Martin, the champion of Aragon, over ownership of the city of Calahorra; this was the duel that won the man the title of Campeador. So far we have historical characters and settings and the love-hate/father murder scenario borrowed from the later Cid legends. In the background Ferdinand (Fernando I) played by Ralph Truman is every inch a king – proud, wise and powerful – but his children are a nightmare. Sancho (Gary Raymond) is trying desperately to be the heir apparent, but ranged against him are Alfonso (John Fraser) and his Machiavellian sister Urraca (Genevieve Page). Interestingly – and I would love to think this was intentional – the *Libro de las Estampas* of the late thirteenth century shows Sancho as black-haired (Raymond) and Alfonso as blond (Fraser).

We have noted already that the film's advisers got it as seriously wrong as the writers of the later legends in terms of accuracy: fifteenth-century woodcuts accompanying the *Mocedades* show Rodrigo in full plate armour. The heraldry, the surcoats, the chamfrons (head armour) of the horses are all late thirteenth century, and in the duel for Calahorra the combatants use two-handed swords that date from the sixteenth century. The scriptwriters found some real history in the sending of Rodrigo to collect the *paria* from unresponsive *taifa* tributaries, but because the ages of Sancho and Rodrigo are reversed the public is left with a distorted image of their relationship. Sancho leads the expedition – which is ambushed by al-Qadir and rescued by Mutamin – but it is Rodrigo who is the guiding hand, now elevated by the king to Campeador. Some historians have doubted whether in fact Rodrigo ever actually became *alfarez*. He was after all Sancho's junior by about five years, having been brought up in his court, and where did the experience come from to win him this post? The answer in the film is his personal victory over Don Martin, but this is simplistic in the extreme.

The celluloid Rodrigo forces Jimena to marry him with Ferdinand's approval, but the relationship clearly cannot work and the Cid's lady goes to a convent, loosely based presumably on the monastery of Cardena. The death of Ferdinand unleashes the blind jealousy of the princes who fight each other with daggers over their father's sarcophagus. The upshot is that Sancho has Alfonso imprisoned (there is no mention of exile in Zaragoza) but Rodrigo intervenes to rescue him from his escort. This is an inversion of the first *cantar* of the *Poema*, in which Sancho is freed by the Cid in a similar way. It is because Alfonso is hiding in Urraca's city of Zamora (Urraca and her sister Elvira, the latter missing from the film entirely, only owned monasteries, not castles) that Sancho besieges it. His death is plain murder, orchestrated by a 'hit man' employed by Urraca, and, oddly, Rodrigo is on hand to avenge him, stabbing the killer by a postern gate as Sancho lies dying. Again, this is a slight variant of the version in the *Poema*.

It is now that the incident of St Gadea takes place, which Menendez Pidal believed was probably historical, but for which there is no actual evidence. Rodrigo forcing Alfonso to swear his non-involvement in Sancho's death appears in the *Poema* but the charters signed by Rodrigo at the time make the whole incident highly unlikely. Furious, Alfonso banishes Rodrigo and he makes his way into a lonely exile. Here the film departs from all known versions. In the *Poema* and later legends Rodrigo has nine days to leave Alfonso's domains and he goes with Fañez and an ever-growing host to camp on the pebble-banks of the River Arlanzon outside Burgos where a memorial to the man stands today. In the film Rodrigo meets a leper named Lazarus; this is drawn from later legends when St Lazarus appears to him in a vision. Reunited with Jimena who has now seen the error of her ways, Rodrigo wanders the northern sierras in search of solitude and peace. The little girl of 9 who appears in the *Poema* is there in the film, although she is rather more helpful, providing a barn in which the couple spend the night.

The dawn, however, brings a host of warriors who have found their hero and insist on riding with them – there will be no peace for men like the Cid. Heston recalled the location shot: 'I mean, it was cold. While they were lighting the shot, two riders simply toppled off their horses, chilled to numbness.'[42] This is a reminder that the Castile of the Cid was still a bleak and barren place, even in the centrally heated twentieth century.

The rest of the film deals with the growing Almoravid threat. Yussuf ibn Teshufin appears as the rather more pronounceable Ben

Yussuf (Herbert Lom), and his black-robed veiled ones with their thundering drums are among the most dramatic and authentic images of the film. Despite the fact that Ben Yussef's Black Guard are garrisoning Valencia, the Cid's siege is causing havoc inside the city. Medieval Valencia no longer exists, so the town of Peniscola was chosen for filming. The film crew built a huge pair of Moorish gates, which they left there as a souvenir.

Heston's view is that the second part of the film is better than the first, 'highlighted with the clash of arms and running horses, the dark betrayals and foul murders [al-Qadir is thrown from his own battlements], the desperate escapes and savage assaults that marked the Middle Ages . . .'.[43] He remembers too the extraordinary experience of taking Valencia. We see none of the real Cid's devastating attacks on the hinterland, burning villages and destroying camps. It is all achieved by the sudden goodwill resulting from hurling bread from mangonels to the starving populace, who then turn on the Black Guard and kill al-Qadir:

> The citizens welcomed [Rodrigo] in preference to weak King Alfonso as the able soldier they needed against the Moors, offering him the crown of Valencia. The Cid, stubbornly unwilling to displace the king who had exiled him and imprisoned his wife and children [twin girls feature as Cristina and Maria], refused the crown, surely one of the outstanding examples of loyalty in history.[44]

Except, of course, that it never happened that way. The film-makers were following Pidal, who accepted the later squeaky-clean legends. Rodrigo's extraordinary loyalty is a theme that runs throughout this celluloid version of the legend but there is no historical basis for it. The Cid took Valencia for himself.

'The gates swung open,' Heston wrote, 'two thousand people screamed welcome. I rode through, Babieca [one of two identical animals used in the production] dancing under my hand, both of us aroused by the roar: "Cid! Cid! Cid!" . . . You don't have to act that. You can't act it. I was there. It happened to me. I know, in my bones

207

and blood, what it is to take a city.'[45] Perhaps the real Rodrigo felt the same.

The astonishing finale, in which the dead Cid is strapped upright in Babieca's saddle, is one of the outstanding, unforgettable moments of film history. It happened by accident as director Tony Mann, lying on the beach to get an 'upshot', happened to see a shaft of sunlight burst over the shoulder of an extra. In an interview Mann said:

God . . . makes such magnificent things that it's difficult not to capture what He has if you go out on location. I'll never forget how I woke up one morning and there was a misty fog over the whole of Valencia [*sic*] . . . the moment when El Cid came out strapped on his horse with his shining armour and his white horse. I was lying on the sand looking up – and a rider passed. It wasn't even Heston. It was just an extra . . . I yelled to Bob Krasker [the cinematographer] 'Look at it, that's what we want, that's God, that's the sun; we've got to get the sun on us.' We were shining Mr Heston's armour and we let him ride out and by God that was how he shone and there was no spotlight or anything . . . it was so white, it was electrifying.[46]

In fact the scene was pure Hollywood. No legend suggests that Rodrigo Diaz was fatally wounded at Valencia; they all agree that he died peacefully in his bed. But Hollywood heroes do not die that way. So Alfonso, now, at last, having learned to 'be a king', rides alongside the Cid under his floating white banner (how his army rode through the Almoravid troops encircling the city is not explained), trampling the evil Ben Yussuf in the process, the dead Campeador sweeping on as Babieca canters into the blur of the horizon along the edge of the bay. This, for nearly fifty years, has been our version of the Cid legend. It is enduring and it is important because it has replaced all the versions that have gone before.

12

What Sort of Cid?

Medieval man was obsessed with the number seven. The Fathers of the Catholic Church conjured seven deadly sins – pride, covetousness, lust, envy, gluttony, anger and sloth – and the great Pope Gregory I condemned them all. As if to balance them, there were seven gifts of the Holy Ghost – wisdom, understanding, counsel, fortitude, knowledge, piety and fear of the Lord. Likewise, there were seven virtues: faith, hope, charity, justice, prudence, temperance and fortitude. In the medieval academic world there were seven linked liberal arts, as laid down by St Augustine from Greek tradition: the trivium (grammar, dialectics and rhetoric) and the quadrivium (arithmetic, geometry, astronomy and music).

When it came to heroes, however, the Middle Ages settled on nine. Three inevitably came from the Bible – Joshua, David and Judas Maccabaeus. Three came from pagan history – Hector, Alexander and Julius Caesar. The last 'triad' was composed of Arthur, Charlemagne and Godfrey de Bouillon. These *neuf preux* appeared together for the first time in literature in Jean de Longuyon's *Voeux du Paon* in the early fourteenth century. This odd and fairly arbitrary mix of heroes was not simply thrown together at random. The Biblical heroes represented the history of the world, God's plan in which the Jews, the chosen people, carried out His word. The 'Romans' stood for the method by which God's peace was carried throughout the civilized world. And the medieval trio symbolized the way in which that tradition had been continued through to what was then the present.

With our more critical approach to history, we can raise serious issues about several of the nine and their inclusion in the list at all. The Old Testament is notoriously allegorical and palpably, in many cases, untrue, so the exploits of Joshua, David and Judas must be taken with quantities of salt. Hector is likely to have been a totally fictional prince (in that there was no single 'Trojan War' in the legendary sense) and in the hedonistic aggrandizement of Alexander and Caesar there is no direct relevance to the Christian god at all. Arthur is a curious blend of legend and myth, with only the thinnest thread of 'truth' to hold the whole together. Charlemagne makes sense as the all-powerful Emperor of the West, who established a huge Christian state of unifying significance. But it is the last of the nine, Godfrey de Bouillon, who is the most absorbing.

The eldest son of Count Eustace of Boulogne, who had fought at Hastings, Godfrey was about twenty years younger than Rodrigo Diaz. He became Count of Verdun and Lord of Bouillon in 1076 when the Campeador was winning laurels under Alfonso VI. A natural warlord, Godfrey was obliged to fight off rivals to his titles and twenty years later was happy to mortgage or sell his estates to finance his expedition to win back Jerusalem in what would become the First Crusade. In July 1099, the month in which the Cid died, de Bouillon was elected Advocate of Jerusalem or 'Defender of the Holy Sepulchre'. He destroyed an Egyptian invasion at Ascalon months later, but he was dead by the end of 1100, when the plan to extend the Christian kingdom of Jerusalem was only partially completed.

The reason why de Bouillon is included as the ninth worthy is that his brilliant capture of the most holy shrine in Christendom (that actually, of course, lay outside Christendom in Outremer) represented the ongoing thrust of Christian chivalry. If we take de Bouillon's achievements and compare them with those of the Cid Campeador, they pale into insignificance. Jerusalem of course, as the place of execution, burial and resurrection of Jesus Christ, was always going to capture the imagination more than Valencia, however 'shining' it may have been, but that apart, the Frenchman could not hold a candle to the Spaniard.

So what of the tenth worthy? The recapture of Jerusalem was a fitting full stop to glory, but of course, as Dylan Thomas noted somewhat cryptically, 'time passes'. Jerusalem was lost again, never to be recaptured by the crusaders, and other great men (and women) grabbed the headlines. Scotland contended that Robert the Bruce should hold the place of the tenth worthy, while France produced not one, but two candidates – the Constable Bertrand du Guesclin and the far less well-known Louis de Sancerre. For Spain, of course, the tenth must be Rodrigo the Cid.

Why has the name of Rodrigo Diaz survived and why has he become the national hero of a country that has, like all countries, many to choose from? This is a hugely difficult question and it goes to the very heart of what history is about. Historian James Sharpe sums it up well with a parallel – the life and crimes of Dick Turpin, the eighteenth-century English highwayman:

> The public's Turpin is not the historically verifiable pock-marked thug. Rather, he is a romantic, courageous, daredevil figure, elegantly clothed and handsome, robbing the rich to help the poor, defying corrupt authority and riding a faithful mare called Black Bess on whom he made his epic journey to York. It is this Turpin who has stalked the pages of novels, nineteenth-century penny dreadfuls and twentieth-century boys' comics. It is this Turpin, instantly recognizable, who appeared in equestrian spectacles, in films, in television programmes, in a modern pantomime and on the signs outside the many pubs that bear Turpin's name, from York to San Remo with Bordeaux in between.[1]

There are no real parallels between Richard Turpin and Rodrigo Diaz, except perhaps that they rode horses which became nearly as famous as they did. Where there is similarity, as Sharpe rightly highlights, is in the cult of celebrity which means so much to us today:

> we are invited briefly [by the media in particular] into the lives of the great and famous, given a peep-show of their experiences, and then, at the end of the allotted hour, shuffled out again into our more humdrum existences. The idea that history is a discipline that involves critical discourse and in which conflicting views

interplay, vanishes. Attempts at confronting the complexity of the past are buried in the production team's agenda and smothered by a desire to replace reflective opinions by sound bites.[2]

But this process has been going on for a long time. The public, be they twentieth-century cinema audiences or eleventh-century listeners to the *Carmen Campi Doctoris*, like their stories simple (the best ones always are) so the complex man who was the Cid Campeador was 'dumbed down' even in his own lifetime.

Historian Richard Fletcher poses the question 'What sort of Cid is wanted today?', but his answer is a little bit of a cop-out – 'I should not pretend to guess.'[3] In terms of the public image of Rodrigo Diaz, as opposed to that of historians, the most recent picture we have is an animated film entitled *El Cid, la Layenda* (El Cid, the Legend). Martin M. Winkler was talking about Anthony Mann's Heston film when he wrote:

The film continues the literary tradition of elevating a historical figure to the level of a mythical hero, a process as old as western culture itself. Tracing such mythicizing in *El Cid*, in the visual medium of the cinema, the most popular art form of the twentieth century, reveals an accomplished example of the transformations which myth may undergo when it supersedes both history and an already existing mythical tradition.[4]

How much more does this apply to *La Layenda*? Brilliant though animated films are, there is a general acceptance that they are made for children and not intended for adults at all. The film took three years to make (2000–3) and involved the work of over five hundred professionals, including one hundred and fifty animators from seventeen countries. A studio in the Cid's Valencia was responsible for some of the creation, and the Bren Team, working on the 3D images, hails from Santiago de Compostela. Since the work has only recently become available outside Spain, we cannot say how successful it is or what it has done for the public's conception of Rodrigo Diaz. The Tizona is faithfully depicted, as is the Mozarabic architecture of the eleventh century. On the other hand, all male characters have huge shoulders and forearms and impossibly small heads, perhaps reinforcing the generic medieval myth that Castilians were thuggish and lacked culture. Babieca is a suitably snorting, magnificent beast and Jimena is a smouldering, dark-eyed gypsy. Quite how the cute badger enters the legend, we do not know!

La Layenda is not, in fact, the first Cid animation. In the early 1980s Spanish television ran a series for children called *Ruy, el pequeño Cid* (Rodrigo, the little Cid) featuring completely fictional adventures. The sort of Cid that Fletcher muses on appears in an alternative-universe medieval Spain in the fantasy novel *The Lion of Al-Rassan* by Guy Gavriel Kay. In that strange parallel universe of Wargaming, he is a character in *Age of Empires II: The Conquerors* and again in *Medieval: Total War*, where his usefulness as a general doubles because he can be bribed – a fascinating glimpse of realism among the hype. Back in the real world, the more adventurous tourist can walk the Cid trail: 'En route we can call in at the Moorish castle, or rather citadel, of Gormaz, on which El Cid led a raid in 1081 which resulted in his banishment. In Burgos, we visit El Cid's tomb in the Cathedral. . . .'[5] Appropriately, travellers stay at the Hotel El Cid. The otherwise inclined could, at least until recently, have watched today's El Cid, the toreador Manuel Jesus, in action in the bullring. He was badly gored on 18 May 2003.

In that year reports focused on the Cid's sword. Still in the Museo del Ejérito, Madrid's military museum, the weapon could not be obtained by Franco or even handled by Charlton Heston (the key to the cabinet could not be found when he and Menendez Pidal visited). In 1999 a piece of the blade was tested and the metallurgical analysis confirmed that it was probably made in Cordoba in the eleventh century. The hilt of course is another matter and we have already expressed our doubts on this. The sword's owner in 2003 was Jose Ramon Suarez del Otero y Velluti, Marquis de Falces, and he offered it for sale to the Spanish government for £4 million. The government offered a less impressive £400,000 on the grounds that the provenance of the Tizona was in doubt. The marquis' claim is that his family has owned the sword since the fifteenth century when it was given to the Falces by King Fernando. His threat to sell it outside Spain was countered by the government, which told him this was illegal under Spanish heritage laws. In the meantime two servants both claimed they had been promised the weapon by the marquis's ancestors!

The sort of Cid we have today engenders merchandise, the curse of the late twentieth and early twenty-first centuries. As a schoolboy in the 1960s I was able to buy a full-size replica of the Tizona from any one of the dozens of shops on the Costa Brava selling Toledo weapons. Beyond my parents' pocket was the *Montante del Cid* (the Cid's tent-pole), which was a 6ft, two-handed sixteenth-century variant.

There is of course a more serious and certainly less commercial side to the man today. Both American and Spanish universities offer 'Cid studies', which inevitably focus on the schizoid Rodrigo, the literary legend and the real man. An international congress met in Burgos in July 2000 in which a series of eminent Spanish scholars explored a whole variety of Cid themes, summed up best perhaps by Manuel Jiminez's lecture 'El Cid, personaje historico, personaje literario' (The Cid, historic character, literary character).

Forty years earlier Anthony Mann and Charlton Heston combined with many other talents to produce the great epic film which we have already discussed at length. Brilliant though this film is, and it is surely among the most beautifully conceived of the epics, it *is* the Hollywood version, made, like so many of the Cid legends that went before it, for public entertainment rather than enlightenment. Above all (and in this respect it differs markedly from earlier examples of the myth-makers' art), *El Cid* is the work of many minds, each with their own take on who Rodrigo Diaz was and what he represented. So, while Charlton Heston sought for a Job-like character as his interpretation of the man from Vivar, Anthony Mann had slightly different ideas: 'We tried to make it all as modern as possible so that it could be related to any society; so that people would understand.'[6]

It would be unfair to accuse directors of the calibre of Mann of 'dumbing down', but had the celluloid Rodrigo been the ambiguous, difficult and sometimes dark figure he actually was, audiences would not have identified with him and box-office sales would have plummeted. In a different sense Anthony Mann is very like the later medieval chroniclers who wrote of the Cid; he was concerned with the 'moral truth of myth',[7] not with the shaded complexities of history.

Only a handful of years before the Heston/Mann film brought the name of El Cid to a worldwide public, Francisco Franco, El Caudillo, had used the man as blatant propaganda. He rode a grey horse, established his headquarters during the Civil War at the Cid's Burgos, officially unveiled the best-known equestrian statue of the hero and frequently saw himself as some sort of reincarnation of the Campeador. The Marquis de Falces remembers family stories of Franco's soldiers stealing the Tizona from Republicans who were trying to smuggle it out of Spain. 'There was a lot of pressure exerted on my grandfather,' the marquis said in an interview in 2003, 'to give the sword to Franco, but he resisted. He gave it to the Army Museum instead.'[8]

This is Rodrigo Diaz as the national hero not of Spain, but of one element of it, and if the Cid was hijacked by Franco in his role as fascist dictator and executioner of thousands, Spain and the world have oddly forgiving natures. The propagandists have gone to work on Franco as they have on the Cid and he has either been forgiven or forgotten or both. As the secretary-general of Franco's party said in 1973: 'Franco was not a monster. He has been demonized by a fictionalization of history. He wasn't a normal dictator. He listened.'[9]

The Cid that Franco stole was that of historian Ramon Menendez Pidal. But if Pidal was a great historian – and his is still the best-known biography of the man – then he was an even greater nationalist. He was also, I suspect, a romanticist. And, consciously or otherwise, the sort of Cid he created was not only larger than life, he was larger than the sources in which he appeared. Pidal's biographer Colin Smith contends that it is the duty of the historian to add a certain creativity for his own generation. Without that, each biography or dissertation would merely be a recognition of what had gone before. Even so, if Pidal was prepared to accept too much of the Cid legend at face value, his was a difficult task in anchoring his opus in reality. As James Fitzmaurice-Kelly wrote when Pidal was still a struggling young historian: 'most of us behold the Cid not as he really was, but as Corneille portrayed him more than five centuries after his death.'[10]

It is possible that, as a young man himself, Fitzmaurice-Kelly would have sat enthralled in the audience at a performance of Jules Massenet's 1885 opera *Le Cid*.[11] It is unlikely he ever saw the earlier version *Il Cid* by the Italian composer Antonio Sacchini, but its existence points up the fact that Rodrigo was seen as a hero during the eighteenth century and not merely in Spain. Whether he was seen as an actual historical character is debatable. All too easily, in the pantheon of cult heroes and legends, the original is very flimsy – England's Robin Hood and Switzerland's William Tell have no hard evidence to prove they ever existed. A number of 'historians' in the early nineteenth century doubted whether Rodrigo Diaz had ever been flesh and blood. The Jesuit Masdeu saw him as a character of fiction and Samuel Dunham in his *History of Spain and Portugal* expressed his doubts. When his Spanish translator Antonio Galiano introduced this work into Spain, however, he was threatened with legal action by a descendant of the Cid, who read the fictional claim as a slur. For a while scholarly debate raged and even produced two Cids, each with a wife called Jimena and a horse called Babieca!

Between the second opera and the doubters, Reinhard Dozy carried out a hatchet job on the reputation of Rodrigo Diaz. He was real all right and he was a mercenary and a despoiler of churches whose word was not reliable. Dozy gives himself away, however, because his view was based on new material discovered in the 1850s and that material was the biased propaganda of the Moors of Valencia, whose way of life had been seriously altered by the Cid. We cannot dismiss these works – they are as valid as the eulogies of Rodrigo that flowed from the pens of the Christian poets and scholars – but we can put them in a context that Dozy seemed unable to do. About ten years after the Cid's death Abu l'Hassam Ali Ibn Bassam (Ibn Bassam) wrote his *Treasury of the Excellencies of the Spaniards*, a series of biographies of the great and good of al-Andalus. He was living in Valencia when the Cid took the city, and writes about him, disparagingly, in his chapter on Ibn Tahir, the amir of Murcia in the 1060s and 1070s. Even here, however, there is a curiously grudging admiration for the man who was his enemy in terms of culture and faith: 'This man, the scourge of his time, by his appetite for glory, by the prudent steadfastness of his character and by his heroic bravery, was one of the miracles of Allah.'[12] Perhaps Dozy did not translate that sentence, but it was carved none the less on the noble plinth of the Campeador's statue in Burgos.

Two years before the Cid's death Abd Allah Mohammed ibn al-Khalaf ibn Alqama (Ibn Alqama) wrote *The Clear Exposition of the Disastrous Tragedy*. A native of Valencia, he took the loss of the city as personally as the various Arab poets who wrote about it. The original work no longer exists, but, like many documents relating to the Cid, a copy was made in the thirteenth century. He is almost the only commentator on the daily government by Rodrigo in the last years of his life.

It was Robert Southey who brought the Cid to England, cashing in (literally) on the fascination with Spain that literate Englishmen felt in the years of the Peninsular War. What Southey was doing was taking a jumble of earlier Cid literature and putting it together as a coherent whole, and in that sense he did us a far greater service than Pierre Corneille, who saw the Cid as a source for human interest. His play, hugely popular in France in the 1630s, focused only on the love-hate relationship between Rodrigo and Jimena in the legends and he even had the *infanta* Urraca expressing her love for the man, thus creating a love-triangle found nowhere else.

Whereas Southey ignored the *Mocedades* of the fifteenth century as so much rubbish – they are bad literature and bad history – Corneille's focus comes directly from them. The Rodrigo of the *Mocedades* is arrogant, proud and overbearing, as if the knightly virtues so extolled as chivalry were somehow inverted and he comes across more like the Heirs of Carrion in the best known version of his 'life'.

Although the *Chronica del Famoso Cavallero* and the *Cronica de España* were both used by Southey, it is the *Poema de Mio Cid* that has seized the imagination of scholars. More ink has been expended on the *Poema* than on all the other Cid literature put together. This is probably justified in terms of Spanish literature – it is the first of its kind in the vernacular – but in terms of history it is less than helpful. We have seen that the first *cantar* is useful in that it can be verified by other sources, but the ill-advised weddings of the Cid's daughters and the subsequent comeuppance of their husbands is pure fiction and can be found in different forms in a whole variety of European folklore. It is a pity then that many commentators claim, with some justification, that it is this work that made Rodrigo Diaz the national hero of Spain, because for two-thirds of it he appears in a less than heroic light. He dupes the Jews of Burgos with blatant dishonesty (however much this notion may have appealed at the time of the *Poema*); accepts decidedly undesirable sons-in-law (which casts doubt on his judgement); and when it comes to pay-back time, it is not the Cid himself who fights but younger champions on his behalf. We are left with the feeling that the real Campeador would have taken on the Heirs of Carrion and their friends single-handed and killed them all; this, too, is the Cid of Pidal and Heston. When the *Poema* was written, however, it was in the days of high chivalry, with knights and banners and fair ladies. It was also the time of the cult of 'St Rodrigo', when his shrine at San Pedro de Cardena was a well-known diversion on the pilgrims' road to Compostela.

Between the *Poema* and the *Historia Roderici* an important change took place in relation to our understanding of the Cid. In Rodrigo's dying weeks Godfrey de Bouillon raised the cross of crusade over Jerusalem and the world would never be the same again.

There is an enduring message in both the Christian Bible and the Muslim Koran that Jack Nelson-Pallmeyer calls the violence-of-God tradition. In relation to the eleventh and twelfth centuries, Isaiah 25:9–10 has a particular resonance:

> The Moabites shall be trodden down in their place
> as straw is trodden down in a dung-pit.

The Moabites of the Old Testament were a tribe in the Holy Land; to Rodrigo Diaz and Godfrey de Bouillon they were Muslims. Out of Africa or Arabia – it made little difference. So the Cid of the post-1099 era – in other words, immediately after his death – was supposed to conform not only to the later medieval ideals of chivalry, but to this black-and-white crusade-versus-*jihad* mentality. And when the original or neo-original documents did not provide this politically correct (for the time) picture, men either ignored them or were shocked by them. So the anonymous author of the *Historia Roderici* who sings the Cid's praises is no wider of the mark than Reinhard Dozy, who saw the man simply as a mercenary.

The notion of the mercenary is notoriously difficult and most discussion of the role in the Middle Ages focuses on the French *jacquerie* and the English freebooters in the Hundred Years War of the fourteenth and fifteenth centuries. As Maurice Keen writes: 'Whole provinces were subjected to the indiscriminate pillaging of soldiery that sought to claim a share on chivalry, but whose manner of living was the antithesis of what chivalry stood for, the protection of the poor, the fatherless and the widow.'[13] The *Historia Roderici* is full of descriptions of such raids, when the Cid rides out across open countryside burning villages and (allegedly) sacking churches.

And so we come at last to the real Rodrigo Diaz, the man of flesh and blood, and find him as elusive as the city of gold his descendants searched for in the jungles of South America. The earliest literature on him is the *Carmen Campi Doctoris*, composed and probably sung with embellishments as time went on when the man was in his 40s and one of the best generals of his or any other age. Later writers, of fact and fiction, tried to portray Rodrigo as the Moorslayer, a Christian hero on a white horse trampling the Moabites and Saracens because they were pagan and it was God's will. Even some modern commentators have dismissed Rodrigo as overrated and somehow 'no better than he should be' because he fought with Muslim against Christian and did it for pay.

This is to misunderstand entirely the political reality of eleventh-century Spain. The country had been Muslim for three centuries by Rodrigo's time and the warlords of the Christian north had been fighting each other for all that time and would go on doing so after Rodrigo's death. If the Campeador went on raids of villages, destroyed towns and took castles, so did his liege lords, Alfonso VI, Sancho II and Fernando I. It was a way of life, however unacceptable we might find it now. In the *paria* system, a sort of bastard feudalism ahead of its time, the weak (various *taifa* states of al-Andalus) had every right to seek protection from the strong (various states of the Christian north), so that Christians ended up with Moorish allies fighting other Christians with Moorish allies. Rodrigo Diaz was not unique in doing that; he simply did it better than anyone else. It made him enemies at the time and it makes him enemies still.

There is much about the Cid that we do not know and cannot explain. From the dust-dry documents that chart his marriage, his ownership of land and his handling of court cases to the overlaid, agenda-ridden nonsense of the legends, we have the ghost of a man, nothing more. 'While he lived in the world,' wrote one who hated him, 'he always won a noble triumph over his enemies; never was he defeated by any man.'[14] Not many of us will have an epitaph like that.

> Here endeth the chronicle
> of that right famous and
> good knight
> The Blessed Cid,
> Rodrigo Diaz de Bivar,
> The Campeador.[15]

Notes

1: OUT OF THE GATES OF HISTORY . . .

1. *El Cid Film Souvenir Brochure* (London, Classics Illustrated, 1961).
2. Ibid.
3. Robert Southey, *The Chronicle of the Cid* (*Cronica del Famoso Cavallero Ruydiez Campeador, Burgos, 1593*) (New York, 1808; New York, Dolphin Books, 1955), pp. 270–1.
4. i.e., 1099. The era system of dating is peculiar to Spain. Until the fourteenth century, all 'Christian' dating began with 38 BC, the official beginning of the *Pax Romana* in Iberia. To convert to the usual AD or CE, therefore, merely subtract thirty-eight years. In the Cid's Castile, the era system was finally abolished by King Juan I on Christmas Day 1384.
5. Anon, *Historia Roderici*, Ch. 75, trans. Simon Barton and Richard Fletcher, *The World of El Cid* (Manchester University Press, 2000), p. 146.
6. Ibid., p. 98.
7. George Macdonald Fraser, *The Hollywood History of the World* (London, Michael Joseph, 1988), p. 40.
8. Ibid., p. 42.
9. Charlton Heston, *The Actor's Life* (London, Penguin, 1980), p. 98.
10. Charlton Heston, *In the Arena* (London, HarperCollins, 1996), p. 242.
11. Ibid., p. 245.
12. *El Cid Film Souvenir Brochure.*
13. Ibid.
14. Anon, *Historia Roderici*, Ch. 75, trans. Barton and Fletcher, *World of El Cid*, p. 98.

2: CASTLES IN SPAIN

1. Laurie Lee, *As I Walked Out One Midsummer Morning* (London, Penguin, 1971), p. 155.
2. Pliny the Elder, *Natural History* xxxii 67–75, quoted in Barry Cunliffe, *Rome and Her Empire* (London, BCA, 1994), p. 236.
3. Even allowing for the notorious Roman exaggeration of figures, this was clearly a sizeable community.
4. Marcus Junianus Justinius lived in the third century AD. He wrote largely on the Greeks and his views on the origin of the world.
5. Justin, quoted in Cunliffe, *Rome and Her Empire*, p. 236. Bilbilis was the Roman town of Tarraconensis, in modern Zaragoza. It was the birthplace of the poet Martial and famed for its

ironworks, producing Greek coins centuries before his birth. Chalybs is the Greek for steel, giving rise to the Chalybeate springs named for their metallic properties and a possible origin of the name of Arthur's sword Excalibur.

6. Gaius Marius (157–86 BC), Consul and defender of Rome, saved the city after destroying the Teutones and Cimbri tribes that were ravaging northern Italy. He reorganized the Roman army to make it the most brilliant war machine in the ancient world and became embroiled in a vicious civil war with his rival Sulla, which spilled over into Spain.

7. Lucius Cornelius Sulla (138–78 BC) was a general who served under Marius but ultimately outgrew and defeated his rival at the Colline Gate outside Rome. He became a dictator with a long list of proscriptions against his opponents. He was known as felix – 'lucky'.

8. Gaius Julius Caesar (100–44 BC) is perhaps the most famous Roman of all. He was probably the Republic's finest general; he conquered Gaul and clashed with Pompey for ultimate control of Rome. He was both dictator and consul, but his high-handed autocracy led to his murder by Republicans in March 44 BC.

9. Gnaeus Pompeius Magnus (106–48 BC) was a dazzling 'boy-general' who supported Sulla against Marius and found himself at loggerheads with Marcus Licinius Crassus and Julius Caesar after their short-lived triumvirate collapsed. He was murdered in Egypt after the defeat at Pharsalia.

10. Miguel de Cervantes Saavedra (1547–1616) wrote Spain's most famous novel in two parts with a ten-year gap. His hero was the tragic anti-hero Don Quixote. Interestingly, in the context of the Cid, Cervantes fought against the Muslims at the naval battle of Lepanto in 1571.

11. Strabo – 'the squint-eyed' – was a Greek stoic born in 60 BC. His great work in forty-seven volumes *Historical Studies* has only survived in fragments, but his seventeen-volume *Geographica* is almost complete. He clearly travelled widely, largely in the East, and quotes earlier Greek writers extensively.

12. Eusebius Sophronius Hieronymus (*c.* 342–420) was an Italian scholar who wrote the first Latin translation of the Bible from Hebrew in the later years of his life, when he was living in Bethlehem.

13. Isidorus Hispalensis (*c.* 560–636) was a Spanish scholar and priest born in Seville. He wrote for the councils of Toledo and a huge encyclopaedia, entitled *Etymologiae*, which was a standard medieval text. He was generally held to be the greatest genius of his age.

14. The Arian Creed took its name from Arias, an Alexandrian who preached that the *logos*, the Word of God,

was not God himself, but an angel-like creature. The whole point of Christianity – that Jesus's life and death was the work of God – was therefore lost and the Creed was branded a heresy.

15. The 'golden century' of Spain was the sixteenth, when the New World was conquered by a relative handful of *conquistadores* and treasure-ships laden with silver sailed home to Cadiz.

16. Barton and Fletcher, *World of El Cid*, p. 2.

17. Lee, *As I Walked Out*, p. 52.

18. The chronicler al-Bakri, a contemporary of the Cid, quoting the tenth-century Jewish traveller Ibrahim al-Turtushi, quoted in M.J. Cohen and John Major, *History in Quotations* (London, Cassell, 2004), p. 312.

19. Laurie Lee, touring Segovia and Madrid in 1935, was told by an Asturian that the area had three 'special kinds of green. The dark green of night, the clear green of water and the pale fresh green of a corpse.' Lee, *As I Walked Out*, p. 103.

20. By coincidence, if that is what it is, one of the more bizarre relics of the Cid is an arm bone on display in the Salon de Poridad in Burgos.

21. Quoted in Paul Preston, *Franco* (London, HarperCollins, 1993), p. 778.

22. Ibid.

23. The grandson of the king allegedly responsible for the slaughter of the innocents, Agrippa was a friend of the insane Roman emperor Caligula. Both men enjoyed persecuting minorities.

24. The name Compostela comes from the Latin *campus stellae*, the field of stars.

25. The ancient name for the Straits of Gibraltar between Spain and Africa.

26. The usual starting places were St Denis, Chartres, Vezaley, Le Puy-en-Velmy and Arles.

27. Purgatory describes the state of souls of those who had died in the Grace of God, but had yet to confess all their sins; a sort of halfway house to heaven. The definition was denied by heretical sects like the Albigensians and Waldenses in the thirteenth century.

28. King of Asturias 791–842.

29. King of Asturias 866–910.

30. Charles the Great, King of the Franks 768–800 and Emperor of the West 800–14.

31. Louis the Pious, King of the Franks and Emperor 814–40.

32. Although Rodrigo was not from this region, the early chronicles refer to his belief in the importance of omens, particularly of birds. This is almost certainly connected with Celtic mythology and the prediction of death.

33. King of the Franks 751–68.

34. The Anglo-Norman chronicler Robert Wace recorded that the minstrel Taillefer, who died in the battle of Hastings, sang the Song of Roland that day to give heart to the Normans.

35. For example, Joan Evans, *The Flowering of the Middle Ages* (London, Thames & Hudson, 1966).
36. King of Navarre 905–25.
37. Ibn Hayan (d. 1076), quoted in Richard Fletcher *The Quest for El Cid* (Oxford, OUP, 1989), p. 49.
38. Andy Symington, *Footprint Guide to Northern Spain* (Bristol, Footprint, 2005).
39. Quoted in Fletcher, *Quest for El Cid*, p. 59.
40. Ibid., p. 61.
41. Fueros of Count Garcia Fernandez, 974, quoted in Fletcher, *Quest for El Cid*, pp. 61–2.
42. Rodrigo is often referred to as an *infanzone*, which is technically incorrect of course, because he was from Castile.
43. Some, like Bishop Jeronimo of Valencia, according to the later Cid legends, positively relished the prospect. At the battle of Cuarte in 1096 Jeronimo asked Rodrigo to give him the honour of drawing first blood against the Almoravids.
44. The name of a religious house – that of St Benedict – after 590. Vitally important in the spread of learning, the Benedictines took the word of God to the furthermost limits of Europe and founded schools and libraries until they were eclipsed in the thirteenth century.
45. Lee, *As I Walked Out*, pp. 70–1.
46. The Anglo-Saxon Chronicle consists of four slightly differing texts of English history compiled at four separate monasteries between the ninth and the twelfth centuries. It is a hugely important source for English affairs, although of course it is distorted by the bias of monkish chroniclers.
47. The Domesday Book, officially *Liber de Wintonia* (Book of Winchester), compiled by the clerks of William I of England between 1086 and 1087. It is an unrivalled source for the economy of eleventh-century England; though incomplete it gives a fascinating and unique glimpse into the everyday lives of ordinary people.
48. From the Fuero of Castro Geriz, 1017–35, quoted in Fletcher, *Quest for El Cid*, p. 62.
49. Lee, *As I Walked Out*, pp. 89–90.
50. Ibid., p. 62.
51. Hilaire Belloc's famous poem 'Tarantella', with 'Aragon a torrent at the door', asks the reader's *alter ego* Miranda whether she remembers the 'wine that tasted of tar'.
52. Lee, *As I Walked Out*, p. 47.
53. A medieval army, with its siege weapons drawn by oxen or mules and an extensive supply train, could probably manage no more than 10 miles a day.
54. Lee, *As I Walked Out*, p. 49.
55. Jim Bradbury, *The Medieval Siege* (Woodbridge, Boydell Press, 1994), p. 52.
56. Verbruggen, *Art of Warfare*, quoted in Bradbury, *Medieval Siege*, p. 71.

3: AL-ANDALUS
1. Robert Krepps, *El Cid* (Manchester, Philips Park Press, 1961).

2. The Third Crusade was launched after a crippling defeat of the Christians by the Muslims at Hattin in 1187, one of the most decisive battles of the Middle Ages. Three European kings – Richard I of England, Philip II of France and Frederick Barbarossa, the Holy Roman Emperor – led three separate armies to converge on Jerusalem to restore the fragile Christian kingdom there. The death by drowning of Barbarossa and the constant bickering between Richard and Philip combined to make the crusade a failure, although a narrow coastal strip was reconquered by the Christians for a while.

3. Richard I, known as Coeur de Lyon, the Lionheart, was the eldest surviving son of Henry II of England. Far more French than English, he spent only six months of his ten-year reign (1189–99) in England and for the rest of the time was at war in France and the Holy Land. Probably homosexual and certainly sadistic, Richard's reputation for courage and military prowess has survived to the present day. He was killed subjugating rebellious French vassals near Limousin.

4. Salah al-Din Yussuf was Sultan of Egypt and Syria and a formidable general. In trying to unite the two portions of his empire, he clashed with the Latin kingdom of Jerusalem and defeated the crusaders at Hattin. Although he lost territory and most of his battles against Richard of England, his integrity and reputation

were immense. Like most Muslim rulers, he was cultured and scholarly. He died in 1193.

5. Roderic of Betica, King of Visigothic Spain at the time of the Moorish invasion.

6. Musa ibn Nusayr, governor of North Africa.

7. Tariq ibn Zayid, after whom Gibraltar was named – the rock of Tariq.

8. Stanley Lane-Poole, *The Story of the Moors in Spain* (1888; Baltimore, MD, Black Classic Press, 1990), p. 13.

9. The Ummayads were essentially a merchant clan of social climbers who established a Muslim dynasty in Syria before turning to Spain. Already entrenched in Mecca before Mohammed's time, they opposed him and spread their rule into Persia with headquarters at Damascus. They abandoned many of the ancient Arab customs and ran what was basically a secular state, employing Christians as administrators and maintaining the Byzantine and Persian systems they inherited as a result of military occupation. By the eighth century, this toleration had given way to aggressive Islamization and Arabization.

10. The Sunni version of Islam is based on the orthodoxy of interpretation of the Holy Koran from the reign of the caliph Uthman (seventh century) and on the *hadith* (theology) of the *ulemas*, the wise men of Islam. From the tenth century onwards the Sunni tradition was centred on the Al-Azhar academy in Cairo.

11. The Shi'ites were originally followers of Mohammed's nephew Ali, emerging as a separatist sect in 661. They rejected the various interpretations of the *hadith*, relying solely on the gospel of the Koran. Between the tenth and thirteenth centuries the sect was most powerful in Persia, where the use of propaganda and terror, via the murderous Assassins, was widespread.

12. Quoted in John Masefield's well-known poem 'Cargoes', the wealth of Solomon was legendary, encapsulated in the exotic nature of what he carried in his ships.

13. II Chronicles 9:21.

14. Livy, quoted in Jan Read, *Southern Spain* (London, Insight Guides, 2004).

15. Anon., *Chronicle of 754*, translated by and quoted in Richard Fletcher, *Moorish Spain* (London, Phoenix Press, 2004), p. 30.

16. Anon., *Estoria de España*, Ch. 559, p. 19, quoted in Cohen and Major, *History in Quotations*, p. 150.

17. Thus making it perfectly feasible for black actors from Paul Robeson to Laurence Fishburn to legitimately play Othello, the Moor of Venice.

18. Quoted in Lane-Poole, *Moors in Spain*, p. 60.

19. Technically there can only be one caliph (successor) to the prophet at any given time. The fact that Abd al-Rahman III called himself this marks a very definite break with Baghdad.

20. Ibn Hawqal, about 990, quoted in Fletcher, *Moorish Spain*.

21. Quoted in Lane-Poole, *Moors in Spain*, p. 129.

22. Ibn al-Arabi, quoted in Read, *Southern Spain*, p. 31.

23. Lane-Poole, *Moors in Spain*, pp. 135–6.

24. The Courts were a kind of feminine chivalry, beginning in Aquitaine and other areas of southern France in the late twelfth century. In complex ceremonies knights and their ladies listened to and composed love songs extolling perfect (platonic) and usually helpless love. The usual pattern was that the knight fell madly in love with a married woman of higher status (for example Lancelot and Guinevere in the King Arthur legends) and it was his duty to fight for her honour and attend her every whim. Sir Walter Scott resurrected this imagery in several of his medieval novels, especially *Castle Dangerous*.

25. Pedanius Dioscorides, from Anazarb in Cilicia, was a first-century scholar who wrote *De Materiae Medica*, which remained a standard work (thanks partly to Shaprut) throughout the Middle Ages.

26. The astrolabe was invented in Cordoba and was used by astronomers and sailors to chart the positions of the stars. Alfonso X of Castile, the most 'scientific' of Spain's rulers in the Middle Ages, prepared elaborate astronomical tables based on the work of the Arab astronomer al-Bitrurgi. Abraham Zaccutti's refining of the instrument led to its being used by Christopher Columbus as he sailed for the New World.

27. Claudius Ptolemaeus was a second-century geographer and astronomer whose influence on medieval cartography was immense.

4: THE HOUSE OF THE SEED

1. Guibert de Nogent, *Memoirs*, quoted in Judith Herrin, *A Medieval Miscellany* (London, Weidenfeld & Nicholson, 2000), p. 141 (trans. Paul J. Archambault).
2. Ibid.
3. *Poema de Mio Cid*, trans. Fletcher, *Quest for El Cid*, p. 107.
4. *Carmen Campi Doctoris*, ibid.
5. Bertrand du Guesclin was a highly skilled professional soldier who fought the English in the Hundred Years War. He was appointed Constable of France (commander-in-chief) by Charles V in 1370, but his relatively humble birth – on a par with that of the Cid – and his guerrilla tactics, which many of the great lords found distasteful, made him enemies among his own people.
6. Which explains the over-simplification in Charlton Heston's *El Cid*. Don Diego (Michael Hordern) is credited as being the king's champion in an earlier generation. The post as such did not exist.
7. Quoted in N. Yapp, *Daily Life in the Age of Chivalry* (London, Readers' Digest, 1993).
8. In *De Rebus a se Gestis*, c. 1220.
9. Quoted in J.M. Brereton, *The Horse in War* (Newton Abbot, David & Charles, 1976), p. 28.

10. The last existing sword manufacturer in Britain – Wilkinson – ceased manufacture in 2006. Until then, all officers of the armed forces in the UK were expected to buy a sword for ceremonial occasions.
11. The Tizona is accepted in all Cid literature as being taken (along with his other sword, Colada) from Moorish enemies, which may explain its ornate drooping quillons, atypical of eleventh-century 'Christian' weapons. It is possible, of course, that the blade is original, with 'modern' hilt replacements added later.
12. Samuel Ibn Naghrila, *War*, trans. Fletcher, *Moorish Spain*, p. 96.
13. Badajoz became synonymous with heavy casualties. In the folkloric ballad *Ben Battle*, the hero loses both his legs, leaving them in the rather sick pun 'in Badajoz's breaches'.
14. So the Cid's neo-contemporary, Macbeth of Scotland, has been made the anti-hero of the 1955 film *Joe Macbeth*, screenplay by Ken Hughes.
15. Anon., quoted in Yapp, *Daily Life*.
16. Anon., *Historia Silense*, Ch. 7, quoted in and trans. Barton and Fletcher, *World of El Cid*, pp. 28–9.
17. Gaius Sallustius Crispus, an historian and politician who lived in the century before Christ. His own career was riddled with corruption (he was expelled from the Senate for licentiousness) but in retirement he wrote three histories of his own time. Sadly only a few fragments now survive.

18. Anon., *Historia Silense*, Ch. 7, quoted in and trans. Barton and Fletcher, *World of El Cid*, p. 24.
19. Ibid., p. 29.
20. Ibid.
21. Ibid., p. 45.
22. Ibid. It may help the film-goer to fix these children in relation to Heston's *El Cid*. Fernando (Ferdinand in the Hollywood version) was played by Ralph Truman, all stern majesty and gravitas. Sancho was Gary Raymond and Alfonso John Fraser, all of them British actors. Urraca was played by French actress Genevieve Page. Elvira and Garcia did not feature at all, as making the script unnecessarily complicated.
23. Ibid.
24. Ibid.
25. Ibid.
26. Ibid.
27. Ibid., p. 47.
28. Ibid.
29. Ibid., Ch. 85, p. 48.
30. The famous comment by King Edward III about his 16-year-old son, the Black Prince, at Crecy in 1346 – 'let the boy win his spurs' – was less heartless than it seems today. Princes had to grow up quickly or not grow up at all.
31. Even today there is a flourishing hospitality trade in monasteries and convents throughout Spain, with a specific brother or sister being given the role of 'hotel manager'.
32. Aymeric Picaud, quoted in George Semler, *Northern Spain*, p. 271.
33. Enzo Musemici Greco.
34. Charlton Heston, *In the Arena*, p. 248.

5: SONG OF THE CAMPEADOR

1. Anon., *Historia Silense*, Ch. 95, quoted in and trans. Barton and Fletcher, *World of El Cid*, p. 56.
2. Anon., *Historia Silense*, Ch. 97, p. 57.
3. Ibid., Ch. 95, pp. 58–9.
4. Ibid.
5. Anon., *Historia Roderici*, Ch. 95, quoted in and trans. Fletcher, *Moorish Spain*, p. 113.
6. Edward, like the Cid, was one of the outstanding military commanders of the Middle Ages. In 1366 he invaded Spain in support of a claimant to the throne of Castile and defeated a superior force (very much his trademark) at Najera. He died of dropsy in 1376 and his magnificent tomb 'of latten gilt' is a superb reminder of the high chivalric code.
7. These were the vows taken by the twelfth century in northern Europe. We do not know how far advanced all this formality was in eleventh-century Spain.
8. Anon., *Historia Silense*, Ch. 105, quoted in and trans. Barton and Fletcher, *World of El Cid*, p. 63.
9. Anon., *Historia Silense*, Ch. 106, p. 63.
10. Ibid.
11. Ibid., p. 64.
12. Ibid.
13. An interesting parallel is the artistic portrayal of the death of the English king Edward the Confessor, which took place ten days after that of

Fernando. In the Bayeux Tapestry the old king is shown sitting up in bed, clearly dying, making his peace with his clergy and nobility. In the next scene his body is being laid out and in the third his coffin is being carried in all solemnity to his church at Westminster, the nobility on foot behind him and mourners ringing hand-bells.

14. Pelayo of Oviedo, *Chronicon Regum Legionensum*, Barton and Fletcher, *World of El Cid*, pp. 82–3.
15. Anon., *Historia Silense*, Ch. 8, quoted in and trans. Barton and Fletcher, *World of El Cid*, p. 30.
16. Anon., *Historia Silense*, Ch. 103, p. 60.
17. Ibid., p. 61.
18. Another example is the fratricidal behaviour of the 'young eagles' Richard, Geoffrey and John, the sons of Henry II of England. These three, however, were fighting each other and their father while Henry was still alive!
19. Pelayo of Oviedo, *Chronicon Regum Legionensum*, Barton and Fletcher, *World of El Cid*, p. 83.
20. Anon., *Historia Silense*, Ch. 9, quoted in and trans. Barton and Fletcher, *World of El Cid*, p. 31.
21. Anon., *Historia Roderici*, Ch. 5, quoted in and trans. Barton and Fletcher, *World of El Cid*, p. 101.
22. Ibid.
23. Flavius Vegetius Renatus was a fourth-century military writer who combed ancient sources to produce a masterly exposition in Roman

tactics, *Institutionem Rei Militaris*, about 380. The work was still being read and followed as late as the fifteenth century.
24. Publius Vergilius Maro was one of the best known of the Roman poets. The Aeneid which charts the ten years of the fictional Trojan War was finished by 19 BC. It established him as one of the greatest writers of all time by the third century.
25. All translations of the *Carmen* are by Eva Campama-Pizarro, 2006.
26. Anon., *Historia Roderici*, Ch. 5, quoted in and trans. Barton and Fletcher, *World of El Cid*, p. 101.
27. Damascening came from the beautiful artistry of the silversmiths of Damascus in the Middle East.
28. Anon., *Historia Roderici*, Ch. 5, quoted in and trans. Barton and Fletcher, *World of El Cid*, p. 101.
29. Anon., *Historia Silense*, Ch. 71, quoted in and trans. Barton and Fletcher, *World of El Cid*, p. 89.
30. Pelayo of Oviedo, *Chronicon Regum Legionensum*, Barton and Fletcher, *World of El Cid*, p. 83.
31. Such acts had two purposes. First, they may have been genuine examples of piety, driven by a fierce Catholic faith few of us today can understand. Second, it was also all about show: Alfonso's contemporaries would have expected him to do this. So, in England at another time, King Henry II walked barefoot to the murder scene of Thomas Becket at Canterbury and had himself whipped by the monks to

atone for the man's death and perhaps exorcize his ghost.

32. Anon., *Historia Silense*, Ch. 12, quoted in and trans. Barton and Fletcher, *World of El Cid*, p. 33.
33. Anon., *Historia Roderici*, Ch. 6, quoted in and trans. Barton and Fletcher, *World of El Cid*, p. 101.
34. Anon., *Historia Roderici*, Ch. 10, pp. 31–2.
35. Ibid., Ch. 5, p. 101.
36. Anon., *Historia Silense*, Ch. 10, quoted in and trans. Barton and Fletcher, *World of El Cid*, p. 32.
37. Ibid., Ch. 11, p. 32.
38. Ibid.

6: THE STORY OF RODRIGO

1. Anon., *Historia Roderici*, Ch. 6, quoted in and trans. Barton and Fletcher, *World of El Cid*, p. 101.
2. Pelayo of Oviedo, *Chronicon Regum Legionensum*, Barton and Fletcher, *World of El Cid*, p. 84.
3. The legal system of eleventh-century Spain was highly complicated, not to say chaotic. Medieval ideology accepted the legalistic doctrine of St Augustine, who arranged law at three levels: divine, which was at once universal and incontestable; natural, which could be understood by all (including animals) and could be improved by philosophy; and temporal, which was man-made. Roman law was undergoing a revival during the Cid's lifetime, beginning in the university of Bologna in Italy, with a modern adaptation of the Code of Justinian. In Castile, however, much of the law was Visigothic for a generation after Rodrigo Diaz and in the south of course the Muslim law of Shariah was practised. To complicate the situation further, Jews were usually allowed to follow their own Talmudic precepts.
4. Anon., *Historia Roderici*, Ch. 6, quoted in and trans. Barton and Fletcher, *World of El Cid*, p. 101.
5. James Fitzmaurice-Kelly, *Chapters on Spanish Literature* (London, Constable, 1908).
6. Quoted in Yapp, *Daily Life*, p. 34.
7. The English term cordwainer, meaning a leather-worker, comes from the renowned skill of Cordoban craftsmen.
8. The 'traditional' Spanish dress of many-layered flounced dresses, short bolero jackets and wide-brimmed sombreros belongs of course to a much later period.
9. Given the influences of the exotic that came from al-Andalus and further afield in Islam, a recent writer on medieval Spain wondered what people had to eat in the Visigothic period!
10. One of the odder sources concerning the rebellion of the gladiator slave Spartacus talks of menstruating women from the slave camp who seem to have been used to lure an unwary Roman army into a trap.
11. Anon., *Historia Roderici*, Ch. 6, quoted in and trans. Barton and Fletcher, *World of El Cid*, p. 101.
12. *Holy Maidenhood*, quoted in Henrietta Leyser, *Medieval Women* (London, Phoenix, 1996), p. 123.

13. Bartholomaus Anglicus, trans. M. Goodich, quoted in Leyser, *Medieval Women*, p. 135.

7: EXILE

1. Quoted in Fletcher, *Quest for El Cid*, p. 125.
2. Anon., *Historia Roderici*, Ch. 7, quoted in and trans. Barton and Fletcher, *World of El Cid*, p. 102.
3. Probably written in exile in Morocco in the 1090s.
4. Abd Allah, quoted in Fletcher, *Quest for El Cid*, p. 125.
5. Anon., *Historia Roderici*, Ch. 7, quoted in and trans. Barton and Fletcher, *World of El Cid*, p. 102.
6. Ibid., Ch. 8, p. 103.
7. Ibid.
8. Ibid.
9. Full marks to the costume designers of the film. Rodrigo and his followers are shown with a black, coiled dragon on a red field. Someone had done their homework!
10. Anon., *Historia Roderici*, Ch. 9, quoted in and trans. Barton and Fletcher, *World of El Cid*, p. 103.
11. Ibid., Ch. 10, p. 104.
12. *Carmen Campidoctoris*, vv. XII–XIV.
13. Anon., *Historia Roderici*, Ch. 10, quoted in and trans. Barton and Fletcher, *World of El Cid*, p. 104.
14. Ibid.
15. Numbers in most chronicles should be regarded with suspicion. The works were written by men who were not present, often years later, and we have no way of verifying them.
16. *Carmen Campi Doctoris*, v. XV.
17. Anon., *Historia Roderici*, Ch. 10, quoted in and trans. Barton and Fletcher, *World of El Cid*, p. 104.
18. In that sense it was very like excommunication by the Catholic Church – and almost impossible to monitor and police.
19. Anon., *Historia Roderici*, Ch. 12, quoted in and trans. Barton and Fletcher, *World of El Cid*, p. 105.
20. Ibid., Ch. 13, p. 106.
21. Ibid.
22. Ibid.
23. *Carmen Campi Doctoris*, v. XXII.
24. Anon., *Historia Roderici*, Ch. 13, quoted in and trans. Barton and Fletcher, *World of El Cid*, p. 106.
25. *Carmen Campi Doctoris*, v. XXVI.
26. Anon., *Historia Roderici*, Ch. 16, quoted in and trans. Barton and Fletcher, *World of El Cid*, p. 107.
27. Fletcher, *Quest for El Cid*, p. 135.
28. Anon., *Historia Roderici*, Ch. 17, quoted in and trans. Barton and Fletcher, *World of El Cid*, p. 108.
29. Ibid.
30. The burial-place of the Kings of Castile and León before Fernando I.
31. Quoted in Fletcher, *Quest for El Cid*, p. 137.
32. Ibid.
33. Anon., *Historia Roderici*, Ch. 18, quoted in and trans. Barton and Fletcher, *World of El Cid*, p. 109.
34. Ibid., Ch. 21, p. 109.
35. Ibid., Ch. 21, p. 110.
36. Ibid., Ch. 22, p. 110.
37. Ibid., p. 111.
38. Ibid, Chs 24 and 25, p. 112.

Notes

8. OUT OF AFRIQUIYA

1. Tertillian, quoted in Cunliffe, *Rome and Her Empire*, p. 230.

2. The fabulously wealthy Solomon of the Old Testament was believed to have had gold mines in Africa. It was undoubtedly the trade routes between the Maghrib and the Roman Middle East that gave rise to this legend.

3. Prester John (John the Priest) was a mythical king of a Christian kingdom somewhere in Africa, long supposed to be Ethiopia. He not only lived for ever but had a magic mirror that allowed him to see any wrong-doing being committed throughout his kingdom. We meet him in legend at the beginning of the crusades and stories about him were still circulating two hundred years later. A letter received by Pope Alexander III in 1177 relates to the 'king of the Indies, the most holy priest', which would imply that his kingdom was in Asia.

4. A similar conversion would occur in eighteenth-century England when John Wesley, already an Anglican parson, met a Mormon preacher on his way back from America and experienced a mystical conversion which sent him on a Methodist mission for the rest of his life.

5. The Templars were a military-religious organization founded in Jerusalem twenty years after the death of the Cid. Under their fanatical leader Hugh of Poyns, the original ten knights swore at the Dome of the Rock to defend the crusader kingdom against all comers. The rules of their Order were written by Bernard of Clairvaux in 1128 and they were officially recognized by the papacy. As time went on they became fabulously wealthy, operating as landowners and bankers throughout Europe to fund their military exploits. Haughty and unpopular, they were tainted with heresy (the worship of the devil Baphomet) and the order was destroyed in 1312. Subsequent notions of the Order bearing the Holy Grail to Scotland and carrying earth-shattering secrets about the marriage of Christ can be dismissed as lucrative nonsense.

6. A much later example was Mohammed Ahmed, the Mahdi or messiah, who vowed in the 1880s to drive all Europeans out of the Sudan. He was initially successful against British generals like Hicks and Gordon but after his death his followers were routed by the British under Kitchener at Omdurman.

7. The Seljuks were a loose confederation of the Turkish tribes who began to conquer lands belonging to the eastern Abbasid caliphs in the late 1030s. Their leader, Tughril-beg, took Baghdad when Rodrigo Diaz was a boy and by the time he was a man the Seljuks had clashed with Byzantium and conquered most of Syria and Palestine.

8. Anon., *Historia Roderici*, Ch. 20, quoted in and trans. Barton and Fletcher, *World of El Cid*, p. 109.

9. Quoted in Fletcher, *Quest for El Cid*, p. 151.
10. Ibid.
11. Pelayo of Oviedo, *Chronicon Regum Legionensum*, quoted in and trans. Barton and Fletcher, *World of El Cid*, p. 85.
12. Ibid.
13. Lane-Poole, *Moors in Spain*, p. 179.
14. Krepps, *El Cid*, pp. 173–4.
15. Ibid., p. 169.
16. Ibid., p. 171.
17. Ibid., p. 177.
18. Lane-Poole, *Moors in Spain*, p. 179.
19. Abd Allah, quoted in Fletcher, *Quest for El Cid*, p. 179.
20. Anon., *Historia Roderici*, Ch. 25, quoted in and trans. Barton and Fletcher, *World of El Cid*, p. 112.
21. This makes it highly likely that he did not own it before; on the other hand it may have been restored to him as an act of good faith.
22. Anon., *Historia Roderici*, Ch. 26, quoted in and trans. Barton and Fletcher, *World of El Cid*, p. 113.
23. Ibid., Ch. 29, p. 113.
24. Pentecost is the feast held on the Sunday fifty days after Easter when the gift of the Holy Spirit is celebrated. Traditionally it is the happiest of the religious services.
25. Anon., *Historia Roderici*, Ch. 30, quoted in and trans. Barton and Fletcher, *World of El Cid*, p. 114.
26. Ibid.
27. Ibid.
28. Ibid., Ch. 31, p. 115.
29. The Ishmaelites, according to the Bible and the Koran, were the descendants of Abraham (Ibrahim) and were usually identified as Arabs, the desert dwellers. In that case the term for Berber invaders is not quite accurate.
30. The Moabites were a tribe living in a mountainous area of modern Jordan, who were in constant conflict with their western neighbours, the Israelites.
31. Anon., *Historia Roderici*, Ch. 33, quoted in and trans. Barton and Fletcher, *World of El Cid*, pp. 115–16.
32. Ibid., p. 116.
33. Ibid., Ch. 34, p. 116.
34. Ibid., Ch. 34, p. 117.
35. Ibid.
36. Ibid., Ch. 35, p. 120.
37. Ibid.
38. Ibid.

9: VALENCIA THE SHINING
1. Anon., *Historia Roderici*, Ch. 36, quoted in and trans. Barton and Fletcher, *World of El Cid*, p. 121.
2. Ibid.
3. Ibid.
4. Ibid., Ch. 38, p. 123.
5. Ibid., p. 124.
6. Ibid.
7. Ibid.
8. Ibid., Ch. 39, p. 125.
9. Ibid.
10. Ibid.
11. Ibid., Ch. 40, pp. 126–7.
12. In other words genets, light saddle-horses.
13. Anon., *Historia Roderici*, Ch. 40, quoted in and trans. Barton and Fletcher, *World of El Cid*, pp. 126–7.

14. Ibid., Ch. 41, p. 127.
15. A mancuse was the equivalent of thirty pennies.
16. Anon, *Historia Roderici*, Ch. 42, quoted in and trans. Barton and Fletcher, *World of El Cid*, p. 128.
17. Ibid., Ch. 43, p. 129.
18. Ibid., Ch. 45, p. 129.
19. Ibid., Ch. 66, p. 141.
20. Ibid., Ch. 45, p. 130.
21. Ibid., Ch. 50, pp. 132–3.
22. The Castilians had no navy until the thirteenth century, so any seaborne enterprise had to be accompanied with mercenary help. The Venetians in particular had a long tradition, inherited from Byzantium, Rome and ultimately Greece, of the galley as a fighting warship. In the case of Alfonso's siege of Valencia it is likely that the ships were merely used as transports.
23. Anon., *Historia Roderici*, Ch. 54, quoted in and trans. Barton and Fletcher, *World of El Cid*, p. 135.
24. Anon., *Chronica Adefonsi Imperatoris*, Ch. 50, quoted in and trans. Barton and Fletcher, *World of El Cid*, p. 185.
25. Anon., *Historia Roderici*, Ch. 57, quoted in and trans. Barton and Fletcher, *World of El Cid*, p. 136.
26. Ibid., Ch. 60, p. 137.
27. Ibid., Ch. 61.
28. Lane-Poole, *Moors in Spain*, pp. 207–8.
29. Quoted in *Southern Spain* (Discovery Channel), p. 40.
30. Anon., *Historia Roderici*, Ch. 62, quoted in and trans. Barton and Fletcher, *World of El Cid*, p. 137.
31. Ibid., Ch. 65, p. 139.
32. Quoted in Fletcher, *Quest for El Cid*, p. 173.
33. Anon., *Historia Roderici*, Ch. 66, quoted in and trans. Barton and Fletcher, *World of El Cid*, p. 141.
34. Ibid.
35. Ibid., Ch. 68, p. 142.
36. Ibid., Ch. 70, p. 143.
37. Ibid.
38. Ibid.
39. Ibid., p. 144.
40. The Nativity of St John the Baptist is celebrated by Christians on 24 June.
41. Anon., *Historia Roderici*, Ch. 73, quoted in and trans. Barton and Fletcher, *World of El Cid*, p. 146.
42. Quoted in Fletcher, *Quest for El Cid*, p. 184.
43. Anon., *Historia Roderici*, Ch. 75, quoted in and trans. Barton and Fletcher, *World of El Cid*, p. 146.
44. Quoted in Fletcher, *Quest for El Cid*, p. 185.

10: THE POEM OF THE CID

1. Charter of Alfonso VI, quoted in Fletcher, *Quest for El Cid*, p. 186.
2. Charter of Jimena, Valencia, 1101, quoted in Fletcher, *Quest for El Cid*, p. 186.
3. Anon., *Historia Roderici*, Ch. 76, quoted in and trans. Barton and Fletcher, *World of El Cid*, p. 147.
4. Chronicle of Morea, fourteenth century, quoted in Herrin, *Medieval Miscellany*, p. 187.
5. *The Chronicles of Matthew Paris: Monastic Life in the 13th Century*

(New York, St Martin's Press, 1984), pp. 63–4.

6. Southey, *Chronicle of the Cid*, p. 268.
7. Ibid., p. 269.
8. Ibid.
9. Ibid., p. 277.
10. Ibid.
11. Ibid.
12. Ibid., p. 278.
13. Ibid., p. 281.
14. Ibid.
15. Ibid., p. 280.
16. Quoted in Fletcher, *Quest for El Cid*, pp. 189–90.
17. Today San Pedro takes in paying guests, as do many of Spain's monasteries, and the monks produce and sell Licor Tizona del Cid, a delicious liqueur made from twenty-eight different herbs.
18. St Eadgyth – M.J. Trow, *Cnut, Emperor of the North* (Stroud, Sutton Publishing, 2005).
19. Quoted in Louise and Jonathan Riley-Smith, *The Crusades: Idea and Reality* (London, Edward Arnold, 1981), p. 40.
20. The Hospitallers were originally those who cared for pilgrims travelling to Jerusalem, the greatest shrine in Christendom. By 1050 they had acquired the church of St John the Baptist in Jerusalem and by the time the Cid died they had added a military bodyguard for protection. This element became more prominent in the early twelfth century and the Knights of St John became as powerful and prosperous as the Templars.
21. Fletcher, *Quest for El Cid*, pp. 197–8.

22. Ramon Menendez Pidal, *Poem of the Cid*, trans. W.S. Merwin (Penguin Classics, 1959), p. 39.
23. Ibid.
24. Ibid., p. 41.
25. Ibid., p. 55.
26. Ibid., p. 57.
27. Ibid., p. 63.
28. Ibid., p. 65.
29. Ibid., p. 69.
30. Ibid., p. 71.
31. Ibid., p. 73.
32. Ibid., p. 81.
33. Ibid.
34. Ibid.
35. 'God Wills It' (i.e. the capture of Jerusalem by crusaders).
36. Pidal, *Poem of the Cid*, trans. Merwin, p. 89.
37. Ibid., p. 91.
38. Ibid., p. 97.
39. Ibid., p. 101.
40. Ibid., p. 103.
41. Ibid., p. 107.
42. Ibid.
43. Ibid., p. 109.
44. Ibid., p. 111.
45. Ibid., p. 123.
46. Ibid., p. 127.
47. Ibid., p. 129.
48. Ibid., p. 135.
49. Ibid., p. 139.
50. Ibid., p. 145.
51. Ibid., p. 155.
52. Ibid.
53. Ibid., p. 156.
54. Ibid., p. 157.
55. Ibid., p. 161.
56. Ibid., p. 205.
57. Ibid.

Notes

58. Ibid., p. 215.
59. Ibid.
60. Ibid., p. 217.
61. Ibid., p. 219.
62. Ibid., p. 227.
63. Ibid., p. 237.
64. Ibid., p. 258.
65. Ibid.
66. Ibid., p. 277.
67. Ibid., p. 279.
68. Ibid., p. 299.
69. Ibid.
70. Ibid., p. 301.

11: ... AND INTO LEGEND

1. Quoted in Melveena McKendrick, *A Concise History of Spain* (London, Cassell, 1972), p. 76.
2. Southey, *Chronicle of the Cid*, p. 269.
3. Maurice Keen, *Chivalry* (Newhaven, Yale University Press, 2005), p. 249.
4. Arcturus in Latin is linked with Ursus the bear. This may have been a nickname for a warrior whose actual name is unknown or it could have been a battle standard.
5. Quoted in Henry Kamen, *A Concise History of Spain* (London, Thames & Hudson, 1973).
6. Preface to Southey, *Chronicle of the Cid*, p. xx.
7. Quoted in McKendrick, *Concise History of Spain*.
8. An exact parallel is the advent on children's television in the late twentieth century, which wove completely fictional stories about slim legends like Robin Hood, William Tell, Sir Lancelot and Ivanhoe.
9. Quoted in Fitzmaurice-Kelly, *Chapters*, p. 2.
10. Technically it is likely that the Cid romances were read in Spanish colonies in America, but that is impossible to quantify.
11. All translations of the *Mocedades del Cid* are by Eva Campama-Pizarro.
12. Corneille, *Le Cid* (1605).
13. Ibid.
14. Wikipedia.
15. Southey, quoted in Wikipedia.
16. Such debates were all the rage at the time, the Romantics seeing flogging as part of the evils of the cruel *ancien régime* which they despised.
17. Wikipedia.
18. Wikipedia.
19. Alfonso X's of the 1270s.
20. Southey, *Chronicle of the Cid*, p. xx.
21. Ibid., p. xxi.
22. And we still do so today. Menendez Pidal in the 1920s and Richard Fletcher in the 1990s both added words and phrases in order to make sense of a Latin or medieval Spanish corruption.
23. Southey, *Chronicle of the Cid*, p. xxii.
24. Ibid., p. xxv.
25. Quoted in Kamen, *Concise History of Spain*, p. 114.
26. Lane-Poole, *Moors in Spain*, p. x.
27. Ibid., p. 192.
28. Kamen, *Concise History of Spain*, p. 125.
29. Pelayo, *Historia de los heterodoxies espanoles*, quoted in Fletcher, *Quest for El Cid*, p. 203.
30. Lee, *As I Walked Out*, p. 91.

236

31. Ibid., p. 159.
32. Ibid., p. 172.
33. Ibid., p. 176.
34. Preston, *Franco*, p. 329.
35. Ibid., p. 345.
36. Ibid., p. 640.
37. Ibid., p. 641.
38. Heston, *In the Arena*, p. 239.
39. Ibid., p. 242.
40. Ibid., p. 245.
41. Mel Gibson has particularly come under fire for this. His *Braveheart* depiction of Scottish freedom-fighter William Wallace portrayed the man as a victim and Edward I, one of the finest kings of medieval England, as a murderous Machiavellian thug. Even more unforgivably, the British officer portrayed in *The Patriot* as a bloodthirsty killer is unmistakably Banastre Tarleton, a gallant soldier in any period.
42. Heston, *In the Arena*, p. 250.
43. Ibid., p. 253.
44. Ibid., p. 255.
45. Ibid., p. 256.
46. Anthony Mann, quoted in Fenwick and Green-Armytage, pp. 187–8.

12: WHAT SORT OF CID?

1. James Sharpe, *Dick Turpin: The Myth of the English Highwayman* (London, Profile, 2005), pp. 211–12.
2. Ibid.
3. Fletcher, *Quest for El Cid*, p. 205.
4. Martin M. Winkler, *Mythic and Cinematic Traditions in Anthony Mann's El Cid* (Winnipeg, Mosaic, vol. 26, 1993), p. 48.
5. Midas Tours Battlefield and Historical Tours: El Cid and the Reconquista, promotional material (www.midastours.co.uk).
6. Christopher Wickering and Barrie Pattison, *A Biographical Dictionary of the Cinema* (London, Secler, 1980), p. 48.
7. Winkler, *Mythic and Cinematic Traditions*, p. 48.
8. Interview in the *Daily Telegraph*, January 2003.
9. Interview in the *Daily Telegraph*, November 2000.
10. Fitzmaurice-Kelly, *Chapters*, p. 2.
11. Rodrigo in this work is one of the favourite parts of tenor Placido Domingo, who first performed it at Carnegie Hall in 1976.
12. Ibn Bassan, *Treasury of the Excellencies of the Spaniards*, quoted in Fletcher, *Quest for El Cid*, p. 185. The line is carved into the stone of the 1955 statue in Burgos.
13. Keen, *Chivalry*, p. 230.
14. Ibn Bassan, quoted in Fletcher, *Quest for El Cid*, p. 185.
15. Southey, *Chronicle of the Cid*, p. 282.

Bibliography

Ali, Abdullah Yusuf (trans), *The Holy Qur'an* (Ware, Wordsworth Editions 2000).

Animation World Magazine, March 2006.

Anon., *Chronica Adefonsi Imperatoris* (Manchester, Manchester University Press, 2000).

Anon., *Historia Silense. The World of El Cid: Chronicles of the Spanish Reconquest* (Manchester, Manchester University Press, 2000).

Barish, Eileen, *Lodgings in Spain's Monasteries* (Scottsdale, Arizona, Anacapa Press, 2002).

Barral i Altet, Xavier, *The Romanesque: Towns, Cathedrals and Monasteries* (Koln, Taschen, 2001).

Barton, Simon and Fletcher, Richard, *The World of El Cid* (Manchester, Manchester University Press, 2000).

Bell, Brian (ed.), *Northern Spain*, Insight Guide (Basingstoke, APA Publishers, 2004).

——, *Southern Spain*, Insight Guide (Basingstoke, APA Publishers, 2004).

Boulton, D'A.J.D., *The Knights of the Crown* (Woodbridge, Boydell, 2000).

Bradbury, Jim, *The Medieval Siege* (Woodbridge, Boydell, 1992).

Brereton, J.M., *The Horse in War* (Newton Abbot, David & Charles, 1976).

Brett, Michael and Forman, Werner, *The Moors: Islam in the West* (London, Orbis, 1980).

Cary, John, *Spectacular: the Story of Epic Films* (London, Hamlyn, 1974).

Clissold, Stephen, *In Search of the Cid* (London, Hodder, 1965).

Corfis, Ivy and Wolfe, Michael, *The Medieval City Under Siege* (Woodbridge, Boydell, 1995).

Corneille, Pierre, *Le Cid*, www.gutenberg.ord/etext/14954.

Cunliffe, Barry, *Rome and her Empire* (London, BCA, 1994).

Daily Telegraph, various dates, 2003.

Duffy, Eamon, *Saints and Sinners: A History of the Popes* (New Haven, Yale University Press, 1997).

Edge, David and Paddock, John, *Arms and Armour of the Medieval Knight* (London, Guild Publishers, 1988).

Bibliography

El Cid Film Souvenir Brochure (London, Classics Illustrated, 1961).

Elliott, J.H., *Europe Divided, 1559–1598* (London, Fontana, 1968).

Evans, Joan (ed.), *The Flowering of the Middle Ages* (London, Thames & Hudson, 1966).

Fitzmaurice-Kelly, James, *Chapters on Spanish Literature* (London, Constable, 1908).

Fletcher, Richard, *Moorish Spain* (London, Phoenix, 2004).

——, *The Quest for El Cid* (Oxford, Oxford University Press, 1989).

Fraser, George Macdonald, *The Hollywood History of the World* (London, Michael Joseph, 1988).

Garate Cordoba, José, *Las Huellas del Cid* (Burgos, Edicions Aldecon, 1970).

Gautier, Leon, *Chivalry* (London, Readers Union/J.M. Dent & Sons, 1959).

Grabois, Aryeh, *Medieval Civilization* (London, Octopus, 1980).

Heath, Ian, *Armies of Feudal Europe 1066–1300* (Worthing, Wargames Research Group Publications, 1978).

Herrin, Judith (ed.), *A Medieval Miscellany* (London, Weidenfeld & Nicholson, 1998).

Heston, Charlton, *In the Arena* (London, HarperCollins, 1996).

——, *The Actor's Life: Journals 1956–76* (London, Penguin, 1979).

Hindley, Geoffrey (ed.), *The Larousse Encyclopaedia of Music* (London, Hamlyn, 1993).

Hutchinson Dictionary of Ancient and Medieval Warfare (Oxford, Helicon, 1998).

Kamen, Henry, *A Concise History of Spain* (London, Thames & Hudson, 1973).

Keen, Maurice, *Chivalry* (Newhaven, Yale University Press, 2005).

Krepps, Robert, *El Cid* (London, Frederick Muller, 1961).

Kybalova, Ludmila, et al., *The Encyclopaedia of Fashion* (London, Hamlyn, 1970).

Lacarra, Maria Eugenia, *El Poema de Mio Cid; realidad historica e ideologia* (Madrid, José Porrúa Turanzas, 1980).

Lane-Poole, Stanley, *The Story of the Moors in Spain* (1886; Baltimore, Black Classic Press, 1990).

McKendrick, Melveena, *A Concise History of Spain* (London, Cassell, 1972).

Matthews, John and Stewart, Bob, *Warriors of Christendom* (London, Brockhampton Press, 1998).

Merwin, W.S., *Poem of the Cid (Poema de Mio Cid)* (New York, Mentor, 1959).

Midas Tours Publicity: www.midastours.co.uk

Montaner, Aberto and Escober, Angel, *Carmen Campi Doctoris* (Madrid, Espana Nuevo Milenia, 2001).

Bibliography

Munn, Michael, *Charlton Heston: a Biography* (London, Robson Books, 1986).

Nelson-Pallmeyer, Jack, *Is Religion Killing Us?* (New York, Continuum, 2003).

Nicolle, David, *El Cid and the Reconquista* (Wellingborough, Osprey Men-at-Arms Series, 1988).

Oakeshott, R. Ewart, *The Sword in the Age of Chivalry* (London, Lutterworth, 1964).

Parker Pearson, Mike, *The Archaeology of Death and Burial* (Thrupp, Sutton Publishing, 1999).

Pelayo of Oviedo, *Chronicon Regum Legionensum* (Manchester, Manchester University Press, 2000).

Preston, Paul, *Franco* (London, HarperCollins, 1993).

Quintana, M.J., *Vidas de los Españoles Célebres* (Buenos Aires, Espon-Calpe, 1948).

Reilly, Bernard F., *The Kingdom of Léon-Castilla under King Alfonso VI, The Library of Iberian Resources Online* (Princeton, New Jersey University Press, 1988).

Scarre, Chris (ed.), *The Times Archaeology of the World* (London, HarperCollins, 1988).

Scott, George Riley, *A History of Torture* (London, T. Werner Laine, 1940).

Sharpe, James, *Dick Turpin: The Myth of the English Highwayman* (London, Profile, 2004).

Smith, Colin, *Ramon Menendez Pidal 1869–1986* (London, Grant, 1970).

Southey, Robert, *The Chronicle of the Cid* (New York, Dolphin Books, 1955).

Symington, Andy, *Northern Spain*, Footprint (Bath, Footprint Handbooks, 2005).

Weber, Eugen, 'The Ups and Downs of Honor' (*American Scholar Magazine*, vol. 68, issue 1, Winter 1999).

Winkler, Martin M., *Mythic and Cinematic Traditions in Anthony Mann's 'EL Cid'* (Winnipeg, Mosaic, vol. 26, 1993).

Yapp, Nick, *Daily Life in the Age of Chivalry* (London, Reader's Digest, 1993).

Index

Index

Index

245

Index

Index